End the Arms Race: Fund Human Needs

*Proceedings of the
1986 Vancouver Centennial
Peace and Disarmament
Symposium*

EDITED BY:
Dr. Thomas L. Perry
and
Dr. James G. Foulks

Gordon Soules Book Publishers Ltd., West Vancouver, Canada
Distributed by the University of Washington Press, Seattle and London

Canadian Cataloguing in Publication Data

Vancouver Centennial Peace and Disarmament
  Symposium (1986)
  End the arms race—fund human needs

Proceedings of the 1986 Vancouver Centennial Peace and Disarmament Symposium, held April 1986.
  Includes bibliographical references.
ISBN 0-919574-96-3

1. Disarmament – Congresses. 2. Arms race – Social aspects – Congresses. I. Perry, Thomas L. (Thomas Lockwood), 1916– II. Foulks, James G. III. Vancouver Centennial Commission. IV. Title.
JX1974.V35 1986   327.1'74   C86-091543-3

Published by:
**Gordon Soules
Book Publishers Ltd.**
1352-B Marine Drive
West Vancouver, B.C.
Canada
V7T 1B5

Distributed outside Canada by:
the **University of
Washington Press**
P.O. Box 50096
Seattle, Washington 98145

ISBN 0-295-96492-8

Typesetting by The Typeworks
Printed and bound in Canada by Hignell Printing Ltd.

VANCOUVER

city of the century

This book was published
in celebration of Vancouver's Centennial

Table of Contents

Acknowledgments

End the Arms Race —Fund Human Needs comprises chiefly the speeches given at the Vancouver Centennial Peace and Disarmament Symposium, held from April 24 to 26, 1986 at the Orpheum Theatre in Vancouver, British Columbia. The production of this book has been made possible only by the generous contributions of work and money from many individuals and organizations.

The Centennial Peace and Disarmament Symposium was probably the most ambitious and successful peace conference ever held in Canada. It was one of the two highlight events in a week-long peace festival organized by the Vancouver Centennial Commission, co-chaired by Mayor Michael Harcourt and Michael G. Francis. The other key event of the week was Vancouver's annual Walk For Peace, organized by End the Arms Race, a coalition of 230 peace-supporting groups.

The Vancouver Peace Festival, including the Peace and Disarmament Symposium, was planned over a year in advance by a subcommittee of the Vancouver Centennial Commission, ably chaired by Alderman Bruce Yorke, who played a major role in organizing the many events of the festival. Michael Francis, Robert Dubberley, Dennis Ottewell, Frank Kennedy, Leonard Schein, Michael Fisher, Foster Fried, Valley Hennel King, Charlotte Baynes and many others worked actively on the committee to make the festival a success. Besides the Peace and Disarmament Symposium, the Peace Festival organized a moving display of artifacts from the Peace Museum in Hiroshima; a large peace tent for cultural events and workshops; a peace film festival; a special one-day youth conference; and an interfaith religious celebration. The committee which specifically planned the Peace and Disarmament Symposium included

Jean McCutcheon, Karen Kruse, Gary Marchant, George Spiegelman, Sheena Lambert, James Foulks, and Thomas Perry—the latter two acting as co-chairpersons.

Many other people played absolutely vital roles in carrying out the meticulous work required to make the symposium and festival run smoothly. We thank especially Sheena Lambert, the Peace Festival Coordinator; Beverly Olds, for publicity and media relations; Paul Branston, for organizing the peace tent; Erika Simpson, for ticket sales; Allen Banner, for poster distribution and publicity; and Michiko Sakata, Sandy Frame and Andrew Milne, for their work on the Hiroshima Artifacts Exhibition. We also thank Lois Roy, Brenda Milne, Thelma Ruck-Keene, Pam Perry, Dan Holmberg and Kathy Abrosimoff, who assisted in various capacities.

Neither the Peace and Disarmament Symposium, nor the other events of the Vancouver Peace Festival, could have taken place without generous financial support. We are particularly grateful to the Vancouver City Council, which strongly encouraged the festival and provided major funding through the Vancouver Centennial Commission. Generous contributions of funds were also received from the Walter and Duncan Gordon Foundation in Toronto, the Arms Control and Disarmament Division of the Department of External Affairs in Ottawa, the government of British Columbia, the British Columbia chapter of Canadian Physicians for the Prevention of Nuclear War (Physicians for Social Responsibility), and from Mr. Harry Walker. Funding essential to produce the book came from generous grants from the Canadian Institute for International Peace and Security, and from the Walter and Duncan Gordon Foundation. We thank the Vancouver Centennial Commission for its continuous help and encouragement during the production of this book.

As co-editors, we particularly thank all of the participants in the Peace and Disarmament Symposium for their contributions to this book. The experts from twelve different countries who travelled to Vancouver to address the symposium, chair the sessions, or draft the Vancouver Proposals for Peace did so often at great personal sacrifice of time and effort. We feel sure that readers will appreciate the worth of their contributions as much as we have. We thank Sheena Lambert and Lori Thicke for editorial assistance in the production of this book. Thanks also to Joy Woodsworth, who typed it and to Chris Bergthorson, who generously contributed his time and talent to design it.

The Vancouver Centennial Peace Festival, with its Peace and Disarmament Symposium and the Walk for Peace, were held to honour Vancouver's 100th birthday, and in recognition of Vancouver's reputation as the peace capital of North America. We hope this book will help in the long and arduous process of ridding the world of nuclear weapons, and achieving multilateral disarmament. If we succeed, all who helped to make the Vancouver Centennial Peace Festival a success may have guaranteed a 200th birthday celebration for their grandchildren in Vancouver, as well as continued life for people all over the world.

Vancouver, B.C.—The beautiful cities of the world must not be destroyed

CHAPTER 1
Introduction: How to Use This Book

THOMAS L. PERRY, M.D. and
JAMES G. FOULKS, Ph.D., M.D.

This book contains the proceedings of the Vancouver Centennial Peace
and Disarmament Symposium which took place in the Orpheum Theatre
in Vancouver from April 24 to 26, 1986. The Peace and Disarmament
Symposium was one of two key events in an eight-day Peace Festival,
held to honour the 100th birthday of Vancouver, the city which calls itself the peace capital of North America. The Peace Festival and the
symposium had been planned for over a year by a committee of the Vancouver Centennial Commission under the able leadership of Vancouver
Alderman Bruce Yorke. The individuals and organizations deserving
great credit for their hard work and financial help in making this enterprise possible are noted in the Acknowledgments section of this book.

Early in the planning of the Peace and Disarmament Symposium, it
was considered important to publish the proceedings of the symposium in
book form so as to make its contents available to a wide group of readers
in Canada and elsewhere who might benefit from the thoughtful presentations of experts from twelve countries who came to Vancouver for the
symposium.

The book is entitled *End the Arms Race —Fund Human Needs,* for two
reasons. Firstly, this is what the symposium was all about. The speakers,
the chairpersons and the audience were all deeply concerned with ending
the arms race, knowing that there can be no effective response to the
deaths, injuries, devastation and environmental havoc which would inevitably and immediately follow a nuclear war. All participants in the
symposium were concerned with the prevention of a nuclear holocaust.
But the participants were also determined to decrease militarism and end
the escalating arms race in conventional, biological and chemical

9

Thomas L. Perry and James G. Foulks

weapons. How can war be made less likely, and security be increased for all of us, West and East, North and South? The symposium participants were also deeply concerned with redirecting the resources of the world to solve the massive economic, social, educational and health problems that affect a majority of all human beings, especially those who live in the underdeveloped countries. The symposium participants passionately wanted to fund *human needs* instead of funding the arms race.

Secondly, the book's title is appropriate because it is the slogan of End the Arms Race—Vancouver's very successful coalition of approximately 230 British Columbia peace and peace-supporting organizations. Each year since 1982, End the Arms Race has organized a Walk for Peace, inviting thousands of Vancouverites to take part in what is the largest annual walk for peace anywhere in North America.

This book is meant for serious reading by Canadians, Americans, and anyone familiar with the English language, who wish to understand better the problems which lead to international tensions, and how they can be decreased. It is packed with useful information and ideas which are clearly presented and can help everyone improve his or her contribution to the peace movement. Much of the information is new, and has rarely been discussed in peace and disarmament meetings, especially the emphasis this book places on the moral aspects of wasting the earth's scarce resources in preparing for war.

The response of the audience at the five sessions of the Peace and Disarmament Symposium, each of which lasted for three and a half hours, testified to the excellence of the presentations. The audience, which ranged from 900 to 1700 people, stayed until the very end of each session, paying strict attention, making notes, submitting questions, and applauding, laughing, or groaning at appropriate points. On a number of occasions, the audience rose to give speakers sustained standing ovations. It is a pity that this book cannot convey the sound effects of the audience's enthusiasm. We hope that some of the exciting ambience of the symposium is reflected in the lively question and answer periods that ended each session. Each speaker's entire presentation is included in the

James G. Foulks, Ph.D., M.D., is a professor of Pharmacology and Therapeutics at the University of British Columbia (UBC), and is a past president of the Canadian Association of University Teachers. He is an active member of Science for Peace. Thomas L. Perry, M.D., a neuroscientist, is also a professor of Pharmacology and Therapeutics at UBC. He works with Canadian Physicians for the Prevention of Nuclear War (formerly known as Physicians for Social Responsibility). Both Dr. Foulks and Dr. Perry are World War II veterans and have been activists in the peace movement for many years.

text with minimal changes made by the editors for grammatical and stylistic uniformity.

The questions answered by the speakers in the panel discussions are only a tiny fraction of those which were submitted in written form by the audience. The shortage of time prevented most questions from being dealt with by the speakers. Their answers have been reproduced with minimal editing for the sake of clarity and to eliminate redundancy.

The book follows the general order of the symposium itself. The first session (part I) was concerned with the current status of the nuclear arms race: where the Geneva negotiations have taken us, and what effect the United States Strategic Defense Initiative (SDI)—"Star Wars"—may have on the arms race. Part I contains individual chapters by Professor Kosta Tsipis, Rear Admiral Eugene Carroll and General Gert Bastian. Kosta Tsipis' presentation in chapter 3 is one of the best explanations we have ever heard about why the Star Wars program is not technically feasible. He clearly describes the technical difficulties of destroying nuclear warheads in the boost phase of missiles, in the mid-course phase, and in the terminal phase where nuclear weapons re-enter the atmosphere. He estimates the enormous amounts of energy generation required for SDI, and shows that the cost for each missile kill, for 1000 to 1500 incoming Soviet missiles, would range between $400 and $2100 million per missile, far more than the cost of effective Soviet countermeasures! Chapter 3 should be essential reading for every person who does not yet understand why Star Wars cannot increase North American security, but actually makes us all the more vulnerable to destruction from a nuclear war. Admiral Carroll's speech (chapter 2) is outstanding for its clarity and perception and is required reading for every person who wants to be more effective at working for peace and security. He emphasizes the mutual security advantages that could be achieved by both West and East from a nuclear weapons test ban, and outlines very logically a sequence of steps for achieving multilateral nuclear disarmament. General Bastian's talk (chapter 4) emphasizes the objections to the deployment of intermediate-range nuclear weapons in Europe, and the goals and activities of the European peace movements. The panel discussion which followed Session I (chapter 5) was extremely lively and informative.

Session II (part II) dealt with the topic of how the arms race is hurting the economies of developed countries, especially the Canadian economy. Both Bishop Remi De Roo and David Werlin in chapters 7 and 8 describe in detail the ways in which social conditions and employment in Canada have suffered from diversion of funding to the military, as does Kathleen Wallace-Deering, chairperson for Session II (chapter 6). In chapters 7 and 8 Bishop De Roo and David Werlin pay a great deal of attention to the need for conversion from military to socially useful production.

Trade unionists, and everyone concerned with improving health care and education, restoring social services and decreasing unemployment in Canada and other countries, will find these two chapters a valuable source of information and ideas. Professor John Kenneth Galbraith in chapter 9 presents a scholarly and sometimes sardonic description of the way the military power controls economics and politics in the United States. Again, the lively question and answer session which concluded Session II (chapter 10) (before an audience of over 1700 people) makes exciting reading.

Session III (part III) was devoted to discussions of the harmful effects of the arms race on the health, social and economic conditions of people in the Third World. This session also laid particular emphasis on what persons of conscience ought to be doing to alleviate the terrible effects of the arms race on the world's poor—the "devastation before detonation," as it has been termed by International Physicians for the Prevention of Nuclear War. The speeches of Bishop Thomas Gumbleton (chapter 12), the Very Reverend Lois M. Wilson (chapter 13) and the session's chairperson, Joanna Miller, (chapter 11) detail the suffering of people in Third World countries because of the waste of money and resources (worldwide, U.S. $800 to $900 billion annually) on war preparations. These contributions are important reading for everyone concerned with the welfare of humankind as a whole. One of us has added material to document how much the world's poor are suffering (chapter 17), and how readily problems of ill health and starvation might be solved by redirection of military spending to funding of human needs. Ambassador Douglas Roche in chapter 14 and Göran Ohlin in chapter 15 present the positions of the Canadian government and of the United Nations respectively on these issues.

The religious and ethical aspects of preparing for nuclear war are dealt with brilliantly by a prominent Protestant churchwoman (Reverend Lois M. Wilson in chapter 13), and by three leading Roman Catholic churchmen (Bishop Thomas Gumbleton in chapter 12, Dom Helder Camara in chapter 16, and Bishop Remi De Roo in chapter 7). These contributions should be invaluable in encouraging churchgoers to take an active part in the peace movement, and we hope readers will encourage wide use of *End the Arms Race—Fund Human Needs* in the religious community.

Session IV of the symposium (part IV) was an action-oriented session. How can individuals work most effectively to prevent nuclear war and promote multilateral disarmament? What can cities and small countries do? Both Joan Ruddock (chapter 20) and Petra Kelly (chapter 21) give eloquent descriptions of what people, and particularly women, are doing in their respective countries (Britain and the Federal Republic of Germany) to promote peace. Mayor Takeshi Araki of Hiroshima describes in chapter 22 the initiatives taken by his city, as well as Nagasaki, to forge an international alliance of city mayors who hope to prevent the tragedies which struck Hiroshima and Nagasaki from ever happening again. Vancouver Alderwoman Libby Davies, who chaired Session IV, and Gary Marchant have added in chapter 23 a description of the peace-related activities of the city government in Vancouver, and a discussion of the legal and moral responsibilities of municipal administrations in Canada to protect their residents from the destruction nuclear war would bring. A highlight of Session IV was James Anderton's stirring speech (chapter 19) describing how New Zealanders made their country a genuinely nuclear-weapons-free zone. Peace-minded people who become discouraged with the apparent lack of progress towards meaningful disarmament will find chapter 19 a real morale booster.

The final session of the Peace and Disarmament Symposium (part V) featured powerful talks by Paul Warnke (chapter 25), Vitaly Zhurkin (chapter 26) and Professor Michael Pentz (chapter 27). The session was chaired by Canada's Ambassador to the United Nations, Stephen Lewis. Each of the speakers discussed what governments can and should do to prevent nuclear war and promote disarmament. There was a surprising amount of agreement between Paul Warnke from the United States and Vitaly Zhurkin from the Soviet Union. The panel discussion which concluded Session V (chapter 28) is especially stimulating.

This book also includes in part VI abridged versions of speeches by Dr. Helen Caldicott (chapter 29) and by science broadcaster Dr. David Suzuki (chapter 30) which were given in Vancouver during the month preceding the symposium. Both of them addressed large audiences in fund-raising and educational events designed to promote the Peace Festival and the annual Walk for Peace. They graciously permitted us to reproduce parts of their speeches to enrich further the contents of this book.

Readers will find much in this book that is controversial. It does not present any single point of view, other than the imperative of preventing nuclear war and formulating strategies for peace. Speakers at the Peace and Disarmament Symposium did not all agree with each other, and careful reading of the questions and answers will show that the audience did not concur with everything they heard.

For instance, this symposium offered illuminating opinions from several leading military and academic authorities as to the forces which impel the nuclear arms race. Along with Admiral Carroll, Professor Tsipis feels that the insistence of the Reagan administration on proceeding with Star Wars (SDI), even at the expense of scuttling existing Anti-Ballistic Missile and Strategic Arms Limitation treaties, will lead to an impasse in negotiations for agreements on nuclear weapons reductions and arms control. In their view, SDI has aroused false expectations which cannot be fulfilled, but instead will lead to an expanded but more unstable and insecure military balance. Professor Tsipis concurs in the conclusion reached by Professor Galbraith that the real purpose of SDI is to provide a reassuring façade of safety in order to dampen the public fears which generated widespread support in Europe and the United States for a nuclear weapons freeze and for arms reductions. They suggest that the illusory but comforting hope for a protective shield has been promoted by an administration whose policies are dominated by those who do not believe that arms control is a desirable goal.

In chapter 9, Professor Galbraith argues that an action-reaction sequence between the great national blocs fuels the arms race under the impetus of an unbridled military power which commands huge financial, material, scientific, and technological resources, and which is no longer subject to effective civilian controls. The necessity for the United States government to maintain the image of an implacable, immoral and threatening enemy in order to justify the enormous appropriations which its appetite for expansion demands, explains the demonology which is practiced by its purveyors. Professor Michael Pentz also identifies the driving force behind the arms race as the military-industrial-bureaucratic-technical-scientific complex, which President Eisenhower warned about in his farewell address. He describes it as self-propelled, successfully feeding on fear and mistrust, in spite of its essential irrationality.

Petra Kelly attributes the drive to attain military power and many other violent and oppressive features of contemporary society to traditional patriarchal values which continue to predominate throughout the world. She advocates the wider use of nonviolent resistance and civil disobedience to safeguard our natural environment and to seek social justice in a disarmed world. She as well as several other contributors are, to varying extents, inclined to see some degree of symmetry in the factors operating to sustain the arms race in both East and West. Bishop Gumbleton characterizes the arms race as an "act of aggression against the poor," stressing the essential immorality of the priority which the wealthy nations give to armaments over the need to redress the suffering of the impoverished multitudes, especially those who live in developing countries. He sees the arms race as a means to protect the imperialistic monopoly of the nations of the northern hemisphere, particularly the United States, in order to preserve their privileged position. This interpretation of the arms race is also reflected in the contributions of Bishop De Roo, Reverend Lois Wilson, and Dom Helder Camara. Others (General Bastian and Professor Zhurkin) assign greater responsibility to the Western bloc, which has generally led the way in introducing new types of weaponry, basing its military policy on an exaggeration of the perceived threat to its security and on the effort to achieve military superiority in order to bolster its worldwide economic and political objectives.

The contribution of scientific research to the technological innovations which are leading toward a precarious, computer-controlled and hair-trigger deployment of nuclear weapons is mentioned by several contributors to the symposium, and receives particular emphasis in the separate presentations of Dr. Helen Caldicott (chapter 29) and Dr. David Suzuki (chapter 30). Dr. Caldicott's suggestion that the time may have come to abandon all scientific research is rationalized by two rather disparate justifications: either because we now know enough to solve all the problems of as-yet-unmet human needs, or because we already know too well how to exercise our capacity to destroy all human life in a nuclear holocaust. In the editors' view, the first proposition is not tenable. For example, numerous outstanding health problems (cancer, atherosclerotic heart disease, degenerative neurological diseases, and mental illnesses) remain to be solved and this can only be accomplished by future research. As for the second, it is difficult to see how arresting the progress of knowledge can help us to close the Pandora's box of nuclear weaponry which science and technology have pried open, although one might reasonably argue that further scientific development in weaponry threatens to make our plight even more dangerous and less secure than is now the case.

Readers may wish to compare Dr. Caldicott's suggestion that scientific progress be arrested with the analysis of the social impact of science and technology presented by Dr. Suzuki. He appeals for society to become more prudent and less precipitous in its haste to find technological applications for all advances in scientific understanding, inasmuch as the consequences often are far-reaching and unforeseen, because of the fragmentary way in which much scientific knowledge is accumulated, which in turn makes a proper weighing of the potential costs and benefits of technology too uncertain for safety.

Both Dr. Caldicott and Dr. Suzuki deplore the willingness of so many scientists to prostitute their talents at the altar of mammon in order to enjoy the blandishments of Pentagon funding for their research endeavors. Dr. Suzuki entertains the hope that a broader education for scientists might heighten their ethical sensibilities. On the other hand, note should be taken of the leading role which many American scientists have played in promoting opposition to the Reagan administration's plans to extend the arms race into space. However, rather than calling for a moratorium on scientific investigation, Dr. Suzuki emphasizes the need for more extensive education of the public and the politicians whom they elect to office, so that they may become more scientifically literate.

We find this approach persuasive. A wide appreciation of scientific principles, increased skepticism in weighing unsubstantiated claims, a more demanding attitude toward the credibility of evidence, and greater rigour in logical reasoning on the part of the general population, might strengthen the political pressures for the steps which can bring the arms race to an end. A more enlightened and scientifically literate public would be more objective in seeing through prejudices, and hence more apt to reject the mythology and the political stereotypes described by Professor Galbraith, which are fostered by the military-industrial complex in order to justify the quest for military solutions to international disputes. Scientific understanding and scientific techniques, which are constantly being improved and refined, also have an indispensable role to play in arriving at the procedures which will be necessary to implement and verify arms control and disarmament agreements. Although platitudinous, it is nevertheless true to say that science is the servant of human purposes. We must all do our part to see that the good ones prevail.

Admiral Carroll, Professor Galbraith, Ambassador Warnke, Professor Zhurkin, and Professor Pentz each specify a sequence of steps which could lead to arms reductions, and each emphasizes the importance of an agreement to ban all further testing of nuclear weapons as the crucial first step which could pave the way for further progress, while arresting the momentum of the otherwise unrestrained pace of deployment of increasingly unstable and destructive weapon systems. Joan Ruddock and Michael Pentz see an important place for unilateral initiatives for disarmament, inviting reciprocity and opening the way for further measures to reduce armaments. Several speakers (Admiral Carroll, Professor Tsipis, General Bastian, and Mayor Araki) also stress the value of expanded programs of exchange and people-to-people communication in breaking down the barriers of fear and mistrust which now divide the world, in order to replace confrontation with co-operation. There is general agreement among the symposium participants that popular pressure, based on a more enlightened public, and expressed through mass peace movements and all levels of government, is required to generate the political will necessary to achieve meaningful progress toward disarmament.

In addition to the publication and distribution of the proceedings of the symposium, the organizers thought it would be useful for the participants to attempt to agree on a brief statement setting forth their joint conclusions as to the most urgent and important practical measures which individuals and governments might undertake to prevent nuclear war and to redirect the talents and resources now wasted on the arms race to the fulfillment of human needs. To this end, two distinguished persons with expertise in drafting documents on peace and disarmament were invited to receive advance suggestions from the participants during the months preceding the symposium, and to prepare a preliminary draft for their collective consideration. We feel exceptionally fortunate that Ambassador Sean MacBride of Ireland, winner of the 1974 Nobel Peace Prize, and Professor Dorothy Hodgkin of England, Nobel Laureate in chemistry and President of the Pugwash Conferences on Science and World Affairs, were willing to accept this responsibility. The participants devoted a full day to a formal discussion of this material, and the document, entitled *The Vancouver Proposals for Peace,* was adopted in its final form after further discussion at a luncheon meeting the following day. A few of the symposium participants (John Kenneth Galbraith, David Werlin, Bishop Gumbleton, Ambassador Roche and Ambassador Lewis) were unable to take part in these discussions.

On the last night of the Peace and Disarmament Symposium, Professor Dorothy Hodgkin dramatically read the Vancouver Proposals for Peace to a large audience in the Orpheum Theatre. They were adopted by acclamation. The next day, April 27, 1986, the Vancouver Proposals for Peace were again read out, by Paul Warnke from the United States and Vitaly Zhurkin from the Soviet Union, to the mass rally ending the annual Walk for Peace. The proposals, reproduced immediately after this introductory chapter, have been sent to the heads of state of the United States and the Soviet Union and all other NATO and Warsaw Pact countries, to the heads of state of the six countries which issued the Five-Continent Appeal, and to the United Nations.

We hope readers will find *End the Arms Race—Fund Human Needs* a stimulating and useful book. We urge you to encourage your family, friends, work associates, church and organizational colleagues, and neighbours to buy and especially to *read* this book. We hope most of all that it will spur people to become involved in the campaign to prevent nuclear war, and to address the real and solvable problems of billions of this planet's inhabitants.

The Vancouver Proposals for Peace

''End the Arms Race—Fund Human Needs''—this is the message of Vancouver's Walk for Peace in the year of its 100th anniversary.

It is natural that this city, which has declared itself to be a nuclear-weapons-free zone and which has, on many occasions, urged the cause of peace, should have chosen this occasion to sponsor the Vancouver Centennial Peace and Disarmament Symposium.

The people of Vancouver and their elected representatives are only too conscious of the threat posed by the arms race to the survival of humanity and of the tremendous waste of resources which it causes. This waste of resources has serious consequences everywhere, and we cannot ignore the fact that in many parts of the developed world there is unemployment, hardship and poverty which, although less severe, is otherwise not unlike that in the Third World.

In the nuclear age, war is no longer a way of resolving conflicts between nations. In 1961, the United States and the USSR came to the conclusion that war could be eliminated only by general and complete disarmament and agreed on eight principles upon which all further negotiations should be based, and this was agreed by the United Nations General Assembly. Eight years ago, the United Nations General Assembly declared unanimously we must end the arms race and proceed to disarmament or face annihilation. Yet, despite this and other resolutions of the United Nations, we face the fact that no progress has been made towards nuclear or any other form of disarmament, despite the fact that most, if not all, of the thousands of nuclear explosive devices that have been piled up are militarily useless.

On the contrary, we are moving into a new phase of escalation and counter-escalation of the nuclear arms race and, if this process is not stopped and reversed, the inevitable outcome will be a further reduction in the security of the nuclear-weapons powers themselves and indeed of the whole world. We are rapidly approaching the point at which there will be equality of security only in the sense that there will be no security for anyone.

The catastrophe we face is not inevitable. There are immediate opportunities to check this suicidal process and gain time to reverse it:

1. A Comprehensive Test Ban Treaty, stopping all further testing of nuclear weapons. We urge the United States to respond to the Soviet initiative by immediately ceasing nuclear testing and urge the Soviet Union to extend its moratorium. We call upon other nuclear states to stop all nuclear weapons tests.

2. A ban on all weapons in space.

3. A freeze on development, testing or deployment of new nuclear weapons and their delivery systems.

4. Immediate and substantial reductions in the existing nuclear arsenals.

5. The establishment of nuclear weapons-free zones in Central Europe, the Nordic and Balkan regions, and the Indian and North Atlantic Oceans, and compliance by the nuclear-weapons states with the newly-established South Pacific Nuclear-Free Zone Treaty.

6. Renunciation by all states, and in particular by the nuclear-weapons states, of the use or threat of force and intervention in the affairs of other states, and a commitment to negotiate an agreement to that effect.

7. Recognition that the arms race is having serious negative effects, both on the nations involved and on the whole world, and that it is

now urgently necessary to reduce substantially all military budgets and transfer the resources thus saved to the promotion of human well-being.

These are steps that can and must be taken now. None of them need wait for long negotiations and formal treaties. The process must be started and independent initiatives are therefore needed. The Report of the Secretary General of the United Nations on unilateral or independent nuclear disarmament measures, adopted in December 1984 by 126 votes to 1 by the United Nations General Assembly requires far more serious consideration and action.

We feel that the proposals made by General Secretary Gorbachev on 15th January, 1986 could lead to significant progress. We urge, therefore, that the existing disarmament forums consider these proposals and develop a mutually acceptable approach to the achievement of nuclear disarmament which can then be jointly agreed and implemented.

The measures we have proposed are essential first steps back from the edge of oblivion and toward a peaceful world. It is within the power of the people of each and every country to exercise their right to determine and preserve their own future, to intervene and compel a change of course. We particularly commend to the smaller nations the positive role they can play in bringing about this change.

Parallel with these changes, new creative initiatives are needed to address the problems of hunger, disease, education, environment and other global problems, and indeed to the establishment of a just international economic order.

From this peaceful city we appeal to our sisters and brothers everywhere:

Let us act together now to end the arms race and to fund human needs.

PHOTO: DAN KEETON

Professor Dorothy Hodgkin

Professor Dorothy Hodgkin has had a brilliant academic career in chemistry at Oxford University, as well as a long history of dedication to the ideals of international understanding and world peace. An expert in the study of complex molecules of biological importance by means of X-ray diffraction crystallography, she was elected a member of the Royal Society in Britain at the early age of thirty-seven, and she received the Nobel Prize for chemistry in 1964. She has been the recipient of many prestigious awards and honourary degrees for her contributions to science. In recent years, Dorothy Hodgkin has served as president of the Pugwash Conferences on Science and World Affairs. These conferences, convened several times each year, bring together eminent scientists and senior government advisors from all over the world for informal discussions of urgent public issues relating to arms control and disarmament. The technical expertise of the participants in the Pugwash Conferences has paved the way for a number of successful disarmament treaties.

PHOTO: DAN KEETON

Sean MacBride

Sean MacBride was awarded the Nobel Peace Prize in 1974 for his life-long support of justice, peace and international solidarity. As a young man, Sean MacBride played an active part in the movement for Irish freedom. He founded the Irish Republican Party, and was a member of the Irish Republican Army from 1920 to 1936. He was imprisoned on numerous occasions for his political activities. Called to the bar in 1943, he appeared in many leading cases before international courts. He served as Ireland's Minister of External Affairs from 1948 to 1951. He was secretary-general of the International Commission of Jurists in Geneva from 1963 to 1971. In 1961, Sean MacBride helped found Amnesty International, the world's most prominent organization for aiding political prisoners, and he received the American Medal of Justice in 1978. He is currently president of the International Peace Bureau, and of the Irish United Nations Association, and he has served as an ambassador for the United Nations in relation to Namibia. He has written numerous books including The Imperatives of Survival *and* Is Nuclear Survival Possible?

PHOTO: JEAN MCCUTCHEON

Drafting the Vancouver Proposals for Peace: left to right, Dom Helder Camara, James Anderton, Göran Ohlin, Marion Dewar, Vitaly Zhurkin, Kathleen Wallace-Deering, Sean MacBride

PHOTO: JEAN MCCUTCHEON

Drafting the Vancouver Proposals for Peace: left to right, Vitaly Zhurkin (with glasses), Kathleen Wallace-Deering, James G. Foulks, Paul Warnke, Sean MacBride, Dorothy Hodgkin

PHOTO: SEAN GRIFFIN

Professor Vitaly Zhurkin and Paul Warnke after reading the Vancouver Proposals for Peace at the public rally ending the Walk for Peace

PART I

Current Status of the Nuclear Arms Race

Rear Admiral Eugene J. Carroll, Jr.

CHAPTER 2
A New Concept For Security In the Nuclear Age

REAR ADMIRAL EUGENE J. CARROLL, JR.

The sovereign nation-states which make up the world order today are distinguished more by their differences than by their similarities. Almost all share one characteristic, however: they assert the absolute right to possess the weapons of war which they use, or threaten to use, in pursuit of their own interests. This right is the quintessential element of sovereignty. Each nation does all that it can afford to do to maintain military forces strong enough to advance its interests in competition with other nations.

Despite the obvious purpose of military force, only the most aggressive nations ever admit that they invest in military power for any reason

Eugene J. Carroll, Jr., Rear Admiral, United States Navy (retired), has had a long and distinguished naval career, including combat duty in Korea and Vietnam. He was promoted to the rank of rear admiral in 1972, acting as commander of Task Force 60, the carrier striking force of the United States Sixth Fleet in the Mediterranean. Subsequently, he was appointed to the staff of General Alexander Haig in NATO, and later became assistant deputy chief of naval operations for Plans, Policy and Operations in the Pentagon. In that capacity, he engaged in American naval planning for both conventional and nuclear war. Since his retirement from the navy in 1980, Admiral Carroll has worked as deputy director at the Center for Defense Information, in Washington, D.C. He is actively engaged in research and analysis on defence issues, and writes and speaks frequently on the need for rational American military programs which will not fuel the arms race and increase the danger of nuclear war.

other than to maintain peace. The Roman dictum two thousand years ago was: "If you would have peace, prepare for war." Almost any extreme of military preparation can be, and is, justified under this rubric, which lives on today in the political slogan "peace through strength."

This simple political phrase sounds eminently reasonable, even commendable. However, it masks a purpose which is far from benign. The slogan as applied in the world today should really be written: "Peace on our terms through superior military strength." The objective of one nation or alliance is to gain enough military superiority to coerce or intimidate another nation or alliance into behaviour which is acceptable to the superior power. The system is often called a "zero-sum game": one party increases its security and control over events by rendering the other party less secure and with less control over events which concern both sides. The pursuit of "peace through strength" produces a win-lose relationship between the contestants.

The entire history of the nuclear age has been driven by the dynamics of "peace through strength." Each side, claiming that it seeks only to deter war, has constantly expanded its nuclear war-fighting forces, attempting to attain levels of nuclear destructive force higher than the opponent's. Because each side sees the adversary's latest nuclear initiative as an increase in relative strength which must be countered, the pursuit of nuclear deterrence has been the engine of the nuclear arms race. The fuel for that engine has been provided by technology, which continuously provides new means of rendering nuclear destruction more efficient, more complete and more certain. Each advance in the technology of nuclear warfare has fuelled yet another round in the competition for superior war-fighting forces.

From time to time the adversaries have shown some interest in moderating that competition through various arms control measures. Unfortunately, that interest has never motivated a successful effort to cut off the fuel to the engine of the arms race. All negotiations have proceeded in what is accurately described as the "talk-test-build" format. That is, talks about controlling, limiting or reducing nuclear weapons are always accompanied by continued testing and production of new nuclear weapons and delivery systems. Talks and agreements develop very slowly; testing creates new weapons far more rapidly. The decade of the seventies produced ten arms control agreements; in the same decade both sides tripled the number of strategic nuclear weapons they aimed at each other. The increases were largely in the form of multiple warheads on new missiles. Both the smaller warheads and the improved missiles became possible only through active test programs during negotiations.

The continuous expansion of nuclear arsenals long ago produced the mutually suicidal relationship between East and West known as MAD, the acronym for Mutual Assured Destruction. This is not a doctrine, a strategy or a voluntary relationship. It is simply a fact of life created by more than fifty thousand nuclear weapons. It is a trap that, created by technology, evolved through testing into arsenals which can destroy all of the adversaries in a nuclear war, and possibly all life on earth. Technology created the trap; now newer and more destructive weapons offer only the prospect of making the trap tighter and more deadly.

It is the recognition of this frightening fact, plus the unrelenting pursuit of "peace through strength," which will soon create an even more dangerous world. Mr. Reagan has turned to defensive technology in an effort to escape the MAD trap built through offensive technology. Calling on American scientists and engineers to make us safe, he has invoked a vision of the world in which nuclear weapons will be rendered "impotent and obsolete."

The president's glorious vision of a world made safe through technology has a seductive appeal, but the military program which would make a reality of his vision falls far short of its goal. It is not the purpose of my talk to document the fatal flaws of the Strategic Defense Initiative (SDI) program; but it is necessary to understand its relationship to "peace through strength" and the grave dangers that SDI will create. "Peace through strength" requires military superiority, and SDI is a desperate attempt to escape the MAD trap by establishing American superiority, both offensive and defensive, over the Soviet Union.

The first evidence to support this conclusion can be found in Secretary of Defense Caspar Weinberger's speech to the United States armed services, in which he told them to prepare nuclear war-fighting capabilities which "will prevail even under conditions of prolonged nuclear war." In implementing this strategy he said that the United States "must ensure that treaties and agreements do not foreclose opportunities to develop these [military space] capabilities." He went on to say that the "DOD [Department of Defense] will accelerate those areas of technology offering the potential for significant military advantage and develop those space systems that have been shown to enhance the U.S. military balance of power."

In that last statement he identifies the fundamental premise on which SDI rests: American technology is superior to that of the Soviet Union, therefore the United States will win a military space race. Clearly, the Soviets concur with that premise, which in large measure explains their eagerness to ban all weapons in space. The United States, on the other hand, calls for reductions in offensive systems, while it develops, and plans to deploy, space-based defences. This basic conflict of priorities between the United States and the Soviet Union explains why SDI cannot succeed.

The United States, proceeding under the premise that it has the advantage in space defence technologies, nevertheless expects the Soviets to co-operate in making major reductions in offensive systems, while both sides develop space-based defences. Both countries have recognized that this shift would clearly benefit the United States: if carried far enough, the Soviets would be effectively disarmed by superior American defences, while still remaining vulnerable to an American attack. In effect, SDI can succeed only if the Soviets agree to co-operate in a relationship which would leave them inferior to the United States. This fundamental illogic in the case for SDI is the ''smoking gun'' which dooms the president's vision to failure.

Also critical is the fact that SDI tests scheduled for 1988 will violate the 1972 Anti-Ballistic Missile Treaty. Three former United States secretaries of defense have said that such actions will spell the end of any form of effective arms control. For all of their shortcomings to date, the arms control measures practiced today do serve to put some effective controls on the American-Soviet nuclear competition, thereby making the world somewhat safer. The alternative, a totally unconstrained arms race, is manifestly more dangerous.

Furthermore, even if the SDI program could come into effective operation in the early twenty-first century, as is envisioned today, the Strategic Defense Initiative would still not eliminate the present MAD balance of terror. Secretary Weinberger reported to Congress: ''With defences, the U.S. seeks not to replace deterrence, but to enhance it.'' The growing United States budget for offensive nuclear weapons makes it abundantly clear that the threat of massive retaliation will remain the backbone of United States deterrent policy into the next century. MAD will remain a fact of life in a world in which nations possess the means to destroy each other.

Finally, SDI looks to the creation of an uncertain balance of imperfect defences and threatening offensive forces which will be totally unstable in time of crisis. The United States Congressional Office of Technology Assessment explains the instability this way:

> There is great uncertainty about the strategic situation that would arise if BMD [Ballistic Missile Defence] deployment took place without agreement between the United States and the Soviet Union. . . . No one could know with confidence whether a situation of acute crisis instability . . . could be avoided. . . . Each would have powerful incentives to ''use or lose'' his system, to

attack before the other side did. The one that struck first might substantially disarm the other side.*

The foregoing discussion suggests that a pursuit of ''peace through strength'' based on technological superiority can never succeed because there is no technological solution to Mutual Assured Destruction. There are no feasible means of building offensive forces which will spare the aggressor from a devastating retaliatory attack. Neither side will permit the other side to gain such a position of strength. Conversely, defensive technology offers no escape from MAD because no adversary will co-operate in a defensive relationship in which it is inferior. The solution to the problem of establishing a stable, enduring, peaceful world order in the nuclear age must be formed through political, not technological, means.

Is there a political solution? Yes, but it does not exist within a ''peace through strength'' concept. In a world with more than fifty thousand nuclear weapons, everyone must be safe or no one will be safe. Security cannot be relative, based on superiority, because efforts to create supe-riority drive the arms race, and that race is fuelled by technological ad-vances. Security must be mutual—that is, each side must be safe—and means must be found to increase the security of both sides equally. In short, safety is not a zero-sum game in which one side wins and one side loses. The only hope for the creation of a secure and peaceful world order is to abandon all efforts to achieve superior military capabilities with which to destroy the adversary. We must, instead, establish a ''mutual security'' system.

There is no possible way to start this process except through positive arms control measures which provide increased safety for all. There is no basis for enduring agreement on any arms control arrangement except mutual benefit. The new arrangements must be fully verifiable, in order to give everyone confidence that all parties are in substantial compliance and that neither side can gain significant military advantage by cheating. And finally, each agreement must lay a foundation for subsequent agree-ments which can successively slow, stop and reverse the arms race.

Given the past history of arms control efforts, it would seem that this prospect is highly unlikely. As stated before, however, all previous ne-gotiations have been in the ''talk-test-build'' format: while negotiating,

---

* Space does not permit full explanation of the many other liabilities of the Strategic Defense Initiative, but those interested may consult a highly readable, useful analysis of the SDI program, *Star Wars: Vision and Reality,* available from the Centre for Defense Information, 1500 Massachusetts Avenue N.W., Washington, D.C. 20005.

the parties have actively sought new weapons with which to achieve military superiority. If the political wisdom and will exist to abandon this dangerous goal, then the logical sequence of arms control priorities is well defined and the first essential step to avert a nuclear war is obvious.

Stop nuclear testing! Such an agreement has already largely been negotiated, including substantially improved verification procedures. The Tripartite Report (United States, United Kingdom and the Soviet Union) to the United Nations of July 31, 1980, outlines all the major elements of an effective test ban treaty. Furthermore, the recent Soviet test moratorium, plus their public commitment to new verification measures, constitute compelling evidence of a willingness on the part of the new Soviet leadership to end all nuclear testing. It is irresponsible, at the least, not to resume negotiations immediately to hammer out the final details of a test ban treaty. Every United States president since General Eisenhower has actively pursued such a treaty through negotiations with the Soviet Union. The Reagan administration is the first in a quarter-century to refuse to take part in test ban talks. Furthermore, both branches of Congress have sent President Reagan a message, loud and clear, to resume negotiations for a test ban. Failure to do so also constitutes a violation of the formal treaty obligations in the Limited Test Ban Treaty of 1963. In this agreement, the parties obligated themselves to end all nuclear tests, by saying that they sought ''to achieve the discontinuance of all test explosions of nuclear weapons for all time, determined to continue negotiations to this end. . . .'' Only the verification issue prevented agreement on a total test ban in 1963; but now many new and improved means of verification are available to guarantee that all parties would remain in compliance with a complete test ban.

If a nuclear explosion ban were adopted, military pressure for new delivery systems would decrease, simply because there would be no new weapons to deliver. A treaty to end the testing of new strategic delivery systems would be easily verifiable using present technology.

With these two agreements concluded, a third treaty to end the deployment of new nuclear systems would logically follow. No military commander wants untested weapons. Not only are they unsafe to use, but there is no way to know how well they might work—or even if they would work at all. It is equally impossible to plan effective uses for untested weapons and to train people to use them. In short, untested weapons are useless and cannot be deployed for any practical military purpose. An agreement to end the deployment of new nuclear weapon systems would be fully verifiable with the technical means already employed. Today, the number and location of deployed weapon systems is verified with great confidence on both sides.

These three agreements lead almost inevitably to a fourth treaty, a ban on the production of explosive nuclear materials and new strategic delivery systems. After all, if you cannot test or deploy new nuclear weapons, why build them at all? With fifty thousand nuclear weapons on hand, we do not need more weapons to destroy each other; and, with no way to test new technology, there is no way to make more destructive weapons, even if they could be deployed. Further production would, therefore, be a pure waste of valuable resources: unreliable, useless devices would be created which would have to be hidden and guarded for no rational purpose. Some unproved verification procedures, including on-site inspection, would be required for this fourth treaty, but both sides would have a strong incentive, and the confidence to agree to enhanced verification procedures at this point in the arms control process.

These four treaties would effectively "freeze" the nuclear arsenals on each side. Neither side could gain any advantage over the other, and further arms control negotiations would no longer be in the "talk-test-build" format. Testing and building would be over, and talks could proceed to produce real reductions in the excessive arsenals which exist today. Reductions could be made in an orderly, balanced way that would actually increase the safety of both sides and make it certain that neither had any intention or desire to plan the nuclear destruction of the other. Highest priority would be given to eliminating MIRVed [multiple, independently-targetable, re-entry vehicle] missiles, both land-based and sea-based.

Despite the tremendous benefits which these arms control measures would bring in terms of increased stability and the reduced risk of nuclear war, no one should regard them as a panacea. Arms control is not a magic wand which will soon, or easily, rid the world of nuclear danger. Instead, arms control agreements, starting with a nuclear test ban, must be paralleled with a broad attack on the many other problems of creating a "mutual security" system based on co-operation instead of confrontation. A system which resolves differences through co-operation and accommodation rather than military force will require foresight, wisdom and years of constructive effort if it is ever to emerge.

Just a brief list of the major problems confronting the world—the North-South economic imbalance, global pollution, water shortages, famine and over-population—suggest the magnitude of the long-term tasks which are at least as important as arms control. But arms control must come first! We must slow, stop and reverse the march to nuclear war, in order to buy time to devise a new system which will solve the other problems. Nuclear weapons are like a fever which must be controlled before the underlying disease of fear and distrust can be cured. In practical terms, progress in reducing military confrontation is also necessary to free the resources needed to attack the world's problems. Today the world spends at least $900 billion a year on weapons and war. Only a very small part of that incredible sum would help us to make rapid progress toward co-operative solutions of most of the world's pressing problems.

The nations of the world must choose soon between the alternatives. Is it to be "peace through strength," or is it to be mutual security for all? Time is running out, because the nuclear powers are now, in the name of peace, taking actions which guarantee the failure of nuclear deterrence. We face a rapidly growing risk of nuclear war—a war which no one wants, a war without winners, even a war without survivors. Arms control is not a panacea, but it can lead, one step at a time, away from nuclear catastrophe toward a world of mutual security. The first essential step to start this process is to end nuclear testing. This is the first step on the path of hope, the path that leads to a safe and peaceful future, while "peace through strength" leads to nuclear war—to a world with no future.

Humankind has faced great challenges in the past and found the solutions which have preserved the glorious, beautiful, fragile world in which we live today. I am confident that once again we will have the wisdom to choose the path of hope.

CHAPTER 3

Technical and Operational Considerations of Space-Based Defensive Systems

PROFESSOR KOSTA TSIPIS

On March 23, 1983, President Ronald Reagan called upon the scientific community to give his country the means to render nuclear weapons "impotent and obsolete." Six days later, in remarks at the National Space Club, Mr. Reagan further explained: "We're *not* discussing a concept just to enhance deterrence, not just an addition to our offensive forces, but research to determine the feasibility of a non-nuclear defence system; a shield that could prevent nuclear weapons from reaching their targets."

This means that whatever the system envisioned by the president, it must be able to intercept *all* nuclear weapons aimed at the United States, since even if a few reached their urban targets the United States would suffer tens of millions of dead and wounded, and the loss of cities worth hundreds of billions of dollars—to weapons that cost just a few million each.

Yet the Strategic Defense Initiative Organization (SDIO), established to implement Mr. Reagan's plan, aims at developing systems to counter only ballistic missiles. No provisions are foreseen for defence against bombers and cruise missiles, which could deliver nuclear weapons against American targets; nor are provisions being made for preventing the clandestine introduction of nuclear explosives into the United States by ship, or even by truck or car—methods by which thousands of tons of narcotics enter America each year. Therefore, even if SDI were completely successful, the United States would still remain woefully vulnerable to nuclear attack.

A more realistic goal, but one which contradicts Mr. Reagan's call for a perfect defence, is promoted in White House documents, and by

Professor Kosta Tsipis

General Abrahamson, the director of SDIO. On October 25, 1984, the general said in a speech: "From the technical viewpoint, we are pursuing this program to increase deterrence and stability." And a White House paper on SDI issued in January 1985, avers that "the purpose of SDI is to identify ways to exploit recent advances in ballistic missile defence technologies that have potential for strengthening deterrence." But in April 1983, the President's Commission on Strategic Forces (the Scowcroft Commission) concluded: "The commission believes that *no* anti-ballistic missile defence technologies appear to combine practicality, survivability, low cost and technical effectiveness sufficiently to justify proceeding beyond the stage of technology development."

An even more pessimistic note was struck by Dr. Richard DeLauer, then Undersecretary of Defense for Research and Development and Engineering, when he said in July 1983: "There is no way an enemy can't overwhelm your defences if he wants to badly enough. It makes a lot of difference in what we do if we have to defend against one thousand re-entry vehicles (i.e., nuclear weapons or decoys that look like them) or ten thousand."

I will try to bring to bear on these conflicting and contradictory statements whatever general considerations physics and common sense afford us, in order to decide which of the above claims will prove to come closest to the pragmatic truth in the future.

A ballistic missile that carries tens of re-entry vehicles and hundreds of decoys takes about thirty minutes to cover the distance from the Soviet Union to the United States. For current missiles, the boost phase during which the missile is accelerated to its required terminal velocity lasts about 200 seconds. At the end of the boost phase, the MIRVed* "bus" begins releasing the individual re-entry vehicles and accompanying

Professor Kosta Tsipis is a member of the Physics Department at the Massachusetts Institute of Technology, where, since 1966, his research has focused on the scientific and technical questions surrounding arms control and the effects of nuclear detonations and nuclear war. He is on the editorial board of the Bulletin of the Atomic Scientists, *and he is also a member of the board of directors of the Council for a Livable World, an influential American organization which strives for world peace. Born in Greece, Professor Tsipis emigrated to the United States in 1954. He studied electrical engineering and physics at Columbia University, and obtained his Ph.D. in high-energy particle physics.*

* MIRV is the acronym for multiple, independently-targetable, re-entry vehicle. A 'MIRVed' missile carries from three to fourteen warheads, each of which can be directed independently to strike widely separated targets. —Ed.

decoys, a process that can last a few minutes. Each re-entry vehicle coasts unpowered toward its target for about twenty minutes in the vacuum of outer space. Influenced only by the local gravitational field, it has an elliptical trajectory that at its maximum distance rises about 1000 kilometres (620 miles) above the earth. Finally, each re-entry vehicle re-enters the atmosphere at a speed of about seven kilometres or four miles per second, where it is violently decelerated and overheated by its friction with air molecules. For that reason, re-entry vehicles are designed and manufactured to resist temperatures of 2000 to 3000 degrees Fahrenheit (1100–1650 degrees Celsius), and to withstand extreme mechanical stresses. Re-entry effectively starts at about 100 kilometres (sixty-two miles) above the earth and lasts another five minutes or so before the vehicle reaches its target.

The Strategic Defense Initiative planners have proposed to erect several different defensive barriers against such weapons. First comes a "boost-phase" defence system which would detect and attack the missile itself during its boost phase as it rises from its silo. Then a second "midcourse" system is proposed, which would distinguish vehicles bearing weapons from decoys and would attack the individual re-entry vehicles during their coasting phase. Finally, a third "terminal" defensive system would attempt to detect and intercept the re-entry vehicles during their passage through the atmosphere on their way to their targets. If the re-entry vehicles were aimed at cities, interception would have to occur 3000 to 7000 metres (10,000–23,000 feet) above the earth. If silos were the target, interception would be possible all the way to the ground.

THE BOOST-PHASE DEFENSIVE SYSTEM

The boost-phase defensive system is considered the most important and also the easiest component of the proposed defence. It is the easiest for two reasons: first, the boosting missile can be detected with relative ease, because of the large infrared signature of its exhaust plume; second, its structure is relatively fragile and quite large, so it is easier to hit and damage than are the re-entry vehicles later released from the missile. This is important, because each missile in the boost phase carries about ten re-entry vehicles and possibly hundreds of decoys; these can be neutralized all at once if the missile is destroyed.

To attack the booster, one must be in sight of it. The most cost-effective approach would be for the United States to place a rapid-firing cannon right next to each Soviet silo and fire at the missile as soon as it is launched. But this system would assuredly be subject to effective Soviet countermeasures and, as a consequence, is not considered viable. Instead, there have been proposals to place weapons on satellites in low-earth-orbit which, during a brief portion of their orbit, could have Soviet silos in sight. The following weapons have been proposed for this role:

1. Neutral atomic hydrogen beams.
2. Large chemical lasers.
3. Small, self-guided rockets; or kinetic energy weapons, which would fire small masses (from approximately ten to one hundred grams [up to 3.5 oz.]) to hit the rising booster at speeds of several kilometres per second.
4. Nuclear-pumped X-ray lasers; either deployed in orbit or popped into orbit from submarines lurking in the Indian Ocean or the Persian Gulf, each laser would be at an altitude to have a line-of-sight view of a Soviet ICBM (intercontinental ballistic missile) rising above the atmosphere, and would shoot it with an intense pulse of soft X-rays, generated by the explosion of a nuclear charge.
5. A powerful laser based in the United States; lethal doses of its light would be shot to a mirror at 36,000 kilometres (22,400 miles) above the equator and reflected to a second mirror in low-earth-orbit, which would then aim the light at a rising Soviet missile.

Each of these proposed weapons suffers from three classes of difficulties: intrinsic technical difficulties; susceptibility to inexpensive countermeasures; and operational difficulties. The first two classes of difficulties will be dealt with specifically as they apply to the boost-phase defensive system. The last class—operational difficulties—will be dealt with at the end of the paper, because operational difficulties plague all three phases of a multi-layered defence system.

Intrinsic technical difficulties. The most obvious technical difficulty in all of the boost-phase defensive systems proposed above is that not one of these systems now exists. There have been demonstrations in principle of large chemical lasers, but these have been of an order of magnitude smaller than that which an actual weapon would require. It is not known whether modular assembly is feasible, and because lasers are nonlinear systems, it is also not known whether these prototypes can be scaled to the required energy and power levels. The advanced high-energy lasers we possess now do not have the proper wavelength to be useful as weapons. Lasers with the right wavelength, on the other hand, are at an embryonic state of technical development, being billions of times weaker than needed.

Particle beam, laser, and kinetic energy weapons deployed in space would require that enormous amounts of energy supplies be carried into orbit. Each lethal shot of laser light or burst of particles would require about a ton of fuel. Each weapon would need to fire at about 1000 missiles, with several shots per missile. So, each weapon-carrying satellite would have to store several thousand tons of fuel. There has been heated debate on how many such satellites would be needed to cover Soviet missile fields at all times, since only a small fraction of the satellites would be over the Soviet Union at any one time. Calculations vary between 422 and 2,263 satellites, depending on what one assumes to be the number of Soviet missiles, their basing configuration, their boost time, and the slew time of defensive weapons (that is the time weapons need for changing aim from one missile to the next). The cost per missile-kill has been estimated to be between $400 million and $2.1 billion, depending on missile boost time and, if lasers rather than particle beams or kinetic energy weapons were to be used in orbit, the size of the laser mirrors. The shorter the boost time, and the longer the time the laser must shine on the missile, the more expensive each kill becomes. Of particle beam, laser and kinetic energy weapons, lasers turn out to be the only conceivable boost-phase weapons. So, since a missile costs only tens of millions of dollars, the Soviets can assuredly drive us to the poor house: by building more missiles, or by placing missile dummies on the ground, they can force us to deploy additional satellites with real weapons overhead. The cost exchange ratio favours the offence by a factor of between ten and fifty.

The ground-based lasers with two families of transmission mirrors — one in geosynchronous orbit, and one in near-earth orbit — would require very large mirrors (at least five metres [sixteen feet] in diameter for short-wavelength lasers to work effectively). Mirrors would also need to be very robust, properly cooled, and would need to incorporate adaptive optics capable of aiming a laser beam with virtually perfect accuracy (within tiny fractions of a degree). It is not known whether such a mirror system could even be constructed from materials presently available. Even if it were possible, when deployed undefended in orbit the system would be vulnerable to a simple attack by the Soviet Union. In fact, since the mirrors both in high and low orbit would be defenceless, an opponent could attack and destroy them prior to launching its own nuclear missiles. Ground-based short-wavelength lasers would be a billion times weaker than is required to destroy an ICBM and would be useless on a cloudy day.

Susceptibility to countermeasures. Effective, inexpensive countermeasures are the most serious difficulty facing a boost-phase defence system. All satellites in orbit can be attacked and destroyed by the Soviet Union. On Monday, April 4, 1983, the *Christian Science Monitor* quoted Dr. Edward Teller, a strong supporter of SDI, as saying that the Soviets can get rid of orbiting systems at one-tenth the cost of putting them there. The Fletcher Commission, which President Reagan assembled to evaluate his "Star Wars" proposal *after* he had announced it, said: "Survivability of the system components is a critical issue whose resolution requires a combination of technologies and tactics *that remain to be worked out."*

Soviet countermeasures (other than direct attack) could include hardening their missiles; hiding or spoofing each missile's infrared signature; blinding the sensors and detectors of the orbiting defensive weapon; and jamming communication between the orbiting system and its command and control computers and/or jamming its communication with other parts of the orbiting system. Both the electronics in a space-based weapon system, and its ability to communicate with its computers, can be destroyed by the electromagnetic pulse from a nuclear explosion in space. In addition, Martin Marietta, an American company specializing in missiles, has shown that missiles with a burn time of as short as fifty seconds are technically feasible now. These missiles would complete their boost phase eighty kilometres (fifty miles) above the earth, while still in the atmosphere. Once above the atmosphere and in the vacuum of space and now largely invisible, the missiles would proceed to dispense their re-entry vehicles and decoys. Particle-beam weapons, hypervelocity kinetic-energy weapons, and X-ray lasers would be unable to attack Soviet missiles which complete their boost phase in the atmosphere within fifty seconds after launch; the atmosphere would attenuate or disperse the laser and particle beams and vaporize the kinetic-energy-weapon projectiles. The other types of proposed weapons—space-borne chemical lasers, or ground-based eximer lasers with two sets of orbiting mirrors—would have only fifty seconds to destroy an ascending wave of from 1000 to 1500 such missiles. The investment cost of each kill would increase to over $2 billion for each missile destroyed.

These countermeasures are as effective and as feasible as those the Soviets could apply against the rapid-firing cannons placed next to their missile silos. Yet, while no one is proposing to install such a preposterous cannon-based missile defence, the Strategic Defense Initiative Organization appears unconcerned by the fact that countermeasures against space-based weapons intended to attack Soviet missiles during their boost phase are inescapably effective.

POST-BOOST AND MID-COURSE DEFENSIVE SYSTEMS
Post-boost and mid-course defensive systems designed to attack either the "bus" during the MIRVing process or individual re-entry vehicles, could consist either of chemical rockets fired from platforms in near-earth-orbit with velocities of a few kilometres per second, or hypervelocity electromagnetic guns firing solid pellets at five kilometres (three miles) per second or faster. These post-boost defensive systems face two classes of extreme difficulties: detection and tracking difficulties and difficulties in discriminating between decoys and warheads.

Detection and tracking difficulties. A re-entry vehicle is a hardened object that can tolerate very large mechanical loads, and skin temperatures of about 1100 degrees Celsius (2000 degrees Fahrenheit). After leaving the missile at the end of the boost phase, the re-entry vehicle has a very weak, evanescent infrared signature. One approach to overcoming this problem would be to attach laser sensors to small rockets, and then illuminate each re-entry vehicle with a laser based in geosynchronous orbit; the rockets would home in on the re-entry vehicles by following the laser reflections.

Decoy/warhead discrimination difficulties. The scheme described above requires that the real re-entry vehicle be recognizable among thousands of decoys. Otherwise, such defences could be easily overcome by accompanying each of the real re-entry vehicles with many tens of light-weight balloon decoys, while enclosing each weapon-carrying vehicle in a similar balloon (a technique called "anti-simulation"). The defence would then have to face 100,000 or more identical-looking objects during an attack: 10,000 would contain real bombs and the rest would be empty decoys.

In testimony presented to the House of Representatives, the Reagan administration's Undersecretary of Defense Research and Engineering, Richard DeLauer, stated: "Any defensive system can be overcome with proliferation, and decoys, decoys, decoys." There appears to be no practical way, either passive or active, to weigh all the identical-looking balloons during their twenty-minute flight in order to discover which contain real re-entry vehicles and which are empty. Such decoys can be built easily, at low cost, and can incorporate spoofing features unsuspected by the defence. There is not even a viable theoretical *concept* at this time for an effective mid-course defence against the projected massive threat of tens of thousands of warheads and perhaps as many as a million decoys. Additional countermeasures could include attacks on the mid-course defence platforms in orbit, and increased background radiation from high-altitude nuclear detonations or infrared-emitting aerosols that would blind or confuse the sensors of the defence. There is no "new technology" on the horizon that could help alleviate these problems. The fact that the offence can present an entirely unforeseen configuration of threats to the defence, by altering its tactics or the observable properties of re-entry vehicles and decoys, makes even less likely the already bleak prospect of an effective mid-course defensive system.

TERMINAL DEFENSIVE SYSTEMS

By contrast, terminal ground-based defences are not plagued by the decoy problem, since the decoys would quickly burn out in the atmosphere. Terminal defences also have been helped by recent technological advances in guidance, homing sensors, very high acceleration rockets, and modular, very fast computers. Yet terminal defences of population and industry are bound to be ineffective, since this defence layer (given the fact that boost-phase, post-boost, and mid-course defences do not appear to have any chance of being effective) would be faced with the threat of thousands of re-entry vehicles descending hidden behind the fireballs of deliberately-detonated Soviet nuclear weapons. A mere handful of these re-entry vehicles, if they leak through, could destroy an equal number of targets. Since high accuracy is not required when attacking cities, salvage-fusing and manoeuvring re-entry vehicles could further exacerbate the difficulties of terminal defences of urban and industrial centres and soft military targets. Therefore, terminal ground-based defences are potentially useful only for the defence of American ICBM silos.

OPERATIONAL DIFFICULTIES IN A MULTI-LAYERED SPACE-BASED DEFENSIVE SYSTEM

All of the difficulties of space-based defences are dwarfed by the third class of difficulties, the operational problems of such a multi-layered defensive system. By the very nature of its mission such a system can never be tested or exercised under realistic nuclear exchange conditions. Neither can these conditions be simulated. The tens of millions of lines of computer code that must support the operations of its massive computational network can never be confidently debugged. The codes can never be tested against the possibility of failure under unforeseen circumstances; therefore, there will always be the probability that with the unexpected, the system as a whole will probably degrade ungracefully. The myriad of command, control and communications links—several orders of magnitude more extensive and complex than those of our current offensive weapons—could be disrupted in a number of ways by the Soviet Union prior to or during a nuclear attack. While the defence has only half an hour to perform its function perfectly, with little or no prior knowledge of the exact configuration of the threat, the offence can prepare for years, devise secret countermeasures, and choose the moment and the form of attack.

Consider, for example, what could happen to the instructions embedded in the computer programs controlling the defensive system. These instructions would supposedly enable the system to recognize a missile, or to discriminate between a decoy and a real re-entry vehicle masquerading as a decoy. The instructions must be written on the basis of imperfect information regarding the complexion of the threat, years before the defence system is called on to perform. At the time of the attack, not only would the instructions not have been tested against a realistic threat, they would most probably be called on to perform while

45

faced with unexpected strategic missile configurations, new decoys, unpredicted background clutter, or radiation. There is no reason to believe that these computer instructions would perform at all, let alone flawlessly. It is not possible to simulate a Soviet attack, since we cannot know how it would look, and we cannot duplicate the nuclear environment in which it would take place. Much less complex computer systems, like those used in the Apollo travel to the moon or by the space shuttle, have required many months of testing and correction of flaws. Even then, despite NASA's ability to delay or postpone launches, it has experienced disasters such as the Apollo 13 accident or the more recent Challenger tragedy. So what are the chances that an untested system would work the first time you pushed its button?

Let me conclude. When we make an engineering judgment regarding the feasibility of Star Wars defences, we must look beyond our capability to manufacture a ten-metre mirror (thirty-three feet), or a twenty-five-megawatt chemical laser. We must look at the required performance of the entire system, and this performance will degrade if an error or flaw appears during the system's brief operational time. In contrast to the Apollo missions and the space shuttle, which had merely to contend with the laws of nature and probability—as exemplified in Murphy's Law (if something can go wrong, it will)—the strategic defence system will have to contend with hostile, unpredictable tactics and actions. So we cannot, in good technical judgment, consider the system outside its engagement environment—which is going to be hostile and unpredictable. Finally, we must consider not only the cost of erecting such a defensive system but also the infinitely larger cost if it fails under attack.

You must suspect by now that Star Wars is not Star Wars at all. It is militarily and technologically absurd. It is instead a political and psychological ploy to weaken demands for arms control in the United States, and a resurrection of the old Ballistic Missile Defence (BMD) scheme in a new, exotic garb—the same BMD which was found unworkable in the early 1970s. Mr. Reagan and his associates are selling us voodoo science, and we must reject it in the name of reason and peace.

CHAPTER 4

From Mutual Assured Destruction to Star Wars: From War Prevention to War Making

GENERAL GERT BASTIAN

NUCLEAR MONOPOLY

One can only regret that at the end of the Second World War the West entrusted the preservation of peace to the nuclear sword. There are many indications that the United States would have been better advised to use the brief period of its nuclear monopoly to negotiate a mutual renunciation of any nuclear weapons with the Soviet Union. The insane concept of preserving peace through nuclear deterrence has ever since been the nightmare of humankind.

Of course, nobody knows if such a treaty could actually have been achieved at that time; the West overestimated the Soviet Union's conventional forces, and this would undoubtedly have hindered any American initiative for nuclear disarmament. However, the fact that the United States, from its position of unilateral nuclear strength, did not make any attempt to relinquish its nuclear weapons in order to achieve a total East-West ban shows the extent to which important decisions in the security policy field can be unfavourably influenced both by exaggerated ideas of the threat posed by the adversary and by efforts to achieve military superiority.

It is difficult to understand why the United States took no political initiative at an early stage to prevent a nuclear arms race; it was predictable that the Soviets would consider the United States' sole possession of nuclear weapons to be an unacceptable risk, and would do everything in their power to develop nuclear weapons of their own. Without a complete ban on nuclear weapons, America's monopoly on these weapons was bound to end sooner or later: the Soviet Union exploded its first

PHOTO: WERNER SCHüRING

General Gert Bastian

nuclear weapon in September 1949, only four years after the bombing of Hiroshima and Nagasaki.

Still, America's clear nuclear superiority continued for many more years, and with it the Western defence concept of "massive retaliation." By adopting this policy, the United States made clear that it was prepared to commit mass murder should a war with the Soviet Union break out. This attitude was bound up with the cynical calculation that in the event of hostilities it would be far easier and more effective to use these powerful new weapons not against soldiers in the field, but against men, women, and children in cities. This policy already implied the intention to make the Soviet people hostage in a state of non-war and ruthlessly to execute their murder should the armistice be broken.

MASSIVE RETALIATION

Advocates of nuclear deterrence said at the time, and still say, that this concept must simply be accepted, and that objections to it are far outweighed by the years of peace which all peoples who are protected by the nuclear umbrella owe to the existence of American nuclear weapons. However, this argument is not convincing. The following statement is the only true one which can be made concerning the effectiveness of deterrence thus far: nuclear weapons have been in existence since 1945, and no new world war has taken place. Nobody knows whether this is only coincidental or whether there is a causal connection between these two facts. One can believe in a connection or deny it, but no more than speculation is possible.

What is certain, however, is that the policy of nuclear deterrence, with its inevitable material, economic and psychological consequences, has deprived the people on both sides of peace and reconciliation, because

General Gert Bastian is a member of the Bundestag, *the national Parliament of the Federal Republic of Germany. He has had a long military career in Germany, beginning with active service on the eastern front against the Russians during World War II. After the war, he rose rapidly through the ranks, was promoted to general, and eventually commanded the German Armed Forces. When NATO decided to deploy Pershing II and ground-launched cruise missiles in Western Europe, General Bastian resigned from the German army to indicate his strong belief that present NATO policies are fundamentally wrong and dangerous. In 1981, General Bastian founded Generals for Peace along with other top-ranking former NATO commanders. This influential organization believes that no rational military use exists for nuclear weapons because they would destroy everything, including those things which they attempt to defend.*

neither side can prosper in the shadow of threatened annihilation. Nor will either side be able to develop fully in the future, as long as nuclear weapons poison the world.

FLEXIBLE RESPONSE
In the late 1960s when NATO replaced the policy of massive retaliation with the strategy of "flexible response," this development did not arise from any moral misgivings about massive retaliation, and did not bring about any fundamental change in the world situation. It was merely NATO's inevitable reaction to the surprisingly rapid growth of the Soviet nuclear arsenal in the 1950s. With every year that passed, the Soviet Union's nuclear arsenal posed a greater threat to the United States and its European allies. The initially one-sided taking of hostages had been transformed into a mutual partnership of death: Mutual Assured Destruction.

So, as an alternative to mutual suicide, the West developed the concept of flexible response—the use of smaller, battlefield nuclear weapons in a crisis situation. Yet inherent in this concept was a logic so extremely unconvincing that it gave the impression of being well-intentioned self-deception. The incalculability of any war (a fact familiar to older servicemen) would make it extraordinarily unlikely that the nuclear escalation triggered by the first use of even the smallest battlefield nuclear weapon could be controlled. A nuclear exchange would become uncontrollable if only on account of the incalculable responses of the adversary, who could hardly be expected to submit meekly to the scenario prepared by NATO. Therefore, when NATO adopted its new strategic concept of flexible response it did not, in essence, abandon the concept of nuclear deterrence, with all its frightful characteristics and consequences. The mass murder and genocide threatened by Mutual Assured Destruction still remained the basis of flexible response, even though the disaster was no longer planned as a sudden horrifying end, but rather as an endless horror which would, at first, afflict only the countries defended by nuclear weapons. This new strategy did not change the fundamental absurdity of safeguarding peace by means of nuclear weapons. It merely made it more difficult to perceive the real meaning of nuclear deterrence, without making it in any way more acceptable.

From year to year, the tremendous growth of both sides' nuclear arsenals has increased the danger of a nuclear catastrophe. However, it must be pointed out that it is mostly the West that has continued to provoke the arms race. Not only has the West invariably had more nuclear warheads, but the most important steps in the armaments field—the introduction of new weapon systems, delivery vehicles and guidance systems—have always been taken first by the United States and only later (in some cases several years later) by the Soviet Union. Unfortunately, the USSR also failed to act in accordance with the obvious fact that effective mutual deterrence requires merely that each side be able to threaten the other with unacceptable damage. The USSR, like the United States, failed to understand that once both sides have this capability it is irrelevant who is equipped with more and who with fewer nuclear weapons, and that consequently there never has been any need to take part in the arms race, nor is there any such need today.

INTERMEDIATE-RANGE NUCLEAR FORCES

One important shift in Western nuclear strategy has occurred because of the needless stockpiling of more and more sophisticated nuclear weapons. As the West has integrated extremely accurate weapon systems—intended for a nuclear first strike—into its arsenal, the original Western strategy for preventing war has been replaced by a strategy of a clearly offensive nature for waging and winning a nuclear war. The deployment of new American systems in Europe, such as the Pershing II and cruise missiles, does not, as is maintained, close a "deterrence gap." Instead, it makes possible one element of the newly-developed American "decapitation" strategy: the ability to launch a nuclear attack on small but politically important targets in Warsaw Pact countries.

It is fundamentally wrong and misleading for the German government to maintain that it promoted the security of Western Europe with its decision to deploy Pershing II and cruise missiles in NATO countries. It is equally false of Chancellor Kohl to brazenly assert that it was only his government's decision to deploy these missiles in the Federal Republic that made possible the resumption of American-Soviet arms control negotiations in Geneva in March 1985, thus establishing a chance for future reductions in the nuclear arsenals of both sides.

As the documented course of events shows, quite the opposite is true. The deployment of Pershing II missiles in the Federal Republic of Germany immediately interrupted the American-Soviet negotiations which aimed to limit the Eurostrategic and strategic nuclear weapons of both superpowers—negotiations which had been conducted in Geneva since November 30th, 1981. A position satisfactory for Europe was within reach with the latest Soviet offer to reduce the number of SS-20 missiles threatening Europe down to the number of existing British and French nuclear systems on submarines.

To interrupt the Geneva arms control talks by deploying cruise and Pershing II missiles just when extensive Soviet concessions were being proffered was a risk-laden and unjustified action. It revealed that the United States and the Federal Republic of Germany were more interested in beginning deployment on schedule than they were in negotiating an agreement that would have made the deployment of new American inter-mediate-range missiles in Europe unnecessary.

Furthermore, the American-Soviet arms control talks which resumed in Geneva in March 1985 (not, as Chancellor Kohl maintained, *because* of NATO's modernization of its intermediate-range nuclear forces, but rather *despite* the modernization and because of worldwide protests against the superpowers' nuclear arms race), are now taking place under far worse conditions than prevailed when interrupted in 1983. The con-tinued build-up of nuclear arms on both sides has added considerably to the complexity of the negotiations, which were already difficult enough.

A second and no less threatening consequence of Pershing II deploy-ment in the Federal Republic of Germany was that to counter it the Soviet Union deployed tactical nuclear missiles in the German Democratic Re-public (East Germany) and Czechoslovakia. This action failed to provide the Soviet Union and its allies with any more security than the initial deployment of American intermediate-range systems had provided for the United States and its allies. Instead, the Soviet reaction, while es-calating the arms race, further destabilized the strategic military situation in Europe, a reaction that had been predicted by critics of the West's modernization of its intermediate-range nuclear forces (INF).

In addition, by deploying, on non-Soviet territory, nuclear missiles characterized by high accuracy and extremely short prior warning times, the Soviet Union indicated that—despite all official announcements to the contrary—it had responded to the changes in American nuclear stra-tegy by creating its own potential for waging a limited nuclear war on the territories of its allies.

A third destabilizing consequence of Pershing II deployment is that now both superpowers, by deploying new, very accurate nuclear weap-ons only a few hundred kilometres from either side of the NATO-Warsaw Pact border (a location which makes these weapons easy to spot and attack), will be forced in a crisis to either use or lose their nuclear weapons. Because of this, should a rapidly escalating political crisis oc-cur, the chances for preventing nuclear war will be drastically reduced.

In addition to the harm caused by modernizing its INF, the United States' intensified effort to develop and deploy extremely accurate strategic nuclear weapons—such as the MX intercontinental missile and the Trident II submarine-launched missile—has created even greater in-stability and risk. Since these systems will be as accurate as Eurostrategic Pershing II missiles, they must also be considered weapons of attack. The development of these strategic weapons, which make vulnerable a major part of the Soviet strategic arsenal, gives the United States a first-strike capability in the strategic, as well as the Eurostrategic, sphere—a development which can hardly be coincidental. Instead, it indicates an increasing American readiness to include the option of a surprise attack with strategic nuclear weapons in political and strategic planning. The previously discernible development of an American capability for a nuclear offensive in the European theatre, has been matched by an equally risky counterpart in the strategic armaments field.

STAR WARS

Unfortunately, development of the so-called Star Wars weapons also points in the same direction. The United States claims that this ''security shield'' will be purely defensive in nature. In his inaugural speech given on January 22, 1983, the American president even said that ''such a shield would not kill people, but destroy weapons; it would not militarize space, but help demilitarize the arsenals of earth''—a statement presumably meant to portray this shield as a purely humanitarian project. Unfortunately, however, President Reagan was not telling the truth.

Parallel to the accelerated development of an efficient anti-missile system in space, the United States is promoting an accelerating development of offensive strategic weapons. In so doing, it is striving to gain the capability to launch a nuclear attack without having to fear a Soviet nuclear retaliation.

One need not be a cynic or a prophet to predict that the final liberation from the risk of a nuclear response by one's opponent by means of an operational anti-missile system would inevitably also strengthen the tendency to use one's own aggressive capability unscrupulously, or at least threaten its use to a greater extent than was possible in the decades of Mutual Assured Destruction. With its Strategic Defense Initiative (SDI) program, the United States is attempting to transform, once and for all, Mutual Assured Destruction into a brutal strategy of not mutual and assured, but one-sided and risk-free destruction. This will, necessarily, create an extraordinarily fragile situation.

The arms control talks between the Americans and Russians which started in Geneva on March 12, 1985, unfortunately do not justify hopes for agreements which could free the world from the fear of nuclear weapons. The greatest disappointment is that calls for a moratorium, which would have frozen the nuclear weapons of both sides at their current levels, and the proposal for a comprehensive nuclear test ban have been rejected by the United States. If both sides actively pursue their armaments programs while the negotiations are taking place, a process which could last many years, this will naturally lead to increasing instability. It is difficult to hope that the talks will reverse all earlier developments and ultimately create an atmosphere as favourable as the one which existed between East and West prior to the commencement of Pershing II deployment. Developments in Eurostrategic and strategic armaments since November 1983, and the likely future developments both in this sphere and in space, confirm, in a most disturbing fashion, the worst fears of the peace movement. Rather than the negotiations giving rise to a sense of optimism, they create a suspicion that the superpowers shamelessly use them to promote further increases in armaments, while portraying each other as the reason for these build-ups.

One last danger which needs to be pointed out lies in the fact that many conservative and even liberal politicians in Western Europe, particularly in the Federal Republic of Germany, are now demanding a European Defence Initiative program comparable to the American SDI. The intention of a European SDI program would be to build up a nuclear-armed Western Europe as a third military superpower. The peace movement in Western Europe rightly rejects any integrated European development of this kind. We certainly do not need any more nuclear-armed superpowers!

PATHS TO PEACE
We need effective unilateral disarmament steps by both the superpowers and their allies in order to turn the insane nuclear arms race into a disarmament race. These steps could be:

1. The renunciation of the first use of nuclear weapons by NATO.

2. The renunciation of all provocative offensive strategies—for example, Air Land Battle, Rogers Plan and Deep Strikes.

3. The withdrawal of all weapons of mass destruction from countries which do not produce such weapons. (At the Green Party's international tribunal in Nuremberg in 1983, the threatened use of weapons of mass destruction was declared to be a crime contrary to international law!)

4. A halt to all Star Wars programs including those proposed for Western Europe.

5. A comprehensive test ban by all nuclear powers.

Having taken these steps, we could then work for:

6. The creation of nuclear-weapons-free zones around the world, following the good examples of New Zealand and the Pacific region.

7. The progressive dismantling of both military blocs, through a series of carefully calculated steps.

8. An end to policies of brutal intervention in the Third World: the Soviets must get out of Afghanistan and the United States must stop intervening in Latin America.

9. The development of concrete models for converting from a war-based to a peace-based economy.

10. An end to the exporting of weapons and of nuclear power plants.

11. An end to the Federal Republic of Germany's use of Canadian terri-

tory belonging to native Indians for military training.*

We need finally:

12. The promotion of nonviolent conflict resolution and the promotion of peace research.

13. Increased co-operation and communication between all independent peace and civil liberties movements in the East and West.

14. A guarantee of human, economic, and social rights for everyone.

For many years détente has been a matter for governments. But it is the people themselves who are responsible for human life and for peace on earth. Generals for Peace and Disarmament, of which I am a member, strongly support the worldwide peace movement. The path to peace will be long and hard. But I am optimistic that the global peace movement will grow and win.

---

* General Bastian refers here to the low-level training flights of German and other NATO military aeroplanes over Labrador, which have been permitted by the Canadian government, and vigorously protested by native groups living in the bush west of Goose Bay. The fearsome noise of the simulated flights has frightened away game and disrupted the lives of Native Indians living in this region. —ED.

PHOTO: MARUSKA STUDIOS

Marion Dewar

CHAPTER 5
Panel Discussion: Session I

MARION DEWAR, EUGENE CARROLL,
KOSTA TSIPIS, AND GERT BASTIAN

Marion Dewar (session chairperson):
Professor Tsipis, given the fact that the "Star Wars" system won't work, why is it that the Soviets feel so threatened by it that they've made its abandonment by the United States a key point in their negotiating strategy?

Kosta Tsipis:
That is an excellent question. But I want to postpone answering it for a second, because I want to share with you this joyful and heartening event: I can see, but you cannot see, that the entire first row of this theatre is occupied by very young people. That is the most encouraging and wonderful thing that I have seen in many years. [*applause*]

And now to the question: I cannot give you a clear answer because I am not a member of the Politburo. But I can give you some anecdotal information. A week ago tonight I had dinner in Cambridge with a very

Marion Dewar was from 1978 to 1985 the mayor of Ottawa, and she is now the national president of the New Democratic Party of Canada. Trained as a public health nurse, she has long been an activist in the areas of local economic development, native people's rights, peace and women's issues. As mayor of Ottawa, she found homes for 4000 Southeast Asian refugees, and later she co-hosted the Women's Constitutional Conference, which resulted in the reinstatement of the equality provisions in the Canadian Charter of Rights and Freedoms. Marion Dewar has played a major part in stimulating the holding of disarmament referenda both in Ottawa and in other Canadian cities.

high-ranking Soviet political leader. He kept excoriating the Americans for doing everything wrong, so we asked him: "Don't *you* do anything wrong?" He thought for a second, and then he said, "You know, we should not have opposed Star Wars so vehemently." So my first answer would be that perhaps they made a mistake in opposing it so strongly.

I have a second anecdote which may shed more light on the question. I was told, this time by a very high-ranking Soviet scientist, that the Soviet scientists, who completely agree with our assessment of Star Wars, *did* go to the Politburo and say: "Star Wars won't work, so don't worry about it." But the Soviet military also went to the Poltiburo and said: "We cannot afford *not* to develop our own Star Wars because we will be perceived as falling behind, as being less competent than they are" — the usual American-Soviet approach to the issues of the arms race.

Clearly, the Soviet political leadership, unlike the Soviet military, does not want to engage in this extraordinarily wasteful and expensive effort to develop Star Wars weapons. So I think the Soviet Union's attempts to convince us not to pursue Star Wars are partly an effort to keep its own military at bay. In fact, a Soviet commentator, whom I highly respect, recently said: "Look, Gorbachev really wants to limit nuclear weapons, but the military won't let him. In order to reduce nuclear weapons he has to give the military something in return."

So, the Soviet response to Star Wars reveals an internal Soviet problem. I know the Soviets realize that SDI (Strategic Defense Initiative) won't work. The question is whether their political leadership will be able to disregard its own hard-liners. In fact, it was announced last August by a Soviet official that the Soviets are not going to institute a Star Wars program. Instead they will work on countermeasures. And they have showed us their countermeasures: I can assure you that they are very effective.

Dewar:
General Bastian, what is the "window of vulnerability?"

Gert Bastian:
This was a term the German government used to prepare the public for the deployment of the Pershing II and cruise missiles in the Federal Republic of Germany. It meant that if the Soviets deployed SS-20 missiles aimed at the NATO countries in Europe, these countries would become vulnerable — a "window of vulnerability" would open. To close it, the government said intermediate-range nuclear missiles aimed at the Soviet Union would have to be deployed in Western Europe. But this reasoning was false. There was already an equilibrium between the Western and Soviet sides. Similar Soviet missiles have been directed toward Western

Europe for the past twenty years, and NATO has not been worried. Therefore, I think that "window of vulnerability" was a propaganda term and not a serious description of the real situation.

Dewar:
I assume that those scientists and politicians who support Star Wars are intelligent. If intelligence is not the problem, what is the basis for the major difference between this group and their counterparts who do not endorse Star Wars?

Tsipis:
Since I am a scientist, I suppose I have to answer this question. If you look at the line-ups of scientists for and against Star Wars, you will find an interesting correlation. All of the scientists I know who support Star Wars—except one—are somehow paid, either directly or indirectly, by the government. This does not prove anything, you know; it is just a mere correlation! All of the scientists who have managed to remain independent of direct government aid seem to have kept their critical faculties intact.

Dewar:
Admiral Carroll, what practical steps can we common people take? We are sick of talk of the dangers. We know these. We need concrete plans for a series of steps to achieve gradual nuclear disarmament.

Eugene Carroll:
In my talk, I laid out what I think is an orderly and practical series of steps, but in order to make these happen, they have to become a political issue at the lowest level of the political process. *Nobody* should be allowed to run for public office, for city council, even for dog-catcher, without taking a position on nuclear testing. [*prolonged applause and laughter*] I should quit while I am ahead.

I often hear the argument that because of the tremendous power of the defence industries the situation is hopeless. It is true that they recycle a portion of their profits back into the lobbying process to ensure the next round of appropriations. But every politician's first imperative is to get re-elected. It doesn't make any difference how many political campaign contributions they get; if enough people turn out at every campaign appearance, and if these politicians come to understand that the votes are against them, and that they won't be re-elected, then they will begin to see the wisdom of your view, and you will have supporters in the legislative process.

Dewar:

I certainly agree that here in Canada we should not allow candidates to run for any public office, even for dog-catcher, without first clearly stating their positions on disarmament issues. And we can do it. We also have had a written request for some comments on the street people, the homeless unemployed in North America. Something that is becoming very clear here tonight is the fact that the huge amount of money being spent in the arms race is enough to make sure that there aren't any street people *anywhere* in the world. That is one of the goals we must work toward.

General Bastian, is there any foreseeable way that the Federal Republic of Germany, either on its own or with other European countries, could negotiate an agreement to remove Pershing II and cruise missiles from the European theatre, even without the United States' approval?

Bastian:

Yes, of course. This would be possible if in the next German elections, in January 1987, we elect a different government. The current opposition has stated very clearly that it is willing to remove Pershing and cruise missiles from our country, and make this matter independent of any agreement with the United States.

Dewar:

Professor Tsipis, some American proponents of SDI claim the Soviets have been working on their own system for many years. Is this your belief, and if so, is their system any more valid than the one the United States is planning?

Tsipis:

We are talking about two things when we talk about Star Wars, and it seems to me that some proponents of SDI have deliberately confused these two separate aspects. I call these "Star Wars I" and "Star Wars II." To start with Star Wars II: I believe that since the 1972 ABM (anti-ballistic missile) Treaty the Soviet Union has been working along lines of research which are permitted by this treaty in order to study possible improvements in ground-based non-nuclear systems that would defend ICBM (intercontinental ballistic missiles) silos or similar hard, reinforced installations. This research is permitted by the ABM Treaty. We are doing similar research. We had an active ABM site in North Dakota, but shut it down when we realized that it was not going to amount to anything. The Soviets also have an active ABM site, around Moscow, and they have been doing experiments and doing research and playing with this system almost since 1972. It's been allowed by the treaty. We have been doing similar things at the Redstone Arsenal in Alabama since the 1970s. Over this period of time, we have been spending a few hundred million dollars a year on ABM research: nothing exciting, nothing new, nothing spectacular—keeping things simmering on the burner, so to speak.

Both countries have been doing what I call Star Wars II research—ground-based systems to protect missiles silos, and stuff like that. To my knowledge, the Soviets have not been doing the kind of research I call Star Wars I—space-based, zappy kinds of weapons with lasers and particle beams. Number one, because I don't think they believe in it. Number two, because I think that in many technologies they are so far behind, that they couldn't do these kinds of research even if they wanted to.

So, when you hear the usual alarmist kind of statement that, ''Oh, the Soviets are ten years ahead, and we'll never catch up with them,'' it is mainly propaganda. And when you hear that the Soviets are doing Star Wars research, what *really* is being referred to is the kind of ABM research that both countries have been doing since 1972, at the level of a few hundred million dollars a year, as allowed by the treaty. The kinds of Star Wars research that Mr. Reagan wants to do would violate the ABM Treaty and this would be an absolute disaster.

Carroll:

May I expand on that briefly. In their testimony to the United States Congress this year in support of their 1987 budget requests, the Armed Services and Department of Defense submitted a report which compared the military technology of the United States with that of the Soviet Union. And they listed twenty areas of basic research with which to compare the two countries. In six areas the Department of Defense reported that the Soviet Union was equal to the United States; in fourteen areas, the United States was superior to the Soviet Union. The Soviet Union was superior in none. And most of the areas of American superiority were directly related to those areas of research most intimately connected with SDI. Of all of them, computer technology is the superb and unmatchable American advantage. And the Joint Chiefs of Staff reported that not only does the United States have an advantage in this area, but it is constantly increasing its advantage.

The other point that I would like to make is that an official of the Department of Defense testified to Congress that present Soviet ballistic missile defence technology is approximately equivalent to the ballistic missile defence we had in the mid-seventies. But we threw ours away, because it wouldn't work and that's what they have now. If that's superiority, I don't understand it.

Dewar:
How does one answer the statement: "The peace movement is nothing more than a communist front"?

Tsipis:
It's not necessary to respond!

Carroll:
I want you to know that at the Center for Defense Information, we haven't taken one *red* cent! [*laughter*] People who oppose the views of the peace movement often make that statement when we try to explain the issues of the arms race factually. It's the response they make when confronted by a logical, developed line of reasoning that leads to a conclusion they don't like. Rather than let the discussion go forward, they try to smear their opponents by dragging in this idea that, "Oh, your motives are wrong." Well I would answer, "Quit worrying about my motives, which I assure you are okay. Start worrying about my facts, and let's argue the issues on the basis of facts, and let everyone make up their own minds. Don't fall for this garbage of slinging mud and innuendos, because there is absolutely *no* evidence that the communists, the KGB, or any other political entity has, in any way, influenced the development of the peace movement and the anti-nuclear movement in the United States or Canada."

Dewar:
Professor Tsipis, if President Reagan and the United States government know that Star Wars is technically impossible, as you have explained, what then are their real reasons for proposing it?

Tsipis:
I believe that their real reasons for proposing it become clear when one looks at what was happening in the United States between 1980 and 1983. In 1980 and 1981, physicists and physicians joined forces to teach the American public about the risks and dangers of nuclear war. And in two years the public was reasonably alarmed. People were realizing that nuclear war is very unhealthy, that it is going to be the last epidemic, and that there is no cure. And cries for arms control and the curbing of the nuclear arms race started to become stentorian and widely spread around the country. By June 1982, the freeze movement had assumed considerable proportions. As you recall, in June of 1982 three-quarters of a million people demonstrated in New York City in favour of the freeze. In the November 1982 elections, a number of congressional elections were de-

cided on the approval or disapproval of the candidate for the aims of the freeze movement.

So by 1982 there was a mounting public demand for arms control—for getting rid of this horrible threat called nuclear war. How does one get rid of this threat? By arms control, by bilateral, co-operative efforts to lower the number of nuclear weapons, and by entering into the kinds of agreements that we have talked about here tonight. But the Reagan administration not only has no desire for arms control, it *adamantly* opposes it. The administration had to find a way to deal with this public demand for arms control. So they provided Star Wars, which in my mind is a superb political ploy, absolutely superb! Ronald Reagan went on television and said: "Now, now children. Don't worry. You don't have to worry about nuclear war, you don't have to worry about nuclear holocaust, we will render nuclear war obsolete. We will put an astrodome of defence over the country. Don't worry about nuclear war"—and it worked!

Star Wars is not a military project; it is not a technological research project: it is a political ploy that has worked superbly well. Reagan and the government know that Star Wars won't work, but they are maintaining that it will because they don't want real arms control.

Dewar:
General Bastian, do you believe that General Secretary Gorbachev's recent arms control proposals are sincere and practical? What do you think of these proposals?

Bastian:
I believe that the proposals for a comprehensive nuclear-weapons test ban, for a freeze, and for a real reduction in strategic missiles have been serious. I am very angry that NATO has made its usual reaction, saying that these proposals are only propaganda and that therefore it won't discuss them seriously.

Dewar:
Why is the United States government so very resistant to Soviet disarmament overtures?

Carroll:
I think the situation is very much as General Bastian and Professor "Tsipsy" have described it—I don't know why I can't pronounce your name. Why didn't you get born in the United States? [*laughter*]

Tsipis:
You can't pronounce it because it's Greek to you. [*laughter*]

Carroll:

This administration wants nuclear superiority. It wants a nuclear war-fighting system which will prevail over the Soviet Union, even under the conditions of prolonged nuclear warfare. And you can't do that by entering into arms-control agreements which surrender what you believe to be technological advantages. In the guidance I read to you, the American Secretary of Defense said, "We will *not* enter into any arms control agreements which prevent us from exploiting our superiority for military advantage." That's what is behind this specious flood of garbage that you hear about what is wrong with the Soviet proposals.

Let me give you one example: their moratorium on nuclear-weapons tests. They announced it over eight months ago, and they haven't tested a nuclear weapon now for about nine months. Now, that wasn't an offer; that was an actual fact. Yet the government of the United States came out with an absolute flood of invective—pure propaganda, just garbage. The United States government said: "They're ahead of us in nuclear testing so we have to keep testing for safety and reliability and credibility." There is not a word of truth in this. The government does not want to negotiate because this would prevent it from developing the new nuclear war-fighting systems which are under development now.

Dewar:

Professor Tsipis, you mentioned the defects of the SDI program, referring to the ICBMs in their various phases of flight, namely boost, post-boost and re-entry. Does the SDI plan make any sense as a zero-phase first-strike weapon system in a plan to hit Soviet missiles in their silos before they can even be launched? And could SDI's various other elements be useful in mopping up surviving missiles as a terminal screen?

Tsipis:

The question refers, of course, to the widespread belief that some members of the Reagan administration may hope to use an effective and workable "Star Wars I" system in conjunction with a first strike against Soviet ICBM silos. This plan would deny the Soviets the capacity to strike back against the United States, and therefore would upset the deterrent situation that we now have. Now, for Star Wars to be used in a first strike, several things would have to happen.

First, an American first strike against Soviet silos would actually have to work. There is good evidence both in the world of physics and the world of mathematics which shows that a first strike probably would not work and that a large number, not a small number, of Soviet ICBMs would survive.

Second, even if, by some miracle, a first strike by the United States were to wipe out all Soviet ICBMS—which amounts to seventy percent of their weapons—and by a second miracle the remaining strategic missiles were wiped out by this semi-working Star Wars I system, this still would not prevent Soviet nuclear explosives from being delivered to the United States by bombers, by cruise missiles, and by some submarine-launched missiles with low trajectories. Therefore, even if a Star Wars defence worked, a substantial number of Soviet nuclear explosives would still land on the United States.

What is a substantial number? My group at the Massachusetts Institute of Technology did a study which we hope to have published by June, in which we look at this issue very carefully. How many nuclear explosions on the United States would collapse its economy? We conclude that it would be thirty-six. Not even the most sanguine admirer of Star Wars can believe that if this system worked, fewer than thirty-six nuclear explosives—out of ten thousand—would eventually land in the United States. I don't believe that anyone really thinks that you can stop 99.74 percent of Soviet nuclear explosives from hitting their targets in the United States. It is an *absolute* physical impossibility. So I don't believe that Star Wars, as envisioned by the Reagan administration, could really be used in support of a first strike. And I don't believe that they are so foolish as to believe it.

Dewar:
General Bastian, how are your proposals in regard to Third World intervention and links to independent human rights groups different from Mr. Reagan's policy of linking disarmamant to other issues?

Bastian:
We must use every possibility to make contact with the independent peace groups on the Eastern side. We do this from West Germany as often as possible, and we are successful in doing so. And this is encouraging to these very brave groups on the other side. Also, if it is not possible to come into direct contact with them, it is encouraging to them if they see that they are not alone, and that we are looking to them and putting public pressure on the governments of their countries, if they are suppressed, which unfortunately happens very often. So I think we can support them very successfully. We don't use every opportunity to do this, unfortunately. And these groups are asking us to help them become more and more successful through direct contacts, and make public the pressures which are exerted on them in special cases.

Dewar:
But surely, that's what President Reagan is saying when he proposes a policy of linkages. And I think that is the argument being given to support groups in other countries that are under oppression and are fighting for human rights. President Reagan is saying that is exactly the position the United States is taking when it is forced to help other countries to defend human rights.

Bastian:
But President Reagan is very one-sided. He is speaking for human rights only in Afghanistan. He is not speaking for human rights in Nicaragua and El Salvador. But the peace movement and the Greens in my country are speaking for human rights in every part of the globe. This is the difference.

Dewar:
Do you think that a ban on the export of uranium by Canada, the West's number one uraniuim exporter, would help to slow down nuclear weapons proliferation, and if so, why? I wish Mr. Mulroney were listening. [*applause*] Would that he were!

Tsipis:
One of the greater difficulties for any nation wanting to develop a nuclear arsenal is procuring the material necessary for building nuclear explosives. Therefore, unguarded, unguaranteed delivery of uranium of a grade that could either be used directly in weapons, or be used in weapons after further purification, helps whomever wants to build a nuclear arsenal. In that respect, exporting uranium without safeguards is an invitation for the proliferation of nuclear explosives. However, exporting uranium thoughtlessly and without safeguards is not the only way to export it. There are ways in which uranium can be exported to countries so that it can be used only in nuclear reactors. You can spike it. You can demand that the other country allow safeguards. You can demand that the importing country allow the United Nations, and the IAEA (International Atomic Energy Agency), which is the agency in Vienna that inspects and monitors reactors around the world, to have access to the reactor that has been fuelled with Canadian uranium and to make sure that the uranium is not being used for any purpose other than the production of energy.

Under these conditions, under conditions mandated by the United Nations, and under conditions that can be clearly fulfilled by Canadian scientists, namely that you can make the uranium unusable in weapons, the export of uranium is not bad. But to export uranium thoughtlessly, and without requiring safeguards on the part of the importing country, is an invitation for nuclear weapons proliferation.

Dewar:
Admiral Carroll, what do you feel are the opportunities for change in American military policy, and global tensions, after Ronald Reagan has ended his second and final term as president?

Carroll:
What are the chances for change after the Reagan administration? Any change will be an improvement! [*laughter*] Having said that, and then trying to figure out in whom and through whom this might be accomplished, it gets much more complex. I am really not aware of a strong candidate on either side. I think it is going to be a terrible dog fight for the Republicans. I am a member of no organized political group: I am a Democrat! And I am just unable to identify the candidate who can lead a very strong, focused campaign which emphasizes a proper concern for defence and at the same time clearly indicates his intention to control the excesses in the arms race. It is a dismal situation for the present, and I don't see the solution in 1988 yet.

Tsipis:
General Bastian says that something worse could happen: Richard Perle could become president of the United States.

Dewar:
Maybe we can start a draft Carroll for president.

Carroll:
If nominated, I will run for the Canadian border! [*laughter*]

Dewar:
Welcome!
　　General Bastian, where does the European EUREKA program and the independent French *force de frappe* fit in with the current arms picture?

Bastian:
Both are dangerous programs. The French *force de frappe* and also the nuclear armaments of the United Kingdom are both in the process of being strongly increased with dangerous new missiles and more warheads. And as to the so-called EUREKA program, our German government is saying to the people that it is primarily a civilian program with a small military spinoff. In truth, it is primarily a military program with a very

small and unimportant civilian spinoff. And therefore it is similar to the Star Wars program. It needs much money, it needs many resources, and it is intended to build up Western Europe, or to start Western Europe on the way to becoming a third nuclear superpower. And therefore, all the peace movements and the Greens in my country and some other Western European countries, are strictly *against* this program.

Dewar:
General Bastian, how did you view the peace movement while you were acting as a general in NATO? How did you develop your current view? To what extent were your opinions or views shared by your colleagues, and what is the best posture the peace movement can take to get those in the military onto our side?

Bastian:
In the last five years of my time on active duty as a general in the *Bundeswehr,* the peace movement did not really exist in Germany. There was silence during this period, and I couldn't gain any real impression then. But the deployment decision was made in December 1979, and I left the army in protest against this decision. The peace movement, not on account of my step, but because of this decision, grew to become very strong. And at this time I came immediately in contact with the peace movement, and I became a part of it.

Dewar:
General Bastian, how can the peace movement influence the military mind today?

Bastian:
There is a very interesting process going on in my country. We have an active group of soldiers, named after a city which has made an appeal to the government to renounce the deployment of Pershing II and cruise missiles. These soldiers on active duty work very closely together with the peace movement. There is a very good and fruitful co-operation between the two. I think that it is very necessary that the peace movement not mistakenly see soldiers as enemies. They are human beings who are misused by governments. We must make them realize how they are misused.

Dewar:
Admiral Carroll, in your expert opinion, would the suggestion by

Bryzinski, President Carter's national security adviser, to mine the Gulf of Sidra instead of bombing Libya have been a safer, more effective and controlled method of dealing with Gadhafi?

Carroll:
Mining the Gulf of Sidra? I hadn't heard that suggestion, and wouldn't believe it if I had. That would have as little to do with controlling terrorism as attacking Libya with aircraft carriers and bombers. You have got to do something that addresses the problem, not something that simply punishes someone and raises the cost of terrorism.

Dewar:
Is it possible that if there is general disarmament, we can safely dismantle and/or destroy the many nuclear weapons that we already have?

Tsipis:
Indeed, this question comes up quite often. How do you effect nuclear disarmament? How do you effect a drastic cut in the number of nuclear explosives? It is quite easy.

A nuclear explosive consists of a little bit of plutonium, you know about three kilograms (6.6 pounds), a little bit of the isotopes of hydrogen, which we call deuterium and tritium, or some chemicals that contain them. And there is also uranium, in a rather unusual configuration. So what you do is, you just unscrew it, and you open it up, and you take out the plutonium. You see, these are nuclides that have not been fissioned. Plutonium and uranium before a nuclear detonation are not very radioactive. Intense and persistent radioactivity is released by various products of the fissioning which accompanies the explosion process. But the plutonium that you take out of a nuclear weapon is not dangerously radioactive. It is toxic if inhaled or ingested, but that's okay; we handle lots of toxic substances safely. And you can just bury it, or you can put it in rods to use in nuclear reactors. You can safely dismantle these weapons without any serious risk of damage, without any significant threat to the health of the country or the people or anything like that. It is an *easy* process, without any scientific or health problems.

Dewar:
Here is an interesting idea. Would any of you like to comment on the proposal to exchange one million college students between the United States and the Soviet Union in a cultural exchange, as a means of preventing nuclear war?

Tsipis:
Why would we condemn the poor Soviet students to our colleges? It would be terrible. [*laughter*]

Carroll:
I think that such exchanges are greatly needed and possibly more needed by Canada and the United States than by the Soviet Union. North Americans need to visit the Soviet Union, to see what is really going on there and whom they are dealing with. If one million Soviet students came over here they obviously also would go home with some good, new understandings. After a period of time it would be awfully hard to perpetuate the image of one nation being evil and preparing to defeat the other. While we fear and distrust one another, we arm ourselves and seek superiority, in an attempt to ensure that the other nation does not destroy *us*. The more constructive exchanges the two sides have—children, college students, scientists, musicians, whatever—the better.

Tsipis:
I agree that any kind of exchange, any kind of bridge, would be useful and constructive, because there is suspicion on both sides—because the Russians think that we are planning to destroy them, and because we are told that Russia is the evil empire. So when people meet and leave the politicians behind there are *always* constructive results.

Bastian:
I have the same opinion. It is very important that people come together more than is possible now. Unfortunately, the boundaries of the East European countries on my continent are very closed. They are not as open as I would wish them to be. And it is also a request of the peace movement that this be changed.

Dewar:
I have one more question. What can the United Nations do for world peace, and how can the United Nations be made more effective? I think that we would like to hear from all three panelists on this one.

Carroll:
The United Nations is founded on the principle of the sovereignty of individual nation-states. In fact, the United Nations recognizes that some nations are even *more* sovereign than others. As it rests on that foundation it has inherent limitations, and I don't think it has the capacity in its present form, with its mode of operation and constraints, to do an awful lot. I think we have to look for a solution which at some point surrenders a de-

gree of national sovereignty to an international body which is empowered with the authority to assist in the resolution of disputes, of differences between states, and where the states are denied the right to use weapons or threaten their use against another state. When we reach that level of wisdom, then an international organization will have a strong and international role. But the United Nations doesn't have it, and doesn't seem about to achieve it.

Tsipis:
Unfortunately I agree with Admiral Carroll; the United Nations in its present incarnation, in its present structure, can really do very little. On the other hand, if we didn't have the United Nations, we would have to invent it, because it is very useful in defusing a crisis. If there is a crisis, you go to the General Assembly, you go to the Security Council, and you can *talk* a lot. It's better to talk than to fight. So in some respects the United Nations is useful. The first response of a country when it feels threatened or attacked is to go to the United Nations. At least it serves as a useful kind of channel for resolving conflict, or for defusing conflict. It doesn't do very much for the larger issues that we are faced with: the threat of nuclear war, the confrontation between the two superpowers, the existence of military blocs. The United Nations does not help there, but it helps in many other ways. Therefore, even though it is not as effective as we would like it to be, it is nevertheless useful.

Bastian:
I think the United Nations can do and *must* do much more to make good resolutions. Why, for example, is it not possible for the secretary-general of the United Nations to enter a plane with a handful of volunteers and go immediately to the centre of a crisis? Perhaps he could go to Nicaragua or to the Middle East in the area where Iran and Iraq are fighting, and make it clear that if they want to go on with their war and their violence, they must first of all kill the secretary-general of the United Nations. This sort of action must be possible. This would be a more creative action than simply passing resolutions.

PART II

Economic Ramifications of the Arms Race

Kathleen Wallace-Deering

CHAPTER 6

The Economics of War and Peace

KATHLEEN WALLACE-DEERING

I'm honoured to be chairing Session II of this symposium, and proud to live in a city which is a nuclear-weapons-free zone, and which sponsors this kind of symposium, the Peace Festival going on throughout this week, and our annual Walk for Peace on Sunday.

I've seen many familiar faces in the theatre during the symposium — faces of people active in the peace movement in Nova Scotia, Quebec, Ontario, the Prairies, and many communities in B.C. I'm grateful that in the theatre tonight so many of you feel the same sense of responsibility that I do, to do whatever each of us can to resist the threat to human survival posed by the arms race, and to build a more just and peaceful world. Working together here in Vancouver and across Canada, we are making our contribution to an extraordinary global movement for human survival, peace and justice. This is the most important activity any of us can be engaged in.

The theme of our session tonight has been advertised in a number of different ways: "The economics of war and peace," "The effects of mil-

Kathleen Wallace-Deering is one of the most effective peace activists in Canada. Educated in anthropology and sociology at the University of British Columbia, she worked from 1980 to 1985 as an organizer for Project Ploughshares. At the 1983 meeting of the World Council of Churches in Vancouver, she organized a Ploughshares Coffee House which served to foster intensive discussion amongst delegates from all over the world interested in peace. She recently participated in the production by the National Film Board of the film Speaking Our Peace, *which interviews Soviet and Canadian women working for peace.*

itarism on the economies of the developed countries, especially Canada,'' and finally ''How to redirect resources from the nuclear arms race to improve the Western, especially the Canadian economy.''

We won't be dealing with the question: ''Regardless of the cost, don't we need nuclear weapons and related weapon systems such as the Strategic Defense Initiative, for our defence? Don't we need them to deter the Soviets from initiating a nuclear war?'' This area was covered very thoroughly in last night's discussion led by Rear Admiral Eugene Carroll, General Gert Bastian, and Professor Kosta Tsipis. The answer given by all three was an emphatic ''NO, we don't need these weapons.'' They clearly explained the ways in which the continuing build-up of nuclear weapons and the development of new systems, such as the Strategic Defense Initiative (SDI), *increases* the likelihood of nuclear war, and *increases* the risk that all of us here tonight will die in a nuclear war. Tonight we'll be building upon the conclusions reached in last night's discussion, that spending on nuclear weapons and SDI does NOT buy us greater security.

Tonight we'll be turning our attention to the economic implications of nuclear disarmament, and to questions such as, ''How much of our economy is dependent upon weapons production?'' and ''Can we afford nuclear disarmament?'' ''Would a Nuclear Freeze Bomb the Economy?'' is the catchy title of an article in which the author asks if a nuclear freeze would endanger millions of jobs in the United States (1).* What would be the impact of a freeze on the American economy, and how would that affect us here in Canada?

We'll also be examining the claims of Canadian government officials —when they announce increased military expenditures and subsidies to companies such as Litton Systems Canada Ltd., which received millions of dollars of public money for its work on the guidance systems of the cruise missile—claims that military expenditures benefit the economy, provide jobs and produce technical innovation. Is that true? Is military spending good for the Canadian economy? Is it good for business? Is it good for labour? Is the Canadian government's policy of providing substantial subsidies to companies through the Defence Industry Productivity Programme of the Department of Regional Industrial Expansion a good *economic* policy? Does our partnership with the United States in the Defence Production Sharing Arrangement, whereby Canadian companies can bid on an equal footing with American companies for Pentagon contracts, strengthen the Canadian manufacturing sector? Are there sufficient technological spinoffs from Canadian involvement in the manufacturing of bits and pieces of United States nuclear weapon systems that we

* These numbers refer to references found at the end of the chapter. —ED.

are through this involvement gaining a place for ourselves as civilian high-tech manufacturers in the world economy? Some government officials and others who support continued and increased Canadian involvement in military production answer "Yes" to many of these questions, but are they right(2)?

Tonight we'll also explore some "how to" questions—how do we convert those sectors of the economy currently dependent upon weapons production to civilian production? How can it be done technologically? How can it be done politically? In a time of high unemployment and slow economic growth, we won't get much support if we are simply shouting, "Close these weapons plants down," without proposing ways for people to keep their jobs and for companies to continue operating. So how do we go about persuading and assisting companies and employees to convert from military production to civilian production(3)?

Finally, in talking about economic conversion, I'm hoping that we might begin to explore the theme of the economics of war and peace in a more global context. Do we in the Canadian peace movement who are working for an end to the nuclear arms race and an end to Canadian involvement in the manufacturing and export of weapons also need to be working for a new international economic order, which will narrow the gap between the rich industrialized countries of the North (in both East and West) and the poor countries of the South? To what extent is our relative affluence in Canada dependent upon the ability of our closest trading partner, the United States, to project its military power around the world to protect its investments, markets and access to raw materials and strategic resources?

Some analysts argue that we need to view the nuclear weapons of both superpowers as simply the apex of their elaborate military systems which span the globe, and which for the Soviets includes their military bases in twenty-two foreign countries, and for the Americans includes their bases in forty foreign countries. They claim that both superpowers are seeking to maintain control over their respective spheres of influence through the arming of client states, and at times through direct military intervention or nuclear gunboat diplomacy. They point to statements by American presidents of their right to use a rapid deployment force in the defence of American "national" or "strategic" interests, which for example have been defined in recent years as continued American access to Middle East oil. To what extent is our affluence in Canada dependent upon the United States' ability to influence world events in its economic favour, using military force if necessary? Is it true, as some would argue, that we are enjoying the privileges of an unjust global economic order which is policed and maintained by military might(4)? In working for peace, must we also then be working for global economic justice(5)? And finally, in working for peace and justice, for a new international economic order, must we be willing to make economic sacrifices, or would we in fact in the long term have greater economic security, as has been argued by the Brandt Commission in their report "North-South: A Program for Survival"(6)?

I've posed lots of questions, and I'm eager to hear the panelists' response. Before introducing the panelists to you, I would like to make a final plea that in our discussion tonight about the economics of war and peace, we remember the human reality which underlies any abstract discussion about the economics of war and peace. Let us keep in mind the faces of the victims of the arms race—the victims in a world where choices are being made to spend vast sums on weapons, while the basic needs of millions of people are unmet. Let us remember that statistic so shocking to many of us, that as we meet here tonight the world is spending roughly $1.5 million per minute on military purposes, while during the same minute thirty children are dying from lack of food and from diseases which are easy to prevent.

Some of us today had the opportunity to visit the United Nations Peace Pavilion at Expo. Among the most striking features of the pavilion, as one approaches and enters it, are the pictures of human faces—of ordinary people from all parts of our world. As we meet here tonight, let us keep in mind the faces of the victims of the arms race which involves economic decisions to allocate money, human talent and resources to weapons production instead of meeting people's basic needs. Let us remember the faces of people in our own country who are unemployed and who are lining up to receive bags of groceries at food banks. Let us remember the faces of people in the Third World who are destitute, hungry, and sick—many of them sick simply because they don't have clean water to drink. Clean water would save the lives of millions of people in the Third World—especially children—and could be provided to all people in the world at a cost of what the world is spending in a few months on the arms race. Let us remember and be challenged by that famous statement by President Eisenhower, when he said that "Every gun that is made, every warship launched, every rocket fired signifies in the final sense a theft from those who hunger and are not fed, those who are cold and are not clothed. The world in arms is not spending money alone. It is spending the sweat of its labourers, the genius of its scientists, the hope of its children. This is not a way of life...under the cloud of war it is humanity hanging on a cross of iron."

References and Notes

1. Bill Hartung, "Would a Nuclear Freeze Bomb the Economy?" *Business and Society Review,* no. 47 (fall 1983): 34–39.

Hartung was the director of a research project on the economic effects of a nuclear freeze, and the results have been published by the Council of Economic Priorities, 84 Fifth Ave., New York, N.Y. 10011. In the article published in *Business and Society Review,* Hartung discusses who are the economic winners and losers of the current arms race, and argues that for most Americans, there are in fact potential economic benefits of a nuclear freeze.

For a more thorough discussion of the ways in which military production has had very negative consequences for the American economy, see Seymour Melman's address entitled, "Military Spending and Job Security: The Economics of Permanent War," published in Project Ploughshares Working Paper 84–85. Melman is Professor of Industrial Engineering at Columbia University. (The working paper is available from the Project Ploughshares office at Conrad Grebel College, Waterloo, Ont. N2L 3G6.)

2. Project Ploughshares Research Director Ernie Regehr answers "No" to these questions. See for example his writings in the following publications:

i. "The Economics of the Arms Race" in *Canada and the Nuclear Arms Race,* edited by E. Regehr and S. Rosenblum. (Toronto: James Lorimer and Co., 1983): 63–84.

ii. "The Military Industry in Canada: Street Vendor to the Global Arms Marathon" in *Canadian Dimension,* (Sept. 1985): 16–88, 33.

iii. "Economic Implications for Canada of the Arms Race and Nuclear Disarmament" in *The Prevention of Nuclear War,* edited by T. L. Perry, Jr. (Vancouver: Physicians for Social Responsibility, B. C. Chapter, 1983): 121–131.

iv. "The Utilization of Resources for Military Purposes in Canada and the Impact on Canadian Industrialization and Defence Procurement," United Nations Document 80-15582 (1980).

A Project Ploughshares Working Paper published in 1986 examines the Defence Industry Productivity Programme. Another researcher examining these questions is Toby Sanger, whose article on Military Spending was published in *The Facts,* (Jan.–Feb. 1986): 8–10. In this article Sanger argues that military spending in Canada doesn't create nearly as many jobs as the same amounts spent by consumers.

3. See the Project Ploughshares Working Paper (Summer 1986) which summarizes the Conference on Economic Conversion which took place in Toronto in the fall of 1985. See also Project Ploughshares Working Paper 84–85 "Peace, Employment and the Economics of Permanent War" in which Seymour Melman describes proposed American legislation for economic conversion.

4. Project Ploughshares Research Director Ernie Regehr makes this kind of argument in the article "Militarization and the National Security State" published by the Canadian organization Ten Days for World Development.

5. Increasingly, churches have been arguing that peace is inseparable from justice. The address at this symposium by Bishop Gumbleton illustrates this perspective. See also, for example, the "Statement on Peace and Justice" adopted by the World Council of Churches at its Sixth Assembly held in Vancouver in 1983. (Published in *Ploughshares Monitor,* vol. IV, nos. 6 and 7.)

6. *North-South: A Program For Survival,* The Report of the Independent Commission on International Development Issues under the Chairmanship of Willy Brandt. (Cambridge, Mass.: MIT Press, 1980.)

Other References

Ruth Leger Sivard, *World Military and Social Expenditures*. Published annually by World Priorities, Box 25140, Washington, D.C. 20007, and distributed in Canada by Project Ploughshares.

Clyde Sanger, *Safe and Sound: Disarmament and Development in the Eighties*. A popular version of the study by the United Nations Group of Governmental Experts on the Relationship between Disarmament and Development for the U. N. General Assembly 1978–81 (Ottawa: Deneau Publishers, 1982). Available from Project Ploughshares.

CHAPTER 7

Our War Economy and Conversion for Peace

BISHOP REMI J. DE ROO

INTRODUCTION

It is appropriate to express my appreciation to all those involved in organizing the Centennial Peace Festival in Vancouver and this particular
symposium on Peace and Disarmament. This Peace Festival has been an
extraordinary cultural experience for all of us. Throughout this week's
cultural and educational events, we have been sharply reminded of our
all-too-human capacity to destroy the earth. We are now actively challenged to search for more creative peace strategies in a nuclear age. I cannot imagine a more fitting way to commemorate Vancouver's centennial,
in a city rightly known as the Peace Capital of Canada.

As I recall, the recent origins of the peace movement in British Columbia date back to the early 1980s. At that time, small groups of people on
both sides of the Canada-United States border protested against the
launching of the Trident submarine base which was strategically located
between three cities, Seattle, Vancouver, and Victoria. Our populations
were apparently considered expendable! The protest movement against
the Trident was gradually transformed into a series of massive demonstrations known as the annual Walks for Peace. In 1983, 65,000 people
marched, followed by 115,000 people in 1984, and some 80,000 again
last year. Effectively, Vancouver has now become the centre of North
America's largest annual Walk for Peace. Indeed, based on the experience of this week, it should be clear to all that the peace movement is still
very much alive and thriving!

As I understand it, this Peace and Disarmament Symposium is designed to bring together people from various backgrounds to share insights, analyses, and strategies for peace in a high-tech nuclear age. In

Bishop Remi J. De Roo

turn, these insights are to be re-formulated in terms of a concrete set of peace proposals for presentation to the United Nations Conference on Peace and Disarmament and to the leaders of the NATO and Warsaw Pact countries. This evening, I am pleased to participate on this panel with two distinguished persons deeply committed to the cause of peace and disarmament, namely, Professor John Kenneth Galbraith and David L. Werlin, president of the Alberta Federation of Labour. From our various perspectives, we have been asked to address the topic of how to redirect resources spent on nuclear weapons and improve our economy.

In making this presentation, I do not claim technical expertise on military affairs, disarmament strategies or economic issues. As a bishop, my contribution lies more in the socioethical dimensions of the economy, peace and disarmament; I view and analyze the signs of the times from the perspective of the Gospel message which emphasizes *opus iustitae pax*—that peace demands justice. Our world today is plagued all too much by structural injustices and ideological conflicts—East and West, North and South—which undercut the search for a true and lasting peace. What we require is nothing less than the building of a new international economic and political order that is clearly based on the goals of justice and peace. This, in itself, calls for a profound conversion—we must convert economically, politically, culturally and spiritually. This is not simply a moral imperative. It is now essential for the very survival of humanity and creation on this planet.

In addressing the topic, ''Our War Economy and Conversion for Peace,'' I propose to share some brief reflections on the realities of our global war economy; the role that Canada plays in it; the resulting moral disorder; the importance of pursuing strategies for economic conversion; and the corresponding need for cultural and spiritual conversion.

Bishop Remi J. De Roo is the Roman Catholic Bishop of Victoria. Bishop De Roo grew up on a prairie farm in the 1930s, witnessing the poverty of the Depression. As a result he has been a passionate champion of the poor and the underprivileged: he has strongly defended the rights of Canada's native peoples, as well as the rights of the oppressed in South and Central America. Bishop De Roo holds a doctorate in theology from the Angelicum University in Rome, and has been the Bishop of Victoria since 1962. He is best noted for the 1983 New Year's statement entitled, "Ethical Reflections on the Economic Crisis," issued by the Social Affairs Commission of Canada's Catholic bishops, which he chaired. This call for a new and ethical approach to economic planning in Canada was seconded by the major Protestant churches. Bishop De Roo has followed up this approach with his new book, published in 1986, Cries of Victims —Voice of God.

GLOBAL WAR ECONOMY

First, we must recognize that we live in the midst of a "global war economy." Since the Second World War, the United States and the Soviet Union have primarily organized their own national economies (and the economies of many of their satellite countries) around the priorities of escalating military production. As a result, vast resources of capital and technology have been directed toward building a global war economy, not only East and West but also North and South.

Today, annual military expenditures throughout the world amount to over U.S. $800 billion, or, in other words, over $2 billion a day.* Indeed, global military expenses are higher than the gross national product of the whole of Latin America and are double that of the continent of Africa. The yearly budget for training military personnel in the United States alone is over twice as much as the budget for educating some 300 million school-aged children in Southeast Asia.

On an East/West basis, economies dependent on military spending have grown enormously. To protect and expand their economic positions (as well as their ideological influence) both the United States and the Soviet Union have sought access to strategic resources and new markets, and so both have rapidly expanded their political security systems. As a result, both sides have built up massive nuclear arsenals—the neutron bomb, the SS-18, the MX missile, the SS-20, the cruise missile—which have brought the world perilously close to a nuclear holocaust. Indeed, Eastern and Western bloc countries today spend an average of twenty times more of their national incomes on military arsenals than on development aid to the Third World.[†]

On a North/South basis as well, economic dependence on military spending has become paramount. To attract investment from industrialized countries in the North, many Third World countries have used military force to repress the poor and control social unrest. Seventy percent of the international arms trade involves Third World countries. Despite food shortages, for example, many Third World countries spend over five times as much importing arms as on importing agricultural machinery. The two superpowers further intensify Third World militarization by seeking to establish military bases and alliances in strategic regions of the Third World as, for example, is occurring today in Central America and Southeast Asia.

---

* Estimates range from $600 to $900 billion. The United Nations Pavilion at Expo 86 indicates $800 billion.

[†]Ruth Leger Sivard in *World Military and Social Expenditures 1985* reports that during the year 1983 the developed countries spent U.S. $547 billion on military expenditures, but only U.S. $30 billion on foreign economic aid.—ED.

As a result, the entire globe has become effectively locked into a war economy. The United States and the Soviet Union, together with the security alliances composed of the NATO and Warsaw Pact countries, constitute the global war economy's strategic centres. This situation, in turn, has led nation-states in the East, West, North and South increasingly to militarize their own economies. It has also created conditions for new forms of state terrorism. As we witness recent events, whether in Afghanistan, South Africa, Libya, or wherever, we must ask this question: is the torture and killing of civilians any less immoral when done by or for powerful governments instead of by terrorist groups?

CANADA'S ROLE

Secondly, we must identify the role that Canada plays in this global war economy. Canada is a member of the Western political alliance through NATO and NORAD. Canada's economy is highly dependent upon that of the United States. The more Canada's economy is tied to that of our powerful neighbour, the more Canada operates as a branch plant of the American military-industrial complex in a high-tech nuclear age.

As a nation-state, Canada has officially rejected the nuclear option. Yet Canada actively participates in the production of nuclear weapon systems. Through the Canadian-American Defence Production Sharing Arrangement, Canadian industries have been directly involved in the production of component parts for nuclear weapon systems, including cruise missiles, Trident submarines, and launchers for the neutron bomb. Canadian scientists and high-tech industries have also been involved in the production of communication systems and related technologies for nuclear weapon systems. Many of these projects for nuclear weapons research are funded in part by the Canadian government under the Defence Industry Production Program.

Canadian territory has also become increasingly important to the United States in the development of nuclear war-fighting strategies. In British Columbia, the coastal waters near Nanoose Bay are probably used for the testing of nuclear warheads as well as for Trident submarine manoeuvres. Parts of Alberta and the Northwest Territories are used for the flight tests of cruise missiles. More importantly, it is highly likely that the Canadian north will play a strategic role in the American "Star Wars" program. As numerous observers have pointed out, the recent renewal of the NORAD agreement, coupled with the decision to rebuild the continental defence system in northern Canada, sets the stage for Canada's involvement in Star Wars and its nuclear war-fighting operations.

At the same time, Canadian arms manufacturers have been actively selling arms to Third World military regimes. Sales include military and police equipment to the Pinochet regime in Chile; equipment and technologies which are probably used for military or police operations in South Africa; and aircraft to the military regime in Honduras. The sales of CANDU nuclear technology to military regimes in South Korea and Argentina also raises serious questions. More recently, a Canadian manufacturing subsidiary supplied armoured vehicles for the new American rapid deployment force, which is expected to be used for military intervention in areas of regional conflict, such as Nicaragua.

In effect, Canada has come to play an increasingly important role in the global war economy, both as a branch plant of the American military economy and as a territorial base for American nuclear strategies. In many ways Canada has become the United States' economic and political satellite. This relationship is likely to be further reinforced if a comprehensive free trade accord is established between the two countries. In any case, the more Canada is tied to the American military economy, the less chance we have of developing an independent strategy for peace and disarmament in a nuclear age.

MORAL DISORDER

Thirdly, we need to clarify the extent to which the global war economy and Canada's role in it constitute a moral disorder. The global war economy poses a real threat to the future of both humanity and creation itself. This, in turn, presents a fundamental challenge to all our religious traditions and categories of moral judgment. For what is at stake is nothing less than the survival of the human race and the earth itself which God created *good*.

From both a religious and a humanistic standpoint, the fact that billions of dollars are spent every day on military weapons, while millions of people are suffering from poverty and starvation in the world, is a scandal of the highest proportions. Under these conditions, human and material resources are being mobilized for the service of death rather than the source of life. The service of death may be a slow process, as in the case of human starvation or military repression in Third World countries. Or it may be a rapid process, as in the case of a nuclear holocaust. In either case, we are confronted with a profound moral disorder in the values and priorities that govern our global economy. The Christian and humanitarian conscience cries out against this evil.

There are some, of course, who argue that the build-up of nuclear weapon systems is morally justified because they maintain deterrence. But strategies for deterrence (as the American Catholic bishops pointed out in their pastoral document on peace) are morally acceptable only if they lead to progressive disarmament. A doctrine of nuclear deterrence based on acquiring and sustaining a position of superiority is not morally acceptable. Yet this is the doctrine that operates in the Reagan administration and its continuing efforts to develop a nuclear war-fighting capability.

In the light of the facts presented to this symposium I am led to question whether the conditions attached by the American Catholic bishops to their highly qualified tolerance of deterrence are being fulfilled. There appears to be no movement toward effective disarmament, no initiative to ensure a minimal deterrent. If the military is indeed intent on acquiring a first-strike capability, or is planning even a limited nuclear war, can we rationalize the morality of deterrence any longer? Must we not draw the logical conclusion which flows from the Second Vatican Council declaration (*Gaudium et Spes,* article 80): "Every act of war directed to the indiscriminate destruction of whole cities or vast areas with their inhabitants is a crime against God and humanity, which merits firm and unequivocal condemnation."

Canada's own involvement both in the production of nuclear weapon systems and in the sale of arms to repressive regimes raises another set of moral issues. The fact that Canada does not have its own operational program of nuclear deterrence and the type of weapon systems required means that Canadian industries produce component parts for American weapon systems designed to further enhance the American nuclear war-fighting capacity. The fact that Canada does not have an independent policy on nuclear strategies means that Canadian territory will be increasingly used, not only for the testing, but in all likelihood for eventual operation of the strategic nuclear weapon systems of the United States. The fact that Canada does not effectively apply human rights criteria when it sells military equipment also means that Canadian arms industries serve to strengthen the hand of repression in some Third World countries.

For Canada, this constitutes a form of "branch plant immorality." As Canadians, we are, whether we like it or not, accomplices in the operations of the American military-industrial machine. However, it is the Canadian workers involved in military production who are the ones most likely to suffer from this moral crisis. Once workers become aware that what they produce with their hands and their intellect can actually be turned against them and used for their own destruction and that of humanity as a whole, the result could be untold anguish, anxiety and fear. It is here that we perceive the deeper human costs of being a branch plant locked into the global war economy.

We Canadians are seriously misled if we act as innocent bystanders in all this. As the United States prepares to "sacrifice arms control on the altar of SDI,"‡ as Rear Admiral Eugene Carroll expressed it, are we not

‡ Strategic Defense Initiative

in some way willing acolytes bowing before the golden idol of military profits? And when public authorities tell Canadian workers in certain regions that they have to choose between jobs in military production or unemployment, is this not a form of inhuman blackmail which must be identified and denounced?

ECONOMIC CONVERSION

Fourthly, we need to make concerted efforts to develop new and effective strategies for economic conversion in Canada. After all, the very existence of a global war economy implies that national economies become increasingly dependent on military production. Any real strategy for peace in a nuclear age requires industrial conversion from military production priorities to more socially useful forms of production. In effect, economic conversion is essential for addressing the moral disorder of a global war economy in a nuclear age.

Economic conversion, however, does not mean simply shutting down manufacturing plants engaged in the production of military equipment: the jobs and livelihoods of thousands of workers are at stake. Nor does economic conversion necessarily entail the elimination of all forms of military production in Canada. Instead, criteria need to be developed for identifying what parts of Canada's industrial system for military production need to be dismantled and/or converted into socially useful forms of production. In Canada, Project Ploughshares, a Church-sponsored organization for peace and disarmament, has begun to develop some of these criteria and strategies for economic conversion in collaboration with labour unions.

In its studies, Project Ploughshares has identified three major industrial conversion targets in Canada: 1) those companies most clearly dependent on contracts with the Pentagon or its suppliers (especially for the production of component parts for nuclear war-fighting systems); 2) those companies which sell military products or equipment to repressive regimes (or which sell products that could be used to repress human rights); and 3) those companies which violate a broad consensus of what an appropriate Canadian defence policy should be.

For Canada, an effective strategy for economic conversion requires reducing the dependence of Canadian companies on American military markets. This dependence could be reduced in two ways: new non-military markets could be found for commodities that have civilian as well as military applications (for example, new civilian markets could be found to replace the military markets for Pratt and Whitney Aircraft engines, which can be used in both military and civilian aircraft); and new, more socially useful products could be developed to replace production of military commodities (for example, the workers at the General Motors plant in London, Ontario could use their skills to produce civilian goods instead of armoured vehicles).

Such strategies for economic conversion require basic changes in the federal policies related to military exports and subsidies for those exports. But even more important is the direct participation of the workers themselves. Workers in industries which serve military needs cannot be expected to put their jobs and livelihoods on the line if they are not directly involved in developing alternative production plans or alternative markets. The most successful cases of industrial conversion outside Canada (for example, the Lucas Aerospace plant in Britain) have been those where the workers themselves helped to develop conversion strategies through alternative-use committees in factories.

These, then, are some of the elements involved in economic conversion. To be effective, however, major structural changes would be required in Canada's political economy, including less economic, political and cultural dependency on the United States; more emphasis on self-reliant models for economic development; more participatory processes for economic planning; and new forms of ownership of, and control over, the means of production (such as community and worker-controlled industries).

CULTURAL CONVERSION

Fifthly, we need to give serious attention to strategies for cultural conversion. Indeed, the kind of economic conversion for peace required in this country is not really possible without a transformation of societal values, ideals and priorities. We have ideologies deeply embedded in our culture and society which serve to rationalize a global war economy and Canada's role in it.

When one reflects on Canada's own history as a nation, one realizes the extent to which a branch plant mentality has been woven into our culture. Our economy has been owned to a high degree by foreign and particularly American-based corporations. In many ways Canada is still highly dependent on the United States economically, politically and culturally. Effective development of alternative peace strategies will require that we end the neocolonial mentality which has promoted our type of branch plant economy.

Another cultural block is the ideology of national security. Canada must participate in this global war economy, we are told, for reasons of national security. But what does "national security" mean in this context? When all is said and done, it doesn't mean securing peace; it means securing profitable investments through military production and expansion. This is largely true whether one is talking about the production of nuclear weapon systems or the fuelling of regional conflicts in Central America or the Middle East. Thus, the real implications of national security need to be unmasked if economic conversion strategies for peace are to be understood and supported.

At the same time, we must challenge the technological rationality which dominates our society today. According to this mentality, peace is treated as a technical problem requiring a technical solution. The true meaning of peace is thereby distorted, and fundamental questions about the causes of war are avoided. Instead of designing policies to get at the root causes of global conflicts and move progressively toward real disarmament, the solution proposed is building ever more sophisticated nuclear weapons and defence systems like Star Wars.

What Canadians really need is a dynamic strategy of cultural education for peace: we need to unmask the dominant myths and discover the true meaning of peace. Through cultural education people could overcome our branch plant mentality, unmask the meanings behind the ideology of national security, and challenge the technological fix approach to the fundamental problems of world peace. Schools, universities, churches, labour unions, women's organizations and a variety of other popular Canadian associations need to stimulate this cultural education.

As the Vancouver Centennial Peace Festival has demonstrated, a wide range of people are prepared to mobilize for the cause of peace. The movement is alive, not only in organizations specifically directed toward peace and disarmament, but also in labour unions, women's associations, the major churches, farmers' groups, student associations, native organizations, various communities, and a host of other popular and professional organizations across the country.

We must learn to live and act together in solidarity through this common struggle for peace and justice. This requires that we open ourselves to other perspectives, transcend narrow self-interests and organizational styles, and see the common links between our various struggles around the economic crisis and the arms race. It is only by creating solidarity between popular organizations and movements that we can forge the kind of moral and political will necessary to challenge Canada's role in the global war economy and bring about economic and cultural conversion for peace.

CONCLUSION

At this point, my personal convictions as a disciple of the Prince of Peace, the Lord Jesus Christ, blend with and affirm the convictions of other people from many religious and humanistic persuasions. All are convinced that peace is a worldwide priority which reflects the aspirations of all peoples, young and old. Peace is a universal value which transcends all frontiers and cultures. Even profound ideological differences must not deter us from facing our responsibilities and expressing our political will for the preservation of human civilization. My Biblical heritage reminds me that we are all brothers and sisters, made in the image of God, members of one family.

War is obsolete as a means of solving quarrels. Only dialogue and solidarity in promoting global justice will provide lasting solutions. Risking the very survival of our own flesh and blood is not only immoral today, it is insane. The nuclear destructive capability now in the hands of so many should open our eyes once and for all. Force can no longer prevail where injustice spawns terrorism. Only international co-operation and justice leading to a civilization of love can guarantee our survival.

Nothing less will suffice than individual and collective conversion expressed through acceptance of spiritual norms above and beyond our national self-interest. The atom bomb and its lethal mushroom cloud is but the shadow side of a newly-emerging symbol which reveals our mutual interdependence as human beings on a fragile planet.

Together let us discern these signs of the times and resolve that we will not cease to voice our convictions until all our leaders join us in our common purpose: we refuse death through war, we choose life through peace!

PHOTO: C. W. HILL

David L. Werlin

CHAPTER 8

Conversion to Peaceful Production

DAVID L. WERLIN

INTRODUCTION

Throughout history, the progressive leadership of the union movement has been opposed to war. Wars are fought at the expense of the working class. Working people make up the armed forces who are sacrificed by all nations during wartime. Prior to the First World War, the Second International Workingmen's Association passed a resolution calling for all working people to prevent an outbreak of war by all means at their disposal, including plans for a Europe-wide general strike. In the latter half of the twentieth century, it has not been just those workers conscripted, coerced or economically forced into the armed forces who have died: since 1945, there have been over ten million war casualties; nine million have been civilians.

Furthermore, wars have given the economic elite and their allies in government an opportunity to attack the gains made by labour during peacetime. In Canada, this has been demonstrably true. In both world wars in this century, union organizers and activists have been jailed un-

David L. Werlin has been president of the Alberta Federation of Labour since 1983, and as such is a member of the Executive Council of the Canadian Labour Congress. He has had extensive experience in the trade union movement, particularly in the Canadian Union of Public Employees, and as a member of the executive board of the Calgary and District Labour Council. David Werlin believes the trade union movement must be at the forefront of the struggle for peace. His actions, such as his representation of the Alberta Federation of Labour at the founding convention of the Canadian Peace Alliance, support that belief.

der sweeping war measures legislation. Civil liberties have been suspended, strikes banned and union activities curtailed. Typically, proposals for wage and price freezes were advanced but seemed to be successful only in freezing wages.

Following World War II, the Cold War and McCarthyism also helped to restrain the trade union movement. The debate within our unions was curtailed by pressure to support the United States; to support rather than to criticize Canada's role in the arms race; to follow American foreign policy; and to follow blindly the old line that the Soviet Union, Soviet system and even the Soviet people are our enemies.

However, the Cold War is being eroded, and the trade union movement is now moving more confidently into the peace movement and becoming a force for peace, détente and disarmament. The Canadian Labour Congress (CLC) helped to organize the founding convention of the Canadian Peace Alliance in Toronto in November 1985. The CLC has now officially joined the alliance and has a representative on its Steering Committee.

Make no mistake though, war has been good for the corporate sector in Canada. Massey Harris, the Weston empire, and Ford Canada Limited are only three of many corporations in Canada that profited immensely from our national war efforts.

The constant escalation of armament production, in terms of both quality and quantity, increases the risk of war. ''Peace through strength,'' or Mutual Assured Destruction, will not prevent war. To claim that the arms race has somehow prevented nuclear war, because we haven't had one yet, is like a heavy smoker claiming that cigarette smoking prevents lung disease because that individual still has apparently healthy lungs. The only sure way to prevent war is universal disarmament. The destruction of the means of waging war is the only logical approach to preventing war.

America, by deploying Pershing II and cruise missiles and developing its Strategic Defense Initiative program, has escalated the arms race and brought us to the brink of nuclear war. The editors of the *Bulletin of the Atomic Scientists* have moved the hands of their doomsday clock to indicate three minutes before midnight. The American Joint Chiefs of Staff are predicting nuclear war by 1990. All the struggles, sacrifices and gains of Canadian working people may well disappear in a radioactive cloud. The fundamental reason for union opposition to the arms race is therefore obvious. Prevention of nuclear war is in itself sufficient reason for people to oppose the arms race. There are, however, other valid reasons for the union movement to oppose military spending.

CANADA'S ECONOMIC CRISIS

On a per capita basis Canada ranks ahead of the United States as an international arms merchant. Sales exceeding $2 billion per year put Canada among the top ten nations exporting military equipment. The federal government actively and falsely promotes arms production as a method of providing job security and economic growth for Canada. Canadian defence expenditures currently consume ten percent of federal government spending and nearly forty percent of federal discretionary spending. Defence spending has risen by an annual average of 13.5 percent compounded over the last six years. Yet for the Canadian people, the last decade has been one of increasing unemployment and a falling standard of living. In no year since 1977 has the increase in average Canadian wages and salaries matched the inflation rate. Between 1978 and September 1985, Canadians have lost over six percent in real income (Table 1).

TABLE 1

LOSS IN REAL WAGES

YEAR	INCREASE IN AVERAGE WEEKLY WAGES AND SALARIES(%)	INCREASE IN CONSUMER PRICES(%)	LOSS IN REAL WAGES(%)
1978	6.2	8.9	-2.7
1979	8.7	9.1	-0.4
1980	10.1	10.2	-0.1
1981	11.8	12.5	-0.7
1982	10.1	10.8	-0.7
1983	N/A	5.8	N/A
1984	3.6	4.4	-O.8
1985 to Sept.	2.7	3.1	-0.5

The National Council of Welfare reports that over 4.1 million Canadians are now living below the poverty line. In 1982 and 1983, over 660,000 Canadians joined the ranks of the poor. That loss in income has been mirrored by a loss in individual Canadian ownership of the assets of our country. Between 1961 and 1984, individual ownership of the total national assets of Canada dropped from 38.4 percent to 32.7 percent. In that same period, corporate ownership of Canada's assets increased from 39.7 percent to 46.8 percent (Table 2).

A deteriorating standard of living and diminishing wages are occurring during the worst unemployment crisis in Canada since the Depression of the 1930s. In a society in which being unemployed is a virtual guarantee of poverty and humiliation, there are now officially 1,347,000 Canadians

TABLE 2

OWNERSHIP OF TOTAL NATIONAL ASSETS

YEAR	CORPORATIONS	PERSONS AND UNINCORPORATED	GOVERNMENT
1961	39.7%	38.4%	12.9%
1984	46.8%	32.7%	10.9%

out of work (Statistics Canada, January 1986). To understand the nature of the problem and obtain some grasp of the real magnitude of our employment crisis, its economic and social costs must be examined. Official unemployment figures exclude "discouraged" workers (those who have given up an active job search), people who are underemployed in a part-time job (because no full-time work is available), students who would work but can't find jobs, and the disabled. Statistics Canada, in a 1982 study, found that if discouraged workers alone were added, the unemployment figures would increase by thirty-three percent. This is in line with the findings of similar Canadian studies.

There are, as of December 1985, 1,780,000 part-time workers in Canada. In fact, half of all new jobs created between 1975 and 1983 were part-time, and all indications are that this trend is accelerating. Fully thirty percent of these workers (Statistics Canada 1984) wanted full-time work but could not find it.

If the 445,000 discouraged workers, and 534,000 part-time workers unable to find full-time jobs are added to the 1,347,000 who are officially unemployed, a more realistic measure of unemployment can be arrived at: a total of 2,326,000 unemployed Canadians. This makes the real unemployment rate 17.9 percent—a far cry from the official 10.7 percent. The social cost to Canada is staggering. A 1982 study by the Canadian Union of Public Employees estimated the total socioeconomic cost of unemployment for that year to be $78.3 billion. The study included estimates of the value of lost production and earnings, unemployment insurance and social welfare payments, lost education and training, lost tax revenues and hidden social costs such as increases in suicides, heart disease and admissions to mental institutions and prisons.

MILITARY SPENDING AND EMPLOYMENT

All through the current economic crisis, federal defence expenditures have increased, yet the government insists on trying to sell defence spending as a cure for unemployment and economic decline. In the current budget, the Mulroney government cut spending and laid off employees in all departments except the Department of National Defence. Furthermore, all other departments are limited to a two percent increase in spending per year. With inflation averaging slightly better than four percent each year, this limitation has produced a virtual hiring and wage freeze across the federal public sector, except for defence. The defence budget will increase by six percent each year for the rest of the decade.

In reality, defence spending is one of the most inefficient ways of spending public money to create jobs. A study in the United States by the United Electrical Workers has shown that far more direct and indirect jobs can be created by directing public resources to more socially beneficial activities (Table 3).

TABLE 3

JOBS CREATED BY THE EXPENDITURE OF U.S. $1 BILLION

INDUSTRY	DIRECT AND INDIRECT JOBS CREATED
Construction	100,000
Education	187,000
Health Services	139,000
Transportation	92,000
Machinery	86,000
Government	87,000
Military	76,000

Source: U.S. Bureau of Labour Statistics

The irony of the situation is plain. Our government, elected on the promise of jobs, jobs, jobs, is actually laying people off, and, with our tax dollars, redirecting public spending to the most wasteful, socially useless form of expenditure. It is important to note that the services being cut back are almost always services to individuals, rather than services to business. Transfer payments from Ottawa to the provinces for health care and education have been reduced, unemployment insurance benefits have been cut back, public housing subsidies, environmental protection programs, and support of cultural activities (most importantly the Canadian Broadcasting Corporation) have all been reduced. Increases in the defence budget have quite simply been made by reducing the budget for public services.

It is the average Canadian who inevitably pays the bill. The corporate share of total government revenue has declined to an insignificant level, while the individual taxpayers have borne an increasingly heavy load (Table 4).

TABLE 4

PERCENTAGE OF TOTAL GOVERNMENT TAX REVENUES (IN MILL-
IONS OF DOLLARS)

YEAR	DIRECT TAXES ON PERSONS	% OF TOTAL TAXES	DIRECT TAXES ON CORPORATIONS	% OF TOTAL TAXES
1955	1,318	22.7	1,135	19.6
1965	3,472	24.6	2,282	16.2
1975	19,193	36.0	7,921	14.9
1985*	54,933	50.8	13,263	10.9

* First three quarters of 1985

Direct taxes on persons now provide more than fifty percent of all government tax revenues, while the corporate share is less than eleven percent. Consumer taxes, which again come mainly from working people, make up the balance. Defence spending, with its lucrative contracts which allow cost overruns and guaranteed profit levels, really amounts to a redistribution of wealth from working people to corporations.

ARMS PRODUCTION INFLATIONARY
Besides being an ineffective way of spending public money to create jobs, and a corporate subsidy at taxpayer's expense, military spending also has other serious effects upon the Canadian economy. It is inflationary, generating spendable income without at the same time enlarging the supply of goods available in the market place. Rapid product change and obsolescence, and cost-plus contracts with no ceiling on final price, all contribute to the inflationary cycle. Rapid obsolescence also contradicts another myth about armaments production in general—that it creates a stable economy. Another problem is the amount of nonrenewable resources used in military production, and more importantly the share of total research and development allocations that goes to the arms race in Canada.

American economist Ruth Leger Sivard has pointed to a striking inverse relationship between a nation's military expenditures and the annual rate of growth of productivity in manufacturing.* Simply put, the more a country spends on arms, the less productive is its economy. For

* Details can be found in *World Military and Social Expenditures 1985* by Ruth Leger Sivard, obtainable in the United States from World Priorities, Box 25140, Washington, D.C. 20007, or in Canada from Project Ploughshares, Conrad Grebel College, Waterloo, Ont. N2L 3G6.—ED.

example, the Japanese and West German economies have consistently grown faster than the American economy in the last thirty years. This highlights another myth about the arms race—that military research produces effective new technologies for industry. While there are some spinoff uses of military technology, generally speaking military research produces only military technologies.

Finally, arms spending in Canada is a major factor contributing to our trade deficit in manufactured goods. Most of the military hardware we use is made in the United States. The McDonnell Douglas F-18 fighter planes cost the Canadian balance of payments between $3 and $4 billion. The claim that offsetting purchases of military component parts would balance this drain is simply not true. Actually, the majority of arms manufacturers in Canada simply produce component parts for American military products. Furthermore, most Canadian production is done by subsidiaries of American corporations, so profits generated are returned to the United States anyway.

WHAT IS TO BE DONE?

The most obvious step Canada must take is to redirect public spending from armaments to much-needed social programs, and to restructure our taxation policies so that corporations pay for a larger share of total taxes. Canada's public roads, bridges, sewers, urban transit facilities, and other public works have deteriorated greatly because of spending cutbacks. The Canadian Federation of Municipalities has estimated that it would require a capital investment of $12 billion simply to bring existing facilities back to acceptable standards. As well, hospitals, nursing homes, day care centres, universities, and many other public services need to be expanded. As indicated, these kinds of expenditures, unlike military spending, would produce a massive increase in employment.

However, it is clear that neither corporations nor employees will support reductions in military spending if income is lessened or jobs are lost. Workable alternatives must be found to enable companies to remain profitable while they convert from military production, and to employ as many—or more—people as they employ now. The key is to convert companies from military to nonmilitary production as smoothly as possible. That means identifying useful and saleable products that can be produced with a minimum of retooling and retraining.

A study in the United States in the 1960s showed that, of 127 occupational groups involved in military production, only six would probably require retraining. Research and development occupations were the most difficult because of their highly specialized nature. The main problem, then, is one of plant conversion, or retooling. The Canadian Union of

Public Employees has suggested the following five steps to facilitate conversion:

1. Legislation requiring every major defence contractor to establish a conversion department to search for alternative civilian uses for existing military technology and to carry out market research on the commercial viability of these conversion projects. Particular emphasis should be placed on the development of technology for medical and other socially useful commodities and services.

2. Establishment of alternative-use conversion committees in all major municipalities. These committees would identify local defence production enterprises, and provide technical, financial and research assistance to facilitate conversion planning. Alternative-use conversion committees should have representation from a wide range of local organizations, including unions, churches and technical colleges.

3. Creation of a national conversion council to sponsor and finance research projects on conversion. This agency should be funded with the money the government now spends to subsidize the export of weapons by defence industries.

4. Negotiation of conversion committees by unions, including those representing workers in defence industries. The function of these committees would be to study how the technology and skills in individual firms could be put to alternate uses.

5. A planned reduction in overall federal defence spending[†], accompanied by a corresponding increase in funding for public and social services.

CONVERSION IS A POLITICAL PROBLEM

The main obstacles to conversion in Canada are corporate opposition and government policy. Military production is immensely lucrative for the private sector, and conversion to nonmilitary production would mean a loss of government handouts, guaranteed sales, guaranteed markets and profits.

Furthermore, the Canadian government has followed a policy of integration of military planning and procurement with that of the United States. Through the Defence Development and Production Sharing Arrangements (DDPSA), Canada has adopted a policy of sharing and supporting American strategic defence policies through NORAD and NATO in return for the opportunity to supply component parts for American major weapon systems. This arrangement stipulates that a rough balance of

---

[†] The current budget calls for Canada to spend $9.9 billion on military preparations in fiscal 1987. — ED.

trade in arms be maintained, effectively forcing Canada to buy American finished weapon systems in order to balance the export of component parts to the United States. This integration has produced Canadian complicity in the American military industrial strategy which was responsible for the Cold War and is now leading the world to the brink of a nuclear holocaust.

Conversion can work, but it requires a government committed to peace and to the economic and physical well-being of Canadian citizens, not to the preservation of corporate profits. Canada has already had experience with a successful conversion of military to nonmilitary production: at the end of the Second World War there was a major shift from arms production to domestic consumer-oriented production. It is clear from that experience that when our government becomes convinced that we have more important priorities, when domestic interests and social needs are recognized as more desirable than military spending, conversion can and will be achieved. We have done it before. We can do it again.

CONCLUSION

For Canadian working people, military production and defence spending only exacerbate the current economic crisis. Defence spending redirects public money from people to corporations. It reduces needed social services and is the least efficient way of spending public funds to create jobs. Furthermore, it increases our balance of payments problems and misdirects critical research and development funds and expertise, contributing to the decline of our manufacturing sector. Military production contributes to inflation, and the high risk of obsolescence makes it a bad risk in terms of job stability and economic growth. It also stands in the way of the development of a strong industrial base. Canada, though rich in natural resources, has a very weak industrial base upon which to build economic security.

Politically, Canadian integration into the American military-industrial strategy has deprived us of part of our sovereignty by compromising our ability to chart an independent foreign and defence policy. We have tied ourselves to an American arms race that daily increases the risk of war, and squanders resources badly needed for socially useful production.

Canada could easily convert from military to nonmilitary production. No major skills-retraining is required, and if each plant were systematically analyzed, alternative products could be developed in a surprisingly short period of time. Unfortunately, the corporate sector will not willingly give up the easy profits involved in arms production, while the current government, like governments before it, has consistently shown itself to be concerned only about corporate welfare.

In closing, I would like to state that the peace movement in Canada should and must share the concern that Canadian trade unions have about the federal government's pursuit, with the support of some of our provincial governments, of a free trade or a sectoral free trade agreement with the United States. Any such agreement would further integrate our economy with that of the United States, which, already firmly under the control of a military-industrial complex, is based squarely on the continuation of the arms race. Canadian economic dependence on the United States would be greatly increased by any such free trade agreements. As our economic dependence is increased, our reliance on a made-in-the-USA foreign policy will increase as well, and we will be less able to resist being dragged into the Star Wars lunacy of the Reagan administration.

We need to convert our economy from an economy for arms to an economy for jobs and services to the people. That requires an independent made-in-Canada foreign policy and Canadian economic self-sufficiency. Free trade would undermine that independence and retard the contribution of the Canadian people to the struggle for peace.

Peace must be won. It can be won. Happily, more and more Canadian unions are committing their organized strength, on behalf of Canadian workers, to the cause of peace, the most critical and noble cause ever undertaken by the inhabitants of this beautiful planet.

CHAPTER 9

The Military Power: Tension as a Servant; Arms Control as an Illusion

PROFESSOR JOHN KENNETH GALBRAITH

There comes a time in the troubled course of human affairs when we must step back and examine the fundamental concepts by which our public attitudes and policies are guided. The weapons race, I am persuaded, now needs this sort of examination.

THE NUCLEAR THEOLOGIANS

No one can look at the present position with satisfaction. The two great powers now deploy weapons of unimaginable destructive power. They plan insouciantly for yet more, and for weapon systems of ever more perilous computer control and hair-trigger tendency. Meanwhile, negotiators come together in Geneva; they talk, and then for weeks or months adjourn. Differences are aired, not compromised or resolved. The differences turn on deeply theological points, and this description is more nearly appropriate to the situation than we realize. Policy on arms control has long since passed into the hands of a small group of specialists, the nuclear theologians. All are subordinate to a higher authority—the military power. In consequence, so elementary a matter as a halt in the testing of nuclear weapons is beyond agreement. From the negotiations we no longer, in our realistic moments, expect any genuine step back from the peril of a suspended death sentence under which we, our children and the planet itself live.

MILITARY POWER: AN INDEPENDENT FORCE

The condition behind this disastrous charade is one which we must now, if we are candid, accept. The military power in our time has become an independent force in the superpower relationship. Arms control negotia-

PHOTO: JIM KALETT

Professor John Kenneth Galbraith

tions are not meant to limit and reduce the threat of nuclear devastation; they have become a cover for the larger expression of military power. They serve it as a design for quieting the public fear of nuclear war.

I am not a unilateralist in these matters. I believe that the military power is now a major force in both of the superpowers—as it is, alas, in numerous of the poor countries of what we call the Third World, where it takes a toll on democracy and, more poignantly, takes a toll, literally, on food, clothing and shelter for the poorest of the world's population.

An interacting dynamic exists between our military and that of the Soviets: each actually supports the other side by taking actions which make the other side respond in kind. One country must act in a certain way because it is what the other has done, or intends to do—and so on, to infinity and the eventual disaster. But as an American, I must speak first of the military power as it now manifests itself in the United States.

The first source of the American military power is the belief—the faith —that any government instrument is subject to democratic process. This belief is strong in our rhetoric; it is what children are still taught in school; but it is, in fact, what no fully informed citizen can believe. The modern military establishment, in the organizations it dominates, the money it controls, the politicians it commands, the scientific community it subsidizes, and under the cloak of patriotism that protects it, has become a polar force in its own right. It embraces and controls the civilian authority that legally and constitutionally is presumed to be the source of its restraint. The president, the secretary of defence and the civilian heads of the three armed services are now the articulate and influential advocates of the military's purpose. No one has recently thought of Mr. Reagan, Mr. Weinberger or Mr. Lehman, secretary of the navy and former weapons lobbyist, as a restraining force on military ambition.

Professor John Kenneth Galbraith is one of the world's best-known and most respected living economists. Born in Ontario, and educated in Ontario, California and Cambridge, England, he served on the faculties of both Harvard and Princeton universities in the United States. He was Professor of Economics at Harvard from 1949 to 1975, and he has been Professor Emeritus at Harvard since then. From 1961 to 1963 Professor Galbraith was the American ambassador to India, an appointment which President John F. Kennedy called one of the best he ever made. Professor Galbraith is a prolific author who appeals to both scholarly and popular audiences. Among his better known books are: The Affluent Society, The New Industrial State, The Age of Uncertainty *and* The Anatomy of Power. *He has been a consistent advocate of multilateral disarmament, and of conversion from military to socially useful public expenditures.*

Mr. David Stockman, recently released from service in the Reagan administration, has just told in graphic terms of Mr. Weinberger's inspired— Stockman says unscrupulous—advocacy of military programs and appropriations. Leaving office almost exactly a quarter of a century ago, President Dwight D. Eisenhower warned of the dangers of the acquisition of power, deliberately or because of neglect, by the military-industrial complex. "In the councils of governments," he said, "we must guard against the acquisition of unwarranted influence, whether sought or unsought, by the military-industrial complex. The potential for the disastrous rise of misplaced power exists and will persist." He could not, were he to return, think his fear unwarranted.

THE NEED FOR A PLAUSIBLE ENEMY
I doubt that many will disagree with me on the matters just mentioned. There are, however, two further consequences of the rise and awesome triumph of the military power that are not so evident.

The first is the need of the military power for a plausible enemy. In the absence of such an enemy, both its influence and, more pertinently, its financial support are gravely at risk.

The second is its need to contend with the main threat to its power in our time—the deep, even urgent, public fear that modern weaponry, by its nature, arouses. In all countries, and not least in the United States, there is a strong political resistance to the idea of nuclear euthanasia. So just as the military power must have a plausible enemy, it also must have a plausible design for countering or containing public fear. This is what arms control negotiations now principally accomplish. But first, the need for an enemy.

The United States in the last century, and again in the years between the world wars, had no plausible military adversary. In consequence, the American armed services had negligible power and resources. Our army in that period was about on a par with that of Portugal. This condition has been remedied. In recent years enemies have been manifestly more available—or have been made to seem so. China, until it was promoted to the role of honourary bastion of free enterprise, for a time so served. North Vietnam, Cuba and Nicaragua have also so served. Nicaragua has recently been hailed as a source of communist infection for two continents—a poisoned dagger pointed directly at a small border town in Texas only two days' drive away. We now have Colonel Gadhafi and Libya. But overwhelmingly and durably, the plausible enemy has been the Soviet Union.

TENSION IN SUPPORT OF MILITARY POWER

The Soviet Union is indispensable to the American military power. Fear of the Soviet Union and tension in our relations directly and overtly serve our military power; any relaxation of tension would damage the resources it commands. From this comes the great fact of our time: tension is actually cultivated to support the military power. Once, military appropriations were in response to external threat. Now, action and response have been reversed, and external threat is in the service of military appropriations. And in a world where military intelligence and enemy intention are extensively in the hands of the military, it would be astonishing were they not made to serve that tension. We accept this fact extensively —and, at budget time, very visibly.

However, as I said earlier, I do not identify this grim development with the United States alone. Although the charge that America is an overreaching imperialist threat comes regularly from the Soviet Union, we can assume that within its enormous organizational complex there is also an influential military community with the power inevitably associated with great bureaucracy. In both the United States and the Soviet Union citizens live perilously because tension and hostility serve military purpose.

They serve it, I must note, in a world where the basic presumption underlying the very word *superpower* is now strongly questioned. That presumption is that the Soviet Union and the United States will relentlessly extend their power: the Soviets presume an unfulfilled imperialist ambition on the part of the United States; the Americans presume a relentless desire for world socialist domination on the part of the Soviet Union.

The highly evident reality, in contrast, is a powerful desire on the part of all the other countries of the world to assert their independence and be free of superpower influence and control. The Soviets have experienced this reality in China, in Egypt, Algeria and Ghana, in Indonesia and, in visible measure, in Eastern Europe—and in Afghanistan. The Americans have experienced it in Central and South America, in Iran, elsewhere in the Middle East, and, perhaps most notably and sadly, in Vietnam. Nonetheless, in spite of these massive retreats, we still speak relentlessly of Soviet expansionism, and the Soviets still speak of the American imperialist design. The purpose of this I cannot think in doubt. The concept of one superpower's relentless will to dominate the world serves the military designs of the other superpower. The hard fact of universal retreat must be kept subordinate to that need. So we have the essence of it: not military need in response to tension and hostility; rather, tension and hostility in response to military need. I come now to the role of arms control.

QUIETING PUBLIC FEARS OF NUCLEAR CATASTROPHE

International tranquillity is not the only threat to the military power. In the age of nuclear alarm and terror there is also the threat posed by massive popular concern and reaction. As I noted earlier, there is strong political support for continued existence. In the United States, of late, this has made itself evident in the freeze movement (which alarmingly invaded the preserve of the nuclear theologians); in pressure for a comprehensive test ban; and in the peace movement in general. This popular reaction was greatly encouraged in the early years of the present administration by compulsive talk of strategies, tactics and survival in nuclear war—of the acceptability of nuclear war, of prevailing in nuclear war, of plans that could deal with protracted nuclear war. There were also some notably insane suggestions as to how individuals and communities might survive nuclear war: "With a thrown-down door and enough earth on top almost everyone will make it."

These communiqués have now stopped. The Reagan administration at last perceived their effect in stirring public reaction. Instead we now have the present round of arms negotiations, and these have been extraordinarily effective in quieting public alarm.

The threat of a major public intrusion on the military power and on behalf of survival has greatly diminished. And in its place we now have a resort to psychological denial—a strong force where nuclear war and the prospect of death is concerned. We turn our minds to happier prospects. In consequence of the resumption of arms control negotiations, the nuclear theologians have been restored to their monopoly of the issue. This monopoly is an extraordinary thing: in the United States we would not readily delegate power over taxes, but we apparently are rather relieved to delegate it over death.

STEPS BACK FROM DISASTER

But let me now turn to more affirmative matters. What are the steps back from disaster?

The first step is, indeed, a better understanding of the role of the military power in our time, and an alert and informed discussion of it. Nothing so clearly demonstrates this power as the tendency of people to avoid the subject. And understanding and appreciating it, we must have a strong, popular and political confrontation of its sources of strength and its purposes. The military power has invaded, dominated and now escapes the democratic process. The answer is not less democracy; it is full and effective democracy. The strong popular will to live is our strength in confronting the military power. We must exploit it to the full.

The second step is to be completely aware of how tension and hostility serve the military power. Let us enlist all democratic processes in seek-

ing to reduce that tension. We must elect politicians who react power-
fully against those who cultivate tension and who vigorously expose the
purpose such tension serves. We must ask the Soviet Union for similar
restraint. But we ourselves must be an example in this regard. There is no
harm or weakness in that. We have sufficiently indicated to the Soviets
that we are less than approving of their economic and social system.
Repetition is unneeded.

Let us now recognize one of the great facts of our time: the nations of
the world do not want to be ruled, or guided, by the great powers—as in
courtesy they still are called. If we accept this, it will ensure that there
will be no collision of American and Soviet policy in Nicaragua, Angola,
the Middle East or Ethiopia. In independence, the people of these countries may not all be well and democratically governed; they may not all
be happy and free. But it is not for us—or the Russians—to alter that
fate.

Next, let us have the strongest possible effort by Canadians, Western
Europeans, Latin Americans, Eastern Europeans and Chinese to minimize the conflict and tension that serves the military power. This is not a
task for the United States and the Soviet Union alone, but for all governments and people.

Finally, having reduced the tension that serves the military power, and
having come otherwise to terms with this force, let us have effective action on arms control. The first step is to arrest the dynamic by which
American actions serve the Soviet military power, and their response
then serves ours. Accordingly, let us have the comprehensive test ban
and the freeze on nuclear deployment and development.

We must bring political and public force strongly to bear on arms control. This means that we must not hesitate to call the present charade a
charade. We must call those engaged in this charade, and their principles, to full political account. We must deliver ourselves of politicians,
great and small, who accept the charade, who are reluctant or ineffective
in the arms control effort. And we must, it goes without saying, reduce
the military claim on the economy and on government budgets. This
would act directly to reduce the military power. These enormous expenditures bear no relation to defence in an age of reciprocal overkill.
Such a transfer of economic and fiscal priorities would have strongly
beneficial effects on the economy. Germany and Japan, the two great
economic success stories since World War II, have chosen the advantage
of using resources not for sterile military production but for refreshing
the capital of civilian industry. This is not a theoretical judgment; the
hard practical evidence, especially in the case of Japan, is there for all to
see. Nor would the transition to a rational use of economic resources be
difficult or traumatic. The present administration in the United States has

promoted a transfer of public resources from social programs to the military power at, it should be observed, some cost to support for the latter. A reverse movement of resources would be far from painful. I am disturbed by the number of intelligent people who believe that the modern economy is somehow sustained by military spending and would collapse without it.

But above all, let us, with Dwight D. Eisenhower, recognize the military power's authority; let us be diligent in seeing that it is brought back under strong and effective civilian and democratic control. Let us especially be sure that it is always under the immediate authority of individuals who serve democratic purpose and not those who serve the military.

Let us be aware of the danger in believing that something is accomplished by speeches, either listened to or given. They may relieve the conscience; it is political action that counts. To this let everyone here be committed. I appeal especially to my fellow Americans. But from all the world let there be a primal thrust against military power.

CHAPTER 10

Panel Discussion: Session II

KATHLEEN WALLACE-DEERING,
REMI J. DE ROO, DAVID L. WERLIN,
AND JOHN KENNETH GALBRAITH

Kathleen Wallace-Deering (session chairperson):
You have overwhelmed us with the generosity of your written questions. [More than 150 were submitted at this session.—ED.] We are sorting them and will try to get through as many as we can. I'm going to ask David Werlin to respond to a series of related questions.

David Werlin:
I have decided to take three questions and convert them into one, since they seem to deal with the same issue. A lot of questions have been directed to me, all the way from why am I wearing a red tie? to are we planning a one-day general strike in the near future to convert our government?

I want to deal with an issue which points to a fundamental problem we have in our society and in the labour movement as a whole. Someone has submitted a question which states: "A few years back the Alberta Federation of Labour refused to take a stand against cruise missile testing in Canada on the grounds that the testing brought jobs to its members. If this is true, has the Federation reversed its stand? If so, congratulations on coming to your senses! If not, how can Mr. Werlin speak about peace, and why was he invited here?" Another question asks about specific policies in the labour movement concerning the problems which would be created in attempting to convert weapons industries into peaceful enterprises, particularly the problem this would constitute for workers who would prefer to be working in other types of industries, but desperately need jobs.

Although the Alberta Federation of Labour has never taken a formal stand against the testing of the cruise missiles, nevertheless informally we have been very vociferous in our opposition to it. The other members of our executive council and I have walked in the marches and have spoken at the demonstrations ever since the cruise missile came to Canada. But there was an incident at our annual convention, I think it was two years ago, where a good resolution on peace was defeated. It was defeated because people who work in the defence industry went to the microphones and made a particular point about how, if that resolution were adopted and acted upon, it would cost them jobs. I have tied all this together because I think it demonstrates what Bishop De Roo said about how people, including working people, should have a whole new view of this question of war and peace and how we fit into it, and what our economies should be about. We really do have to come to grips with the entire issue of conversion and of our whole attitude to peace and the significance of what our economy is involved in. These three questions capture a struggle which has been going on in the labour movement for many years.

One of the problems that we are just beginning to overcome in the labour movement is the tendency to think and believe that there is an enemy out there somewhere, an enemy which has never really been described to us, and about whose economic and social system we learn very little in our newspapers, the media, or the trade union movement. Because we know so little about this enemy we are easily convinced that all the wrong is on its side, and therefore all the right is on our side. Therefore we should not even try to come to grips with the issues because we are being soft on some evil regime somewhere. And if you are an American, you are accused of being a liberal, and if you are a Canadian you are accused of being a leftist, NDP commie-fink or something vile.

This is the struggle that has been going on in the labour movement ever since the Cold War began, ever since the days of McCarthyism. And we are just now beginning to get away from that. It is just now becoming unpopular to use that kind of psychology against people who raise real, important issues about war and peace.

Wallace-Deering:
Bishop de Roo, how would Canadian business react to not being able to sell military equipment to repressive regimes such as Chile? How do we overcome the powerful business lobby in order to change the federal government's position on this question?

Remi De Roo:
I can't speak for business, but I think most of us have a pretty good idea of how business would react. But the real question lies in the second

aspect. I am very grateful to Professor Galbraith for having touched on this point and reminded us of something absolutely fundamental: you and I have to reclaim our democratic responsibilities. Thank God we still live on a continent where we can hold assemblies like this without fear of political, cultural or military reprisals.

And let's face the consequences of our own principles. If we really believe we are responsible then let's make sure our democracy works — which means that each one of us must start accepting our own responsibility. As Professor Galbraith stated, and as other speakers have said, we must make sure that nobody represents us in public office who is not willing to take a stand on this profound moral question.

Wallace-Deering:
Here are a couple of questions for Professor Galbraith. Do you feel that Canada and other small powers should abandon alliances like NATO and NORAD? Is the basic problem military control, or American corporate control?

John Kenneth Galbraith:
I am delighted to respond to both of those questions. I would certainly urge Canada to stay in NATO. The NATO meetings are not intellectually taxing. Nothing new has been said at any of them for some years. And there is, as Paul Warnke has said, and I trust will be saying later in this symposium, the real hope that in the future Canada will be a voice of reason in NATO seeking to ease tension and quiet down the more belligerent tones of the other participants—whose names I won't mention. Canada has much more influence being in than being out.

As for the second question, "Is the basic problem military control or American corporate control?", this is a very important question. The left in Canada, and the left in the United States and around the world, has been transfixed over the years by the notion that somehow the corporations are the ultimate source of all evil.

I don't think the telephone company or the Canadian Pacific Railway or similar civilian corporations should be the major focus of our attention. The major, specific, and defined object of our attention should be the relatively small number of corporations, and the relatively huge bureaucracy, that work together in the military structure. If we spread our efforts over all corporations, we will dissipate our energies and engage (as somebody in the audience just did) in an outrageous exercise of self-gratification. We need to concentrate our energies in a highly practical way on those corporations that are working in direct conjunction with the military.

Wallace-Deering:
David Werlin, in your speech you referred to the reluctance of the corporate sector to support conversion, because of the likelihood of decreased profits. If conversion is a viable economic alternative, why should there be fewer economic profits?

Werlin:
Maybe I should have handed that question to Professor Galbraith. Perhaps he'll bail me out after I'm through. I think the point has to be made—and it follows from what Professor Galbraith has just said—that not all corporations are our enemies. When we discuss conversion, we have to single out certain corporations.

It is a fact that only few corporations make the high rates of profits that the major corporations make producing arms. But when we talk about whether conversion is viable—when it would reduce the profits of arms manufacturers—we have to remember that no other industry has the taxpayers as a means of financing itself. And no other industry can accuse taxpayers of disloyalty if they refuse to finance it. No other industry operates in the secret manner that the military and the so-called defence industries do; they are able to conceal their profits, and the kinds of deals they are making with the government from public scrutiny—even from the scrutiny of the law.

So the massive profits corporations make from arms production would be reduced by conversion. But the economy as a whole, when you redirect all that money and energy and labour and resources into socially useful products, would get a general lift. The economy wouldn't suffer by converting from military production. It is just that a handful of corporations in the defence industry would suffer.

Wallace-Deering:
Professor Galbraith, because the production of unusable weapons does *not* add to economic well-being, wouldn't the shutting down of the American industrial-military complex *increase* the purely economic well-being of the United States by freeing up resources?

Galbraith:
There is no doubt in my mind, and in any reasonable view of this matter, that a drastic cut in our military spending would be economically good. As we heard earlier from the panel, the employment efficiency of the weapons industries is very low. A lot of the money goes to a relatively small number of high-priced people. Or a certain amount of the profits goes, as we have discovered this year, to $650 toilet seats! I don't know

why the United States Defense Department allows itself to be scatologically so vulnerable.

So I do not think that conversion to civilian production and civilian well-being would be difficult. And as I told my colleagues on the panel: I am a little bit concerned about our frightening people too much about the difficulties of conversion. I don't think that this is a subject for great concern. And over the longer run, the economy is more vigourous when capital is used for improving the efficiency of civilian production—as the Japanese and Germans and the Koreans have shown—rather than siphoning it off into sterile military purposes.

De Roo:
I think we should give Dr. Galbraith an honourary degree in theology.

Galbraith:
I already have one. From Loyola, a university in Baltimore.

De Roo:
Good for them! It restores my confidence in my Jesuit professors.

Galbraith:
I was afraid you would object if you knew it came from the Jesuits.

Wallace-Deering:
Here are a group of questions for Bishop De Roo, either about the absence of church people from the peace movement—a lot of church people are not participating in the peace movement—or about the active work of some people who are Christians directed against the peace movement. Specifically, there have been a lot of questions about the evangelical right in the United States which supported President Reagan and the military strike against Libya which he ordered.

De Roo:
In response to your first statement: we do have to address the fact that there seems to be a reluctance on the part of a lot of Christians, and specifically on the part of Roman Catholics, to support the peace movement. Part of this comes from a very painful aspect of Roman Catholic history—belief in what we call the theory of the "just war." The popular impression of this is that the Roman Catholic church has justified war. People forget the fact that the classic scholars who spoke about a just war posited so many qualifications that effectively a just war could rarely be found. There were some pretty sophisticated analyses behind their arguments which I am not going to bore you with. However, it is one thing to

live in the past and try to explain why we persisted so long with a just war theory. It is another to live in the present and realize that since the atom bomb was developed, the very nature of war has changed.

It was a totally different story when a few hundred soldiers could run at each other with swords or shoot a few arrows into one another, and in most cases survive the ordeal: after a period of fever, they might possibly regain good health. The situation then was profoundly different from the situation now, where the very use of the arms at our disposal means the obliteration of all life, and where there are no longer any winners and losers. The nature of war has changed: there is no longer such a thing as a just war. A lot of Christians and Roman Catholics are also going to have to face the question of whether or not they should support the peace movement, because it is *perceived* as being somehow under the influence of any number of nefarious and evil people.

Let me go to the second question, which concerns the wing of Christianity that seems to support the idea that a nuclear war would somehow be a purification of the human race—a visitation of God upon sinful people—out of which apparently some little, select elite would escape in this phenomenon of "rapture." You have probably seen the bumper stickers on cars: "when Rapture comes, this driver's seat will be empty." It is a horrendous travesty from two points of view.

First of all, can you imagine the notion—the image—of God that lies in the back of the head of a person who would say that? Can you imagine that somehow God is a ferocious monster just waiting for a chance to use the atom bomb on us, just waiting to destroy a great part of humanity in favour of some self-defined little elite which believes it somehow conforms to that absolute idea of who God is? This image is not only a total travesty of the Jewish and Christian concept of God, but also of the concepts of most major religions—which have seen God not as an evil force, but as a beneficent being.

Another travesty committed by certain fundamentalists—so-called evangelicals—is that they use the Bible to somehow justify the use of the atom bomb as the instrument of Armageddon. This is happening particularly widely in the United States, but also here as well. I say this with sadness in my heart, but we are very much influenced by this way of thinking right here in Canada, because many of our myths and persuasions come via the American popular press: we are all listening to the Bible thumpers. A very dangerous and sad phenomenon is occurring: the total distortion of the fundamental Biblical symbols and myths.

Let's not forget that the American nation was founded by a people who called themselves "Pilgrims," escaping like the Israelites from what they called a form of persecution and slavery in Egypt into the Promised Land where they were to build a new kingdom. And I understand that most of the discourses of the early American presidents were laced with these Biblical references. And indeed the Pilgrims were successful, and through a very narrow understanding of Christianity they began to confuse their success in this new land with a direct blessing from God. Mind you, there is a partial truth in that, but there is also a very dangerous error. Because they then slipped unconsciously, but very effectively, into the most dangerous Biblical trap there is, and one from which very few people have escaped: namely, to identify God's purpose for humanity with one's own particular ideology or political system.

So now one finds the Bible, and the most profound Biblical myths—like liberation, and freedom and the kingdom and all that—being used to explain a particular political project. The result of this error is that anyone who disagrees with the present political policy is seen as the infidel, whose destruction can be justified in Biblical terms. Because "God is on our side" we can identify the "commies" (all those evil people out there who don't happen to follow our political system) as infidels whom we can legitimately and peacefully lay to rest with the atom bomb. This is the most dangerous travesty of religion that has ever existed. And it brings us to the very heart of what fanaticism is all about. Fanaticism, basically, is the temptation to identify my particular viewpoint with God's, and to consider evil all other human beings who don't agree with me. This attitude is the most dangerous evil we face today.

Wallace-Deering:
Professor Galbraith, what do you think of the ideas of Alvin Tofler on the need for new, democratic institutions and the power of the popular imagination?

Galbraith:
I would like to suggest that in an exercise such as the one in which we are engaged this evening, there are two possible purposes. One is recreational—and that carries us off into the realm of ideas like those of Alvin Tofler. I don't object to them: everybody needs to have a general retreat from real life once in a while. But let us not be in doubt that on the serious issues with which we are concerned this evening we will be successful only when political leaders sense the danger that if they don't follow our views, they will soon be out of office.

I was associated for a long ten years of my life with the matter of Vietnam. The end of the Vietnam War was really a great triumph in the history of people who have lobbied for political change. It was the first time in history that a great country, the United States, said, "We have had enough,"—and pulled out. America made a terrible mistake going into Vietnam, but it showed enormous virtue in getting out. But I have to tell you: this did not happen as a result of the philosophical condemnation of war; and it didn't happen because of the speeches some rejoice so much to make. It happened when the people in Washington, including the president, became aware of a voting population so opposed to the war that it made them fear they would be turned out of office. Let us not lose sight of that very important fact.

Wallace-Deering:
I might just add to Professor Galbraith's comment that at the Walk for Peace on April 27 there is going to be a pledge sheet for Canadian citizens to sign, which says that voters will only consider candidates who support—with words and actions—an end to the nuclear arms race and a commitment to work for peace with justice. Copies of that pledge sheet will be sent to the person's member of Parliament.* Here is a question for David Werlin. Do the labour unions have a policy that their pension funds will not be invested in military-related industries?

Werlin:
The short answer is that many unions have such a policy. The longer answer is that we have very limited control over pension funds and even less control over how they are invested. First of all, most of the pension plans the unions are involved with are private pension plans. Workers can negotiate what goes in from their own pay cheques and their employers' contributions, but they don't have very much say beyond that. Then there are public pension plans. In Alberta, my very conservative province, sixty thousand Alberta government employees are on pension plans which are controlled by the government. Their money goes into whatever investment the government chooses. And by legislation the provincial government does not have to disclose where pension funds are invested. So there is certainly a lot of political work to be done on this issue, and some people in the labour unions are working now to make sure that we do address this issue. It is a question not only of our pension funds being invested in arms manufacturing. Many also are being invested in South Africa and in Chile; and many were invested in napalm during the Vietnam War (most of which, by the way, was made in Canada, and exported to the United States).

* Kathleen Wallace-Deering was referring to the Peace Voter Pledge Campaign, a major initiative planned for the two years or so before the next federal election, and designed to get a very different sort of politician into the Canadian Parliament in Ottawa. Readers who want to see peace candidates elected from their ridings may want to write for Peace Voter Pledge Cards to: End the Arms Race, 1708 West 16th Ave., Vancouver, B.C. V6J 2M1.—Ed.

Galbraith:
Don't you think, though, that it is important here to distinguish between issues that are symbolic and issues that are real? I don't entirely deplore symbolic issues. I have voted for years to have the Harvard University Corporation divest itself from investment in South Africa. I always did it because of the pain and sorrow it caused the Harvard treasurer, rather than the *real* political effect that I ever thought it would have. Now, isn't something of the same thing true as regards your pension funds?

Werlin:
Yes, there is a certain amount of purely symbolic importance in raising the pension issue; but this issue gets working people to think about the whole question of war and peace and investments. It's one issue that working people can honestly feel they have a *right* to address.

Wallace-Deering:
Professor Galbraith, would you comment on the Libyan air strike?

Galbraith:
I have already declared myself on that in this past week. I think that it was entirely wrong. I'm not, as I think probably few here are, an especial admirer of Colonel Gadhafi. I think that concealed terrorism is one of the important problems of our time. But I don't think that the American air strike did anything to check it. It probably strengthened Colonel Gadhafi. It certainly resulted in the deaths of uninvolved people and it caused the United States very great difficulties with its friends in Europe, and with European public opinion. It set a bad precedent. And I must say, I didn't particularly care for the modified support it got from Canada.[†]

Wallace-Deering:
This related question is addressed to the man of the cloth. Bishop De Roo, how do you turn the other cheek to blatant acts of terrorism?

De Roo:
First of all, I think we have to do some serious thinking about this whole question of terrorism. So far, we have mostly defined terrorism ideologi-

---

[†]The Canadian government had generally condoned the American air raid carried out against Libya ten days earlier. Stephen Lewis, Canada's ambassador to the United Nations, reportedly endorsed the American military reprisal against Libya in a speech he delivered at Simon Fraser University on the same evening that Professor Galbraith addressed the Centennial Peace and Disarmament Symposium (*Vancouver Sun,* April 26, 1986). —ED.

cally. In other words, we consider somebody a terrorist who disagrees politically with us and takes some effective action. I am not in favour of terrorism: far from it. But I am inclined to agree with what Professor Galbraith has said about the Libyan situation: the American response will only make things worse and it sets an extremely dangerous precedent.

Pacifism is a very significant Christian issue. It forces us to consider the real nature of power. In the Western world, pretty well throughout contemporary civilization, we have defined power as the ability to dominate and destroy. We have forgotten what lies at the very heart of the Christian message; namely, real power is the power of love.

You will never bring about a conversion by fear, by hatred or by power. Human beings can never change until they feel trusted, appreciated for who they are, dealt with truthfully, and are ultimately called to become more than they themselves realize they are. Now, I am *not* saying that we should condone terrorism. But I am saying, the answer to terrorism by relatively small terrorists is not terrorism by big guys; that merely confirms and justifies the fanaticism of the small terrorists. It is also interesting to note that even in the face of terrorism it is very difficult to get countries to agree to certain effective sanctions such as economic sanctions, or sanctions forbidding planes to land in certain areas. Ultimately countries decide whether or not to apply sanctions after they consider who is going to make or lose money. Which brings us back to the basic problems: money and power. As long as we are in a competitive world where the ultimate values are making money and exercising power, we will never even agree on how to handle terrorism.

This is a profound and complex issue. But when all is said and done, the Christian answer of forgiveness and reconciliation is ultimately more powerful than the answer that comes out of a gun. We still have to use a certain amount of international discipline, even power, to protect the innocent from those who are obviously evil; but we are never going to solve the problem, and will probably make it worse, if we don't get at the roots of the situation—injustice.

Werlin:
I'll try to be brief. This whole problem of terrorism and the responses to it is a very important question. But I think that the United States lost an awful lot of ground getting into the Vietnam War and then having to pull out of Vietnam. And I think that this raid on Libya and the invasion of Grenada in 1983 were more for domestic consumption: to re-establish Reagan and his administration as being capable of defending their so-called national interests anywhere around the world. The raid on Libya had very little to do with resolving the whole question of terrorism. If

they want to resolve that problem, they are going to have to resolve the Palestinian question, and a whole number of related questions.

Wallace-Deering:
I am really sorry that this has to be the last question. We are surrounded here at the table by literally dozens more. Professor Galbraith, would you like to comment on Dr. Edward Teller, who is often considered the father of the hydrogen bomb. He recently stated in a discussion about social systems that, "We might be able to survive a nuclear war, but we won't survive without one."

Galbraith:
Oh yes, I can comment on that. I heard a few weeks ago a discussion about Ed Teller. Someone said, "He is a disgrace to the human race." And somebody else got up very angrily at that statement and said, "I just want to take issue with that. Ed Teller does not belong to the human race!"

PART III

Ethics, the Arms Race, and the Third World

Joanna Miller

PHOTO: DAN KEETON

CHAPTER 11
The Arms Race and Suffering in the Third World: One Problem

JOANNA MILLER

In the past two days we have heard a very sobering message about the dangers of the arms race and the urgent need for us to change if we are to avoid the holocaust that so many people fear. We have been warned that time may be running out. This morning's sessions will give us new insights into the changes that must occur soon if we are to avoid the disaster which may now be just over the horizon.

In 1981, Inga Thorsson, a very distinguished Swedish diplomat, presented to the United Nations a report it had commissioned on the links between disarmament and development. This report represented three years of work by a committee of twenty-seven experts from around the world, including Canada's Bernard Wood of the North-South Institute. The report concluded that the arms race and underdevelopment (by which we mean the poverty, deprivation and suffering that is experienced by so much of the world) are not *two* problems, they are one: *they will be solved together or neither will be solved.*

Joanna Miller has been deeply involved for many years in working for peace and justice. She is a board member of the Canadian Institute for International Peace and Security and a board member of Project Ploughshares. She was president of UNICEF Canada and served as a member of the board of directors of the United Nations Association. For the past two years Joanna Miller has served on an advisory committee on issues relating to arms control set up by Douglas Roche, the Canadian ambassador for disarmament. Joanna Miller has also served as a special advisor on disarmament to the Canadian delegation to the United Nations.

What was the response? The nations of the world read the report, nodded their approval, and then went right back to their bad old ways: increasing their military budgets to the point where they now approximate $1 trillion annually, misusing the world's resources and the talents of its people in the pursuit of ever larger military establishments, and showing decreasing concern for the disadvantaged whose future is being sacrificed to the demands of those military establishments. Primary responsibility for this lies with the rich, industrialized nations (the North) and especially with the two superpowers, who alone account for two-thirds of the world's military expenditures. Those who suffer most are the people of the developing world (the South), whose hopes for economic and social development have been sacrificed to the world's obsession with militarism.

Yet the impact of our actions is not understood by many North Americans. This lack of understanding was epitomized by President Reagan shortly after his election when he told the world leaders assembled in Cancun, Mexico, that it was time for the developing nations "to pull themselves up by their bootstraps." He seemed unaware that the very policies he was then putting in place would undermine their ability to do so. By massive increases in his military budget, he has driven up American deficits and with them *real* interest rates, thereby adding to the debt-servicing burden of the developing world. With Third World debts now approximating $900 billion, any increase in interest rates adds billions of dollars to these debts. In addition, high interest rates drain capital from the nations of the developing world at a time when they desperately need it for their own development plans. And so, ironically, those nations which can least afford it find themselves helping to finance the American military build-up. It is ironic too that often the very weapons they have financed are then exported back to Third World nations and turned against their people to silence their demands for a fairer share of their nation's wealth. This is but one example of the way in which the arms race victimizes those who are already most at risk.

If we are honest with ourselves, we will admit not only that we have been indifferent to the needs of the developing world, but that we in the North have used our military power to protect our privileges and to maintain the status quo—to retain access to the resources, the agricultural lands and the investment opportunities of the South. We have kept on reaping the benefits associated with the arms race even when it involved us in supporting unjust economic structures.

This weekend we have heard the personal anguish of people who were in Hiroshima when the bomb was dropped in 1945, where tens of thousands died in an instant. If we acknowledge what is happening in the world of the 1980s, we must know that tens of thousands, even millions,

126

are dying in the South every year from wars and the deprivation that accompanies the relentless militarization of our planet. And they die, not in a blinding flash as at Hiroshima, but one by one. UNICEF states that every two seconds a child pays the price of the world's indifference with its life. Forty thousand children die each day from the effects of poor nutrition and inadequate medical care. Yet most of these deaths are unnecessary—the world has the resources to meet the basic needs of all its people.

We in the North have been trying to have it both ways: we talk of the urgent need to stop the arms race, but we don't really want to give up our weapons and the privileges they defend. And now we are afraid—afraid that we may have to pay the price for the choices we have made.

I believe it is time to focus, not on our fears for *our* survival, but on what we in the North are doing to our planet by our addiction to military power. And since they suffer most, we should focus first on the peoples of the Third World. Shridith Ramphal, secretary-general of the Commonwealth, recently described their situation in these graphic words:

> The Third World, by and large, is in distress and disarray. Its governments are demoralized. Its people despair. Human suffering has not diminished but hope for relief from it has. Internationalism is in decline. Crude power is ascendant. International morality is in retreat. A new militarism holds sway. The moral corruption of absolute power has become for our international community—our global state—a common way of life.

Unless we in the North understand our role in this, unless we stop blaming others for the arms race, I believe that our efforts to save ourselves will be doomed to failure. Peace and justice are indivisible. That is the lesson we must learn and learn quickly. I know that our very distinguished speakers in this session will help us to understand these issues.

Bishop Thomas Gumbleton

CHAPTER 12

The Arms Race Protects the Power and Wealth of the Privileged

BISHOP THOMAS GUMBLETON

Some time ago I read a truly shocking account of what absolute poverty means. It comes from Cairo, a city that contains one of the worst slums in the world. A visitor to Cairo describes the slum:

> It was raining mud in the city of the dead. A freak midwinter sandstorm had mixed with a rare desert rain to drop fat pellets of wet dirt on the one thousand acres of ancient underground tombs and mausoleums that some five hundred thousand homeless people have converted into a bustling city. . . . These carved gravesites, situated in the shadow of the Mohammed Ali Mosque in southeastern Cairo, were once the sacred resting places for the caliphs and the Mamelukes. But because of a crippling housing shortage, the government has allowed poverty-stricken Egyptians to squat inside the miles of cemeteries.

Bishop Thomas Gumbleton is the Roman Catholic regional bishop of innercity parishes in Detroit, Michigan. Ordained as a priest in Detroit in 1956, he has gained a reputation as an eloquent and outspoken advocate for the rights of the poor and underprivileged, and the causes of nuclear disarmament and world peace. In 1973 he investigated the political imprisonment situation in Vietnam, and in 1979 he represented the National Conference of Catholic Bishops on a visit to the American hostages held in Iran. Bishop Gumbleton is the president of Pax Christi, USA, and the vice-president of Pax Christi International. He was one of the drafters of the important American Catholic Bishops' pastoral letter, "Challenge of Peace: God's Promise and Our Response."

This reporter goes on to tell what it is like to exist in this "City of the Dead." Then he concludes by saying:

> It was dusk in the city of the dead, and the young girl seemed glued to the damp dirt behind her father's donkey. The animal's hind legs kept inching toward her face. She began to pick through the excrement. Finding a few kernels of undigested corn, she placed them in her torn pocket, and crawled on all fours back inside her tomb.

I have seen people picking through garbage to find some little bit of food. I have seen people sleeping in the streets in the winter. But I hardly know how to react to the stark reality of a child so hungry that her only food is found in the excrement of animals.

Yet, in fact, she is one of the two billion people who struggle to exist on an income of less than five hundred dollars a year. She lives in "absolute poverty," which means "barely surviving on the margins of life, afflicted by disease, illiteracy, malnutrition and squalor—a condition of life so degrading as to insult human dignity." Almost half of these people are children, and their suffering is profound: eleven million children die each year before their first birthday. In fact, forty thousand children die every day from hunger or hunger-related causes. That is fifteen children every minute. Is it any wonder that some have described what is happening as "silent genocide?"

And the most tragic fact is that we live in a world where God gave us all the resources we need so that every person could live a fully human life. Why do we have a world in which so many suffer and die from hunger, even though the resources are there? Obviously, there are many reasons for this, but in this paper I will look at the problem in relationship to the arms race.

And for me, there is a very real, causal connection. We choose how to use our resources, and we make a choice for armaments instead of for people. We do this for the ostensible reason of guaranteeing our national security. But, I contend that we, in fact, choose armaments over people because these armaments support an economic order in the world that benefits a few of the world's people, while the vast majority remain desperately poor. Our arms protect our privileged place in the world. Surely this is a harsh judgment. But I think that the facts will bear me out.

The arms race long ago went out of control. We are living on a planet where more than $800 billion are spent annually on armaments. This money is buying nuclear weapons capability for more and more nations. Today, the estimate is that about twenty nations possess, or will soon be capable of developing, nuclear weapons. Even more costly is the constant development of militarism in most countries and the increasing use of military action to deal with international conflict. Since World War II, there have been approximately 120 wars or military conflicts. Of these, 115 took place in the impoverished Third World, which has become the battlefield in which the so-called "developed" nations resolve their economic and territorial disputes.

But it is important to note that the arms race itself is, in a sense, "an act of aggression against the poor," as the 1976 Vatican statement to the United Nations described it. Our judgment on the arms race is made in the light of the inestimable human suffering and loss of life which occurs right now, every day, as a direct consequence of the global choice to spend hundreds of billions of dollars on arsenals of death and destruction. John Paul II, bishop of Rome, made a strong point about this in his first encyclical letter: "We all know well that the areas of misery and hunger on our globe could have been made fertile in a short time, if gigantic investments for armaments at the service of war and destruction had been changed into investments for food at the service of life" (*Redemptor Hominis* No. 16).

One of the ways this attack on the poor happens is through the continuing rise in global unemployment. There are as many as six hundred million people who have no jobs or are underemployed. Add to these another six hundred million—the elderly and children who are dependent on them—and ask who can comprehend their suffering. Although military expenditures do create jobs, the studies of the United States Bureau of Labour indicate that many thousands more jobs would be created if the government were to spend the money for civilian purposes. Dollar for dollar, in the developed, developing and underdeveloped nations, more employment is created through such public endeavours as construction, transportation, health services, and education than by expenditures for military purposes. One must conclude that unemployment is not just some necessary fact of life, but a conscious choice being made by governments, including our own.

Closely related to unemployment is underdevelopment. This, too, is a choice being made by the governments of the world. The deplorable drop in American foreign assistance in recent years and the more recent cutting back on social programs to assist our own poor are well documented. In the face of current military expenditures, our governments cannot afford food, clothing, shelter, vaccines and education for the poor at home and abroad.

Again, I must insist: such underdevelopment is not just some fact of life, but a conscious choice being made by the United States government—and, sadly, by so many other governments.

To me it is clear that unemployment, hunger, poverty, and underdevelopment are the direct consequences of the choice to spend money on armaments. Are our governments run by cruel tyrants who enjoy the sufferings of others? Of course not. But their priorities are not with the poor of the world. The American government has military pacts with forty-two nations; it also has treaties, executive agreements, arms sales accords, military associations and alliances with almost one hundred countries. The United States generates fifty-six percent of the world's arms trade—more than the Soviet Union, France, Britain and China combined. This is "big business" and means huge profits for a few, while the majority suffer.

Another very sad aspect of this military policy relates to the countries which do benefit from our military assistance programs. Many believe that the United States engages in military and economic assistance programs to preserve freedom and democracy. But the reality is that the top recipients of American military and economic aid are, according to Amnesty International, among the world's top ten violators of human rights. These include South Korea, Indonesia, Thailand, Chile, Uruguay, Brazil —and, of course, we supported the Shah in Iran and Ferdinand Marcos in the Philippines. According to our own United States Senate, sixty-nine percent of the nations receiving military grants from the United States are classified as "repressive regimes."

It is true that these nations allow American air and naval bases on their soil. And for many, this is sufficient justification for our economic and military assistance. But, in fact, what seems even more important to our policy makers is that these nations offer what is called a "favourable investment climate" for corporations: low wages, no unions, no strikes, cheap raw materials, no health and safety regulations and no restrictions on the treatment of workers. In order to maintain this favourable investment climate, the governments of these nations often co-operate with the corporations by politically repressing their own citizens. And many times this repression is maintained through terror, torture, imprisonment and murder—much of which the United States government pays for. It is hard to escape the severe judgment on this situation made by Archbishop Raymond Hunthausen a couple of years ago. He maintained that we support the arms race "to protect our privileged place in the world" or, as Pope John Paul described it when he spoke in Edmonton just over a year ago, to protect the "imperialistic monopoly" of the nations of the North over the nations of the South.

Is this something new? No, it is really consistent with American policy over the past thirty-five years. In 1948 a "top secret" State Department document stated bluntly: "We have fifty percent of the world's wealth, but only 6.3 percent of its population. . . . In this situation we cannot fail to be the object of envy and resentment. Our real task is to devise a pattern of relationships which will permit us to maintain this position of disparity without positive detriments to our international security."

Lately much attention has been focused on the conditions in Central America. Militarism in Central America—again, paid for largely by the United States—serves the power elite. And the testimonies from there have revealed to the world that every possible means will be employed to protect the power and wealth of the privileged. Money continues to flow to the military establishments of Central America. President Reagan has tried to persuade the world that Central America is awash in a sea of red. He may be right. But Mr. Reagan identifies that red with communism. I identify that red with the blood of the thousands who have died there at the hands of a ruling elite's military establishment. Central America is haemorrhaging to death. I fear that history may well record that North Americans sat by as a kind of holocaust went on around us.

In Central America and other countries of the poor South, I see two especially cruel ways that our "pattern of relationships," supported by our arms policy, has permitted us to maintain a "position of disparity without detriment to our national security." The first is the system of concentrating agriculture on crops primarily for export which is common to so many of the poor countries. It can be clearly identified as a major cause of hunger and malnutrition. In Central America, for example, the richest five percent of the population get over half of the nation's income, while the poorest twenty percent receive less than four percent of the total income. Fifty percent of the area's eighteen million inhabitants have annual incomes of less than one hundred dollars per person. And prices for food and essential goods are not much different from those in the United States.

Even more serious is the fact that hunger and malnutrition among the poorest segments of the population are getting worse instead of better. A recent study by the Pan-American health organization shows that in a ten-year period malnutrition rose by sixty-seven percent among children under five years of age. In Nicaragua alone, the number of severely malnourished children doubled during that period. Some observers have pointed to the rapid population growth in Central America to explain this increase in hunger. Others have suggested that farm output has simply not risen fast enough to keep up with the population. In reality, total food production per person has risen in every country, except Honduras, since the early 1960s. The hunger problem is clearly related to the fact that more and more of the region's agricultural products are exported, rather than being used to feed the local population. This increase in exports has dangerously lowered the nutrition level of many of Central America's poorest people. Most of this increase has gone to the United States.

The way the system works is that a small number of people control most of the land and make the decisions about how that land is used—what crops are grown, where they are sold, and who makes the profits. And the decisions are not made for the benefit of the people, but for the sake of profits. Profits determine what will be grown and where it will be sold. In Nicaragua, prior to 1979, the Somoza family owned over one-fifth of the arable land in that country and accumulated great wealth from that land. In El Salvador, fourteen leading families control most of the land. Sometimes multinational corporations are the major landowners.

I can hardly think of anything that would cause greater rage in the heart of a parent than this cruel system of exploitation. Put yourself in such a situation. You work long hours in the field every day. Your children probably work alongside you. This is the only way you can barely eke out a living. You grow the food. But then you have to watch while that food is taken away, sold outside the country, while your own children are starving to death. Can you think of anything more cruel? More evil? Is it really any mystery why these countries are in revolutionary turmoil, and why there is a constant demand for land reform?

Of course, now, after the Sandinista revolution in Nicaragua in 1979, the Somoza family is gone. The land is being redistributed, and a new economic model is being established. But in the United States we continue to support those regimes where the few still dominate and exploit the many, where the regimes continue to protect the massive American investments that guarantee a continued flow of wealth into the United States and provide our "privileged place in the world." And it is clear to me that our heavily-armed superpower status is what makes it possible for us to continue to protect our "privileged place."

John Paul II at Edmonton spoke clearly—if somewhat harshly—about the evil of this situation: "The poor people and the poor nations . . . will judge those people who take these goods away from them, amassing to themselves the imperialistic monopoly of economic and political supremacy at the expense of others."

The "pattern of relationships" which maintains our "position of disparity" is the system of international trade. At a Commonwealth conference a few years ago, Mr. Julius Nyerere, president of Tanzania, provided a damning indictment of the world economic order as it was organized in trade relationships. He spoke with great feeling of the hundreds of millions of people existing in absolute poverty. He cited one of the clear causes of this evil: the control maintained by the rich nations, not only over the prices of goods they sell, but also over the market in which developing nations must sell the commodities they produce.

> The price at which cotton is bought and sold in the world is determined by the workings of the international free market. . . . Countries in the South learn what the prices will be by listening

to reports from Britain, the United States and Europe. The cost
of producing that cotton is completely irrelevant; so is the cost of
living of the worker or peasant in the cotton fields. . . . On the
other hand, the prices of lorries, tractors, fertilizers, etc., are all
determined by the producers, the transnational corporations and
other firms. The result is that poor countries almost always buy
dear and sell cheap.

Of course, such a system guarantees that the rich nations keep getting
richer and the poor nations poorer, and that the rich nations have a very
privileged place. And, again, our heavily-armed superpower status
makes it possible to protect this privileged place. In the light of these
connections between the arms race and the situation of the poor, must we
not conclude, with the 1976 Vatican Report to the United Nations cited
previously, that the arms race must be "condemned unreservedly?" It is
so clear that "the arms race itself is an act of aggression against the poor,
causing them to starve." Or, as John Paul II said: "We all know well . . .
and yet we continue to choose armaments at the service of war and destruction instead of food at the service of life."

Why do we make this choice? Why is this evil situation allowed to go
on? This is the hardest question. Of course, some will say, as I suggested
earlier, that we need the armaments for our national security. But arms
levels are not only sustained but expanded—expanded to the point where
we have the combined capability of destroying the whole world seven
times over. One Trident submarine is able to destroy 240 cities, and the
proposed Trident fleet will consist of thirty submarines with an incredible
capability of 7,220 nuclear warheads. Do we really need this kind and
size of arsenal, even for national security? Is it not rather the case that the
ever-accelerating arms race results in less and less security as both sides
rapidly develop the weaponry that will put us into a first-strike posture?
The claim is made that we make these vast expenditures on the arms race
in order to protect our democracy, our system of free enterprise, our capitalism, and the fundamental concepts taught us in our constitutions and
our religious traditions. But is this really true? If, in fact, it were ever to
come to a nuclear war, what would be the difference between "them"
and "us"? The war would be controlled by our military establishment
and by their military establishment. What would it matter that we have
elections and checks and balances? In the end, it would be the military
professionals on both sides who would make the decisions that would
cause the all-out nuclear exchange and end the world as we know it. No,
it is not really for any of these reasons. My reluctant judgment is that we
do it to maintain that disparity—to protect our privileged place. And I
sense deeply the evil of what we are doing. With John Paul II, I see the
poor nations of the South rising up in judgment against the North. The

arms race results in untold and immeasurable suffering, especially for the poor, the elderly, the ill and the children of the world. But as we have seen, it is not some natural disaster to be coped with, but rather a conscious choice—a deliberate policy—and is, therefore, a direct attack upon innocent people. Such an attack is decidedly immoral. There is only one way to change this situation. If enough of us decide, whether out of fear or love or both, that the arms race must be stopped, and if we join with others who similarly insist that the arms race must be stopped, I believe it can be stopped.

But such a decision, taken seriously, will have its consequences. As John Paul II declared when he visited the United States in October 1979, it will require "profound reforms of attitudes and structures . . . in order to recreate the conditions needed by the disadvantaged, if they are to have a fresh chance in the hard struggle of life." Changes in attitudes and structures will also mean changes in our lifestyle. It will mean less consumption, living more simply. It will take our public witness, which may also mean a change in lifestyle.

What we have to decide is this: which do we value more, our lifestyle, or the very life of our brothers and sisters in the human family? I hope we choose in favour of our brothers and sisters. I hope we have the courage to say no to the "gigantic investments for armaments at the service of war and destruction" and, finally and convincingly, say yes to "investments for food at the service of life."

CHAPTER 13
Blessed Are the Peacemakers

THE VERY REVEREND LOIS M. WILSON

THREATS TO SURVIVAL

We are now living in the dark shadow of an arms race more intense, and of systems of injustice more widespread, more dangerous and more costly, than the world has ever known. Never before has the human race been so close to total self-destruction. After August 6, 1945, the threat to the world's survival became qualitatively different from anything known before in human history. In an incredibly short time, humankind moved from the horrors of Hiroshima and Nagasaki to the likelihood—unless we act courageously—that life on the whole planet will be totally devastated. A moment of madness, a miscalculated strategic adventure, a chance combination of computer errors, a misperception of the other's intention, an honest mistake—any one of the foregoing could set off a nuclear holocaust. And even in the absence of declared war, nuclear weapons claim victims through nuclear weapons testing and the dumping of nuclear wastes. Is it any wonder, then, that so many have committed themselves to working for human survival by focusing their attention and priorities on stopping the arms race?

Yet for millions in the Third World, on whatever continent they live, the most immediate threat to survival is not posed by nuclear or conventional weapons. A nuclear war is not required for thousands to perish daily, in nations both rich and poor, because of hunger and starvation. Human misery and suffering have reached unprecedented levels. Conflicts between East and West and between North and South intersect in the Third World to cause massive injustice, homelessness, starvation and death for many, as well as oppression and despair. Millions are left homeless, expelled from their native lands as refugees or exiles, as wave

PHOTO: WOLF KUTNAHORSKY

The Very Reverend Lois M. Wilson

after wave of agony sweeps over the world. Is it any wonder, then, that so many have committed themselves to working for human survival by focusing their attention and priorities on food and clean water in the Third World? And so Barbara Ward said, "I would put clean water at the very forefront of the possibility of getting a stable world in the next thirty years."

DIFFERENT INTERPRETATIONS OF SECURITY AND PEACE

Some people feel that peace can be secured and maintained through a system of threats. Security, they believe, lies in deterrence, and in always having weapons superior to those of the enemy. Defined as the primary objective, security must be achieved by any and every means. Sometimes this definition is applied to *national* security; then, any new military strategies and increases in military spending are justified because they lead to greater "national security." National security becomes an all-consuming goal.

Other people feel that peace can be secured and maintained only through the creation of a just, participatory and sustainable society. They speak more often of collective security than of national security. Their priority is not more money for arms, but food for their children and clean water for their villages. They would claim that only by sharing the world's resources in a more equitable and just way, on a sustained basis, can security be offered to all. Security, they believe, is the product of a social, political and spiritual environment, based on love and justice, which serves the welfare and security of all. Ultimately, we must see the true security of individuals and nations as the consequence of global justice.

Let me remind you at this point of a statement made by the World Council of Churches when it met in Vancouver in 1983.

The Very Reverend Lois M. Wilson is president of the World Council of Churches. She is also a national board member of Amnesty International, CUSO, the Canadian Institute for International Peace and Security, and the United Nations Refugee Status Advisory Board. Since she was ordained a minister of the United Church of Canada in 1965, Lois Wilson has worked on many issues within the United Church, the World Council of Churches and the United Nations. These issues have included world peace initiatives, the North-South dialogue, human rights, the changing role of women, and ecumenical and inter-religious dialogue. Since her election in 1983 as president of the World Council of Churches, Lois Wilson has travelled extensively in many developing countries. She is an expert on social and economic conditions in the Third World.

The arms trade is a new form of intervention maintaining and developing dominance/dependence relationships and encouraging repression and violation of human rights. Militarism leads to massive allocation of human and material resources to research and production in the military sector of all countries at the cost of lowering the priority of meeting the needs of human development. We believe the time has come when the churches must unequivocally declare that the production, deployment and the use of nuclear weapons are a crime against humanity, and such activities must be condemned on ethical and theological grounds.

These differences in interpretations of peace and security are not new. One of the first conferences on disarmament was held at the Hague in 1907. But what is significant is what happened *around* that conference. Korea had sent a representative to plead Korean independence from Japan. But Britain, France and America (in alliance with Japan) refused the Korean plan for independence and self-development. The consequent suicide of the Korean delegate in a hotel in the Hague demonstrated to the world the anguish of a colonially-exploited people.

One person who continued in the tradition of understanding that there is no peace unless one has rice to eat and a roof over one's head, was Dietrich Bonhoeffer, later martyred under the Nazi regime. Speaking at a peace conference in 1935 in Denmark, out of the German context of that time, he maintained that there is no path to peace through armed security, but only through just and equitable economic and social relationships. His speech did not please those who attended.

EFFECTS OF THE ARMS RACE ON THE THIRD WORLD

The attention given to the arms race by the developed countries has grossly distorted their economic and social priorities and put an enormous drain on their finite resources; both of these developments have had a major effect on the Third World. The arms race is now predominantly a race in modern technology. Weapons research is driven by the pursuit of a final technological solution to the goal of security. Weapon improvements have led to new military strategies and have dramatically increased the probability of nuclear war.

Moreover, military research has grown more and more beyond political control. The massive allocation of human and material resources to military research and development (fifty percent of all natural scientists work directly or indirectly for military purposes) has distorted the developed world's perception of what is socially useful and necessary. Very little scientific or technological inventiveness is concentrated on disarmament or development: many electronic gadgets that we use in every day life (such as pocket calculators) are offshoots of military research; yet, no safe and reliable technological method of birth control for women has yet been developed.

The growing gap between the rich and the poor, exacerbated by the cost of the arms race, alienates the poor and hungry even more, and robs them of any hope of survival. UNICEF stresses the need for a "revolution in child survival to improve the state of the world's children." And I want to emphasize that what is happening to children is *abominable*. They are *sinned against*. But it is the mothers of these children who are the key to change. In relation to hunger, the essential role of women is rarely recognized. In Africa, women do between sixty and eighty percent of all agricultural work. They bear the children, carry the water, produce the food and gather the fuel. It should then be obvious why people become intensely angry when resources legitimately expected to be used to train and support these women are instead used by industrialized countries to continue to dominate the world and preserve their prerogatives of power through escalating arms production.

There is a growing anger among the poor of this planet. They are angry because we of the industrialized nations are not angry enough. They are angry because producing arms to fuel the conflict between East and West takes precedence over their profound needs for basic human necessities. And unless global priorities are changed, that growing anger will develop into a major threat to peace and security for the whole world. Already at a crucial point, the escalating arms race deepens the social and economic crises in the Third World. By imposing unbelievably heavy debts on the Third World to support trade for industrialized countries; by militarizing space, which results in a scarcity of resources for the Third World; by developing military technology rather than appropriate technology for a hungry world; and by supporting a war culture based on violence (which concentrates its power through political, economic and military might), the developed world denies human beings in the Third World the legitimate aspiration of a peaceful, prosperous future.

THE ROOTS OF VIOLENCE

A desire to grab and maintain economic advantage is at the roots of the use of violence. Certainly, the expansion of trade and the growth of the developed countries' standards of living would have been impossible without the raw materials from the colonies and dependent nations. The history of colonialism is a history of world expansionism, colonial exploitation, slavery and the grabbing of land and resources.

I'll never forget my first visit to Westminster Abbey in London. I had been taught that it was a wonderful place; but most of it was statues of people who had slaughtered other people in this war or that war. History for me in school was a series of dates of wars. It was the history of violence that we were taught. And until we recover our whole history as human beings, including our history of peaceful co-operation, all of our rhetoric is going to be in vain.

Present militaristic efforts to "defend our way of life" (i.e., our place in the global hierarchy) are in reality aimed at maintaining the status quo, which is arranged in favour of the industrialized countries. They exploit cheap labour in Third World countries; they keep the prices cheap for raw materials by establishing prices through the creditor's club; they give tax-free incentives to those doing business in Third World countries; they assure themselves access to fuel and markets upon which their economic prosperity depends; and they support military dictatorships to keep the lid on it all politically. Because investment is simply not profitable in an unstable environment, repression and human rights violations usually accompany efforts to keep a politically unstable situation on an even keel.

Since World War II, there has been a frightening internationalization of wealth and power. Five hundred companies account for from eighty to ninety percent of international trade. Important lobbies are created by transnational corporations to maximize unfettered free trade and to take profits whenever they can. Power and wealth have interpenetrated the world like a cancer. And so the power elites have made the militarization of Third World societies a priority, in order to maintain the stability that investment requires.

Usually the media is also used as a tool for social control, both to promote consumerism and to mesmerize unsophisticated people into social apathy. I recall a visit made to one of the desperate slums on the outskirts of Santiago, Chile. Those same slum dwellers who had not enough calcium in their diet to retain their teeth gathered to watch the community television promote electric tooth brushes for all. Later, we watched Dallas and the Flintstones with dubbed Spanish sound tracks: bread and circuses to assist the military in keeping an ordered society! I have seen small clumps of people in Third World countries watching television, and they *know* how we live. There is a growing anger among the poor on this planet, and that growing anger will escalate and continue to be a major threat to peace and security unless the global priorities are changed.

According to the Canadian Churches' Task Force on Corporate Responsibility, the price the Ford Motor Company paid for the privilege of operating in South Africa was to sign an agreement with the South African government to support the military forces protecting the status quo (i.e., pro-apartheid) in case of a black uprising. Ford signed a contract with the South African police and military to supply vehicles in case of an emergency and to allow weapons to be stored on its premises in case the military needed them suddenly. For all of this, Ford would receive a tax deduction as part of "normal operating expenses." When I questioned the president of Ford about signing such an agreement, he answered, "But we had no choice." The translation of this is: "Support of the military in South Africa was the price we were willing to pay to protect our lucrative investments and support our way of life." All of this, and more, goes on.

Canadians are only dimly aware of the connections between militarism, the build-up of arms on a global scale and the poverty and oppression of the Third World. While militarism continues unchecked throughout the world, the deprivation of hundreds of millions of people in the Third World increases. A direct connection between militarism and deprivation lies in the arms trade. Canadian military exports to the Third World now amount to about $150 million a year. It would be a step forward if Canada were to place the neglected issue of the arms trade on the international agenda, and show its support for curtailing the arms trade by supplying its own detailed statistics to an international arms trade register. Then we would begin to be aware of the extent of the arms trade and who Canada's customers are.

THE COST OF THE ARMS RACE TO A STABLE GLOBAL DEVELOPMENT

The world spends the equivalent of nearly U.S. $2 billion each day for armaments. This does not include the enormous projected costs of developing the Strategic Defense Initiative (SDI). The disparity between defence expenditures on the one hand and expenditures on behalf of a stable global development on the other are so wide that it boggles the mind. The real dimensions of the coming peace and security crisis include vital issues relating to population, environment, and the economy.

Population. By the year 2000, the world's population will be six billion. It continues to double every thirty years. The growing population will mean greater competition for scarce world resources. Growing poverty will increase the likelihood of unrest and war, adding to the chances that the superpowers themselves may become militarily entangled in an effort to protect their economic interests. But the greatest crisis in population growth is the toll on the earth's resources and life support systems. Billions of people will have to struggle just to get enough resources to stay alive.

Environment. During the past four decades, half of the world's forests have been felled. By the year 2000, half of what remains will be gone. Tropical rain forests will have disappeared, although they are the lungs of the earth. At least ten thousand tons of radioactive waste is awaiting disposal—somewhere. (People of the Pacific tell the rest of the world: "Bury it in your own backyard, if it's so safe.")

The Economy. And then there are the hopeless debts that the countries of the South owe the banks of the North—about U.S. $800 billion—with little hope of repayment. There is a decided reluctance on the part of the creditor nations even to sit down around the table with the debtors to re-schedule the debts. Yet common sense and equity require that developing countries be helped, not penalized further, when they are buffeted by economic shocks completely beyond their control. Rich nations must make concessions. There is an immediate need to re-evaluate the debts, to limit interest rates and lengthen repayment periods, or possibly to cancel debts outright for the least developed countries. There is an urgent need to co-operate with and strengthen United Nations institutions in order to create a new international economic order. There is a pressing need to restructure the international financial system according to the principles of universality, equitable representation, accountability and fair reward for labour.

AN INTEGRATED APPROACH

We desperately need to reverse the trend toward disintegration and disorder in the multilateral trade and financial systems on which the world depends for survival and prosperity. Solutions will require an integrated, co-operative, global approach. Developed countries, for example, will find it hard to enforce pollution controls if industries simply move their operations to countries where controls are nonexistent. And Third World countries are unlikely to make pollution controls a priority in the face of their most pressing problems of poverty and debt repayment.

THE OTHER COSTS

We are accustomed to thinking about the costs of the arms race in terms of military spending alone. That is, annually, about $10 billion for Canada, and about $1 trillion for the world. But we need to be equally aware of the other costs:

1. International institutions, because of our inability to renew or reform them, have been paralyzed by the military build-up and lack of trust between countries.
2. The entire globe faces environmental dangers and damage because the arms race has taken precedence over ecology.
3. The people of many countries have suffered privations because their governments have spent more money on arms imports than on food imports.
4. The world's economy has suffered structural damage as a consequence of the war system.
5. National policies exist which fail to reflect the link between disarmament and development.

THE ROLE OF A PERSON OF CONSCIENCE

As citizens of Canada, we should support these policies through the political processes available to us:

1. The long held goal of 0.7% of GNP for development assistance should be retargeted for 1990 rather than delayed until 1995 and be focused more clearly on helping deprived people to meet their own basic needs, including food, clean water, health, education and employment.

2. This expenditure should no longer be tied to items of Canadian origin, so as to permit tenders from developing countries and, in due course, allow for general international competitive tenders.

3. Canadian government funds should not be used, directly or indirectly, in association with export credits to secure capital contracts for Canadian firms. It is shabby to present as *aid* funds which are spent in promotion of Canadian exports in *trade*. Export subsidization and development assistance are not the same thing. The "Aid-Trade Fund" should be removed from the official development assistance account.

4. Food aid should be employed only for emergency relief. Its use in other areas is fraught with dangers, particularly when it competes with local production.

In addition to supporting the above policies, we should read widely from the literature, poems, songs and expressions of despair and agony that come out of the Third World. "Songs of the Unsung" from a Malaysian poet speak of unpoetic subjects like war, poverty and hunger. We should subscribe to magazines and publications coming directly out of the life of the common people of Asia, Africa, Latin America.

We need to be conscious of being part of the larger peace movement in the world. The particular issue we are working on is connected to many global issues in this interdependent world. We should turn our backs on isolationism.

We should challenge the violence in our own culture by choosing creative alternatives. Bear in mind that the essence of being human is to take part in caring human relationships. This is not optional for a human being. Caring for another and for the whole of creation is what defines us as human beings.

We must remember that every utterance of faith in weapons of mass destruction—every justification of violence and oppression—is a litany of death. Every unjust law, every untimely death, every use of human talent to create more weapons is a litany of death and contrary to God's purpose in creation. So sing a litany of life. Blessed are the peacemakers.

Ambassador Douglas Roche

CHAPTER 14

Canada and the International Year of Peace

AMBASSADOR DOUGLAS ROCHE

What is meant by the United Nations proclamation declaring 1986 as the International Year of Peace (IYP)? And what does it mean to Canada? IYP is essentially a challenge to the governments and peoples of the world to focus more clearly on the multi-dimensional nature of peace — conflict resolution, economic and social development, human rights, elimination of racial discrimination, as well as the traditional issues of arms control and disarmament.

Peace can no longer be defined as the absence of war, though disarmament measures are essential. Peace demands the attainment of true human security so that people everywhere can live free of the threat of war, free of violations of their human rights, free to develop their own lives to attain economic and social progress. Peace, then, is a multi-splendoured goal.

No one expects that this goal can be achieved by December 31, 1986. That is not the idea behind the International Year of Peace. Rather, IYP highlights the broad international agenda that must be advanced as the

Douglas Roche was appointed Canada's ambassador for disarmament by the Mulroney government in 1984. One of Canada's authorities on North-South relations, he has served as a Canadian delegate to the Economic Commission of the United Nations. From 1972 until 1984, Douglas Roche was a Conservative member of Parliament for Edmonton South, and while an MP he joined Parliamentarians for World Order (PWO) and was elected its international chairman in 1980. He was given the 1983 World Peace Award by the World Federalists Association for his work in PWO.

world continues to evolve into a global community with increasingly closer relationships among all peoples. This growing recognition that the planet is a place of common ground, with common vulnerability and common opportunity, is the real message of IYP. It establishes peace as a system of values. This is clearly an advance in global thinking. And this advance constitutes a signal of hope to a humanity that has for too long been fractured and frustrated in the attainment of enduring human security. All this is a subject critical to Canada's interests in the modern world as was indicated by Canada's co-sponsorship of the IYP resolution at the United Nations.

It seems as if the world has two political axes—East/West and North/South. The East/West axis has been characterized by forty years of tension, of escalating armaments and declining understanding. East-West relations have come to be defined in terms of the nuclear arsenals of overwhelming destructive potential possessed by the two superpowers. The North/South axis is characterized by decades of deprivation, famine, homelessness and disease. North-South relations have come to be defined in terms of the stark disparities in resources and opportunities which exist between a privileged minority of the world's population, who enjoy great prosperity, and the vast majority afflicted with utter destitution.

The management of these two sets of relationships is the starting point on the route to peace. East-West relations focus on the negotiated limitation and reduction of arms and the building of confidence and trust; North-South relations focus on the sound economic development of the most impoverished nations in the world.

The United Nations' 1985 *Report on the World Social Situation* reveals how far we have to go to achieve these goals:

1. In 1984, global military expenditure was U.S. $800 billion—approximately $130 for every man, woman and child in the world. This is equivalent to more than the average income of many developing countries.

2. In 1980, military spending by developed countries represented more than ten times the amount spent by developing countries on health programs.

3. The cost of a single nuclear submarine equals the annual education budget of twenty-three developing countries with a total of 160 million school children.

The field of arms control is itself highly complex, technical and, above all, political. It is easy to advocate ridding the world of nuclear weapons. Numerous proposals have been put forward since the Baruch Plan of 1946, but it has been very difficult to find a way of negotiating them down to acceptable levels on the basis of equality and equal security.

A significant step was taken in this direction at the November 1985

Summit meeting between General Secretary Gorbachev and President Reagan. In their joint declaration, the leaders agreed that "a nuclear war cannot be won and must never be fought." As well, they identified several areas in which the United States and the Soviet Union had a common interest in progress. These included:

1. Accelerated work at the nuclear and space talks which began in March 1985.

2. The further enhancing of the Non-Proliferation Treaty.

3. Accelerated global efforts to conclude an effective and verifiable convention banning chemical weapons.

4. Agreement to work for positive results at the Vienna Mutual and Balanced Force Reduction Talks (MBFR) and the Stockholm Conference on Confidence and Security Building Measures and Disarmament in Europe.

Establishing and sustaining political dialogue at the highest level in order to build on the common ground between East and West is a step of fundamental importance. This approach has been a consistent element of Canadian foreign policy. At the conclusion of his visits to many world capitals in 1983, former Prime Minister Pierre Trudeau suggested ten principles of a common bond between East and West:

1. Both sides agree that a nuclear war cannot be won.

2. Both sides agree that a nuclear war must never be fought.

3. Both sides wish to be free of the risk of accidental war or of surprise attack.

4. Both sides recognize the dangers inherent in destabilizing weapons.

5. Both sides understand the need for improved techniques of crisis management.

6. Both sides are conscious of the awesome consequences of being the first to use force against the other.

7. Both sides have an interest in increasing security while reducing the cost.

8. Both sides have an interest in avoiding the spread of nuclear weapons to other countries, so-called horizontal proliferation.

9. Both sides have come to a guarded recognition of each other's legitimate security interest.

10. Both sides realize that their security strategies cannot be based on the assumed political or economic collapse of the other side.

These principles, reflected in the Gorbachev-Reagan Summit statement, broaden the perspective of East-West relations and stimulate greater international effort in the search for a durable peace.

In his first speech immediately after assuming office in September 1984, Prime Minister Brian Mulroney reiterated the commitment of the Canadian government to work effectively within the world's multilateral forums to reduce tensions, alleviate conflict and create the conditions for a lasting peace. He said:

> There can be no let up in our efforts to reduce the threat of war. No matter how frustrating or difficult, negotiations must be pursued. . . . The exercise of political will is nowhere more important than on this issue on whose outcome the lives of our children and humanity depend. . . . No matter how much we may accomplish here in Canada, I will have failed in my most cherished ambition if under my leadership Canada has not helped reduce the threat of war and enhanced the promise of peace.

External Affairs Minister Joe Clark carried the government's commitment into the global community when he stated in an address to the 39th General Assembly of the United Nations:

> Canada, for its part, is determined to continue to play a leading role in the search for peace and disarmament. We believe the nuclear build-up threatens the life of every Canadian, and the existence of human society. Countries like our own must use influence to reverse that build-up and reduce the danger of destruction. That will be a constant, consistent, dominant priority of Canadian foreign policy.

Canada has a long, constructive history of active engagement with the most important global issues. This tradition was outlined by Mr. Clark in the foreword to the government's Green Paper on foreign policy:

> We assisted at San Francisco in the creation of the United Nations. We were at Bretton Woods when the post-war monetary system was designed. We were at Havana and Geneva as well, where the international trading system was conceived. We have worked diligently ever since to improve international order — Lester Pearson and peacekeeping, Howard Green and the Partial Test Ban Treaty, Paul Martin and membership in the United Nations for newly independent states, Pierre Trudeau and co-operation between North and South and between East and West.

Although 1986 is designated by the United Nations as the International Year of Peace, every year is a year to work for peace, and Canada will go on pushing and probing for viable ways to stop the spread of nuclear weapons with the motivation and spirit described in the 1984 Throne Speech: "Patience and perseverance we will need, for in this endeavour even the smallest progress is worthy of the greatest effort."

Thus Canada, along with its allies, works to influence and assist the bilateral negotiations in positive, constructive ways in order to achieve radical reductions in nuclear weapons. This is done through a great deal of unpublicized effort. Though there is only room for the two superpowers at the Geneva negotiating table, Canada constantly stresses that the conduct of these negotiations will have an impact on every nation on earth. The ongoing negotiations—with their series of offers and counter-offers—indicate the scope and complexity of extensive systems of nuclear arms possessed by both sides. Though agreement still seems a long way off, most experienced observers are now reflecting cautious optimism.

Canada has traditionally taken a broad approach to security—defining it not simply in terms of military might, but in a way which places it in a wider context. There are four components of Canada's security policy: 1) arms control and disarmament; 2) defence; 3) peacekeeping; and 4) conflict resolution.

The government has identified six specific objectives on the arms control and disarmament agenda:
1. Negotiated radical reductions in nuclear forces and the enhancement of strategic stability.
2. Maintenance and strengthening of the non-proliferation regime.
3. Support for a comprehensive test ban treaty.
4. Negotiation of a global chemical weapons ban.
5. Prevention of an arms race in outer space.
6. The building of confidence sufficient to facilitate the reduction of military forces in Europe and elsewhere.

How does Canada advance these objectives?

Canada warmly welcomed the announcement in January 1985, made by the United States and the Soviet Union on the resumption of bilateral talks. In this past year we have used all channels open to us to actively encourage, support and facilitate the conduct of serious and constructive negotiations. Canada has had an ongoing series of consultations and discussions with the United States—bilaterally and along with our allies in NATO—on the progress of these negotiations. Prime Minster Mulroney and President Reagan have had several meetings and conversations in which Canada's concerns and interest in the negotiations have been stressed. Within NATO, we have encouraged regular, detailed discussions of the Geneva talks and their implications for alliance policies. As well, Canada has engaged in an active dialogue with the Soviet Union. The Prime Minister has written to General Secretary Gorbachev outlining Canada's views and priorities on arms control questions, and Canada has conducted bilateral arms control and disarmament discussions with Soviet officials in Ottawa and in Moscow. Similar consultations have already occurred, and others are being planned with selected East European countries.

Canada has practical contributions to make to the bilateral and multi-lateral arms control process. The government's activity will be focused in three directions: 1) encouraging compliance with existing treaties; 2) developing verification mechanisms; and 3) building confidence between East and West.

Compliance with existing treaties remains key to a credible and viable arms control regime. Mr. Clark recently reaffirmed Canada's firm support for the regime created by the ABM (Anti-Ballistic Missile) Treaty and the existing SALT (Strategic Arms Limitation Treaty) agreements on limiting strategic forces. He said: "Our stance towards SDI (Strategic Defense Initiative) research is rooted in the need to conform strictly with the provisions of the ABM Treaty. We will continue to urge the parties to these treaties to do nothing to undermine their integrity, but rather work to reinforce their status and authority."

Canada has long considered the Non-Proliferation Treaty (NPT), now signed by 131 nations, as an essential component of international security. It is an important security lynchpin which benefits all countries by reducing the risk of nuclear proliferation and facilitates the peaceful use of nuclear energy. The third review of the NPT, held last September in Geneva, produced a consensus document which reaffirmed the importance of the NPT. Canada's own objectives at the Review Conference were clearly met—the maintenance of the NPT as a basic element of the non-proliferation regime and a reaffirmation of the purposes and provisions of the treaty. Canada will continue to work to strengthen and enhance this treaty, to maintain the impetus of the Review Conference in the letter and spirit of the treaty.

The achievement of a Comprehensive Test Ban (CTB) remains a fundamental objective for Canada. Recognizing that there remain outstanding political and technical difficulties in the negotiation of a CTB, Canada is working steadily within the Conference on Disarmament to move forward on this important item.

There are few weapons of mass destruction as horrific as chemical weapons. Canada has been an active participant in the work now under way in the Conference on Disarmament to negotiate a multilateral, verifiable convention banning chemical weapons.

Canada is also engaged in the discussions at the Conference on Disarmament aimed at the prevention of an arms race in outer space. Canada submitted a detailed study of international law relating to arms control and outer space. This survey identifies a number of important themes for examination if an international treaty on preventing an arms race in space is to be successfully written.

The building of confidence in East-West relations is of great concern, for it is a prerequisite to arms control and disarmament. In both the

Stockholm Conference on Confidence and Security Building Measures and Disarmament in Europe and at the Vienna Mutual and Balanced Force Reduction Talks, Canada is working with its allies to find ways of achieving agreement on this issue.

The diversity of Canada's participation in the multilateral arms control and disarmament forums reflects the complexity of the problems as well as the need to construct a productive political atmosphere in order to negotiate equitable, durable and verifiable arms control agreements. One way of growing importance that Canada contributes to this process is with its extensive verification research program. Verification is not, of course, an end in itself, but it does enhance the effectiveness of treaties by promoting confidence and compliance in negotiated texts. A solid body of verifiable arms control treaties in which nations placed a degree of confidence would go a long way toward easing tensions and mistrust. Verification, Mr. Clark recently pointed out to the House of Commons, "is an area where Canadian expertise and diplomacy come together."

Canada's verification program supports our arms control and disarmament priorities by: 1) undertaking research studies for problems applicable to international negotiations; 2) promoting specialized training programs; 3) hosting international symposiums of experts on specific subjects; 4) providing liaison with national and international bodies outside Canada engaged in verification work; 5) presenting to the public the issue of verification.

Since the program's inception in 1983, nearly one hundred projects have been undertaken directly in support of Canada's ongoing work in the Conference on Disarmament. As well, the verification program supports the Vienna talks and the Stockholm conference. Some of the program's more recent activities include:

1. The planned $3.2 million upgrading of the Yellowknife seismic array as a major contribution to research into monitoring an eventual Comprehensive Test Ban.

2. The presentation to the secretary-general of the United Nations of a detailed handbook for use in investigating allegations of chemical or biological weapons use.

3. The ongoing "Paxsat" projects designed to determine the feasibility of remote sensing from space-to-space or space-to-earth in the verification of an eventual treaty prohibiting weapons in space.

4. A series of comprehensive compendiums of statements made in the Conference on Disarmament and its predecessors, on the subjects of chemical weapons, radiological weapons, outer space and verification.

This body of knowledge and expertise on verification issues is shared widely with the international community. In this way Canada is furthering, in a very practical way, the global arms control process.

Canada's credentials in this sort of serious background work on verification have been well-established and are now widely recognized in the multilateral forums. This may account, to some extent, for the unprecedented success Canada had in having the 40th General Assembly adopt by consensus a resolution on "Verification in all its Aspects." This resolution gained the unanimous support of the international community on the legitimacy of verification as a genuine, necessary and integral component of the arms control process. Nations from the East, West and neutral-non-aligned world noted that, if disarmament measures are to be effective, they must be "fair and balanced, acceptable to all parties, their substance must be clear and compliance with them must be evident." The resolution calls upon member states to "increase their efforts toward achieving agreements on balanced, mutually acceptable, verifiable and effective arms limitation and disarmament measures."

As well, it invites member states to communicate to the secretary-general their views and suggestions on "verification principles, procedures and techniques to promote the inclusion of adequate verification in arms limitation and disarmament agreements and on the role of the United Nations in the field of verification." The resolution has clearly helped in establishing common ground on the issue of verification, which is a basic component of multilateral and bilateral arms control work.

The General Assembly's proclamation of the International Year of Peace goes well beyond the more traditional issues of disarmament and the peaceful settlement of disputes. It recognizes that efforts to improve the conditions of life for people around the world and the natural environment can alleviate tensions and thereby make for a more peaceful world. It is obvious that flagrant inequality between rich and poor is a potential source of instability; that incarceration, torture and murder of persons by their own or alien governments breeds bitterness and violence; that continuing desertification of vast tracts of Africa may force entire communities to move into the territory of others, with serious potential for conflict.

Canada has for many years made substantial efforts to alleviate such problems, and we will remain active and persistent in seeking long-term solutions for them. Canada's development assistance programs recognize our humanitarian duty to help the world's poor, illiterate and afflicted; they also recognize the benefits for our own economic well-being of a more widely-shared prosperity. We are, therefore, committed to advancing issues of concern to the less-developed countries in a number of ways:

1. Arriving at a better definition of growth and adjustment in developing countries, through discussions underway in the World Bank and the International Monetary Fund (IMF).

2. Strengthening the international trading system through the promotion of a new round of multilateral trade negotiations.
3. Participating in the special United Nations discussions on African development problems.
4. Strengthening the international economic negotiating machinery of the United Nations Conference on Trade and Development (UNCTAD).
5. Improving the definition of international agricultural policies and seeking to make the Food and Agriculture Organization (FAO) and the World Food Program work better.

Canada also helps to protect human rights through our participation in the Commission on Human Rights (currently in session in Geneva), the Economic and Social Council and the General Assembly's Third Committee. Work is proceeding to allow Canada to ratify the international Convention Against Torture. We have been especially heartened by recent political developments in Guatemala, Haiti and the Philippines, which point to new policies and better respect for human rights of the people of those countries.

Canada has long striven to persuade the South African authorities of the injustice and short-sightedness of the system of apartheid. Last July, the government announced a series of measures designed to stiffen the pressure on South Africa and to signal our profound dissatisfaction with its failure to put an end to institutionalized racial discrimination. Prime Minister Mulroney played a key role at the most recent meeting of Commonwealth heads of government in developing a Commonwealth plan of action. We are using every avenue to urge the South African government to summon the courage to dispense with this unjust and backward system. The Anglican primate of Canada, Reverend Edward Scott, is a member of the Group of Eminent Persons now seeking a more open dialogue with South Africa in an effort to avert a major tragedy.

For more than a decade, Canada has been in the vanguard of international efforts to improve the management of the world's natural environment, but mankind is still witnessing the disastrous results of careless neglect. Acid rain is damaging our forests and the aquatic life in our lakes; the Sahara advances perceptibly into the hitherto fertile lands of the Sahel; cities are defiled by smog and undrinkable water. Efforts to combat environmental damage must be based on the realistic premise that, though this is a long-term problem, action must start now.

Progress has been registered recently through international collaboration to reduce pollution in the Mediterranean and the signing last July of an international protocol on sulfur dioxide emissions. In 1986, we will continue to combat acid rain and Great Lakes pollution; in the Economic Commission for Europe, discussions are continuing to reduce nitrous oxide emissions from industrial sources, power plants and motor vehicles; in the United Nations Environmental Program, negotiations are under way on an international protocol on the protection of the earth's ozone layer. The World Commission on Environment and Development will visit Canada May 22–31 to examine environmental problems and better ways and means of resolving them. Groups and private citizens will have an opportunity to present views to the Commission.

It is highly appropriate that the International Year of Peace will provide the backdrop for a United Nations-sponsored international conference this summer on one of the most important issues of our time—the relationship between disarmament and development. There are few issues that cut so broad a swath across the concerns of both developed and developing countries than the disarmament/development linkage. In concluding its 1981 study, "The Relationship between Disarmament and Development," the United Nations Experts Group stated:

> The world can either continue to pursue the arms race with characteristic vigour or move consciously and with deliberate speed toward a more stable and balanced social and economic development within a more sustainable international economic and political order. It cannot do both. It must be acknowledged that the arms race and development are in a competitive relationship, particularly in terms of resources but also in the vital dimension of attitudes and perceptions.

One of the most important contributions of the Experts Group study was to broaden the scope of the disarmament/development relationship to place it in the context of a triangular interaction between disarmament, development and security. The study noted that the range of contemporary challenges to the security of nations is far broader than the military power of potential adversaries. In outlining some of the nonmilitary challenges to security, the report pointed to:
1. The scarcity of vital raw materials and commodities.
2. The long-term effects of environmental degradation.
3. The present inequality in the distribution of the world's wealth and opportunities.

Canada looks upon the conference as an opportunity to undertake a practical, in-depth examination of the questions raised in the disarmament/development relationship. For example: what resources are presently devoted to armaments; how has this spending affected development; what resources might be diverted from military spending; what would be the possible problems, costs and benefits of this diversion?

As well, Canada believes the approach to the discussion must be a global one—encompassing developing and developed countries, nuclear and conventional disarmament—keeping security, in its broadest definition, as the touchstone.

The raising of world-consciousness and recognition of the importance of the disarmament/development relationship during this, the International Year of Peace, will mark an important step in the right direction toward creating a peaceful world. Canada is well placed to assist the international community in its first full and open discussion of the relationship between disarmament and development. As a developed country, with a tradition of deep involvement with the developing world, and as an active participant in all the multilateral arms control and disarmament forums, Canada will bring special expertise and sensitivities to the discussions.

In addition to Canada's diverse ongoing work for peace, we will be undertaking a program of activities designed to highlight the themes of the International Year of Peace and to engage Canadians across the country in this special international year. Canada's program of activities will include:

1. Support of the United Nations International Year of Peace activities through a $10,000 contribution to the IYP Voluntary Trust Fund which forms part of our overall $100,000 commitment to the objectives of the United Nations World Disarmament Campaign.

2. A cross-Canada tour and regional meetings of the Consultative Group on Disarmament and Arms Control Affairs by the ambassador for disarmament on the dual themes of IYP and the question of the relationship between disarmament and development.

3. The preparation, in book form, of a selection of essays written by distinguished Canadians and dealing with the broad theme of IYP from their individual perspectives.

4. A national essay competition on the theme "What is peace and what can I do to achieve it?" and a poster competition on IYP which will be organized by the United Nations Association in Canada.

5. The issuance of a commemorative stamp by Canada Post Corporation to mark IYP.

As well, other government departments will be undertaking their own programs which are linked to the themes of IYP. For example, as part of its ongoing activities, the Department of National Defence will be highlighting the IYP in its publications, exhibitions and speaking tours. The role of the Canadian Armed Forces in contributing to peace and Canada's ongoing commitment to peacekeeping will be among the featured themes. For many Canadians, the IYP proclamation confirmed what we had already known. It has served to remind us that peace without development is not peace, that peace without racial equality and harmony is not peace, that peace without a reasonable quality of life is not peace.

It is, therefore, the fullness of Canada's programs—from development assistance and active support for human rights to the protection of the environment and the promotion of a better standard of living for people across the country and, indeed, around the world—that constitutes a meaningful contribution to peace. The spirit, determination and commitment generated by IYP must be carried forward into the years ahead if we are to create a truly peaceful planet. Canada and Canadians can use IYP as a catalyst in our ongoing work for peace. If we can infuse others with our hope and belief in true human security, we will have accomplished a great deal.

CHAPTER 15

What Is the United Nations Doing to Promote Peace?

GÖRAN OHLIN

Much has already been said by other speakers about the enormity of the injustices and inequities in the world, and it has been said with great eloquence and passion. On the other hand, there are also some strands in our proceedings that worry me slightly. One is the tendency to argue that the threats to peace in the world stem from evil forces, that the problem is one of the struggle between good and evil, or perhaps between evil and evil. It seems to me dangerous to forget that the real tragedy of the conflicts of the world throughout history is that so often they are conflicts between people with good intentions which just happen to clash. This is also why the work of resolving such conflicts is in practice so difficult.

A second observation that may be appropriate is that we must make distinctions among the various threats to peace in the world today. The point has already been made that while we sometimes talk about forty years of peace since the Second World War, the fact is that there have been well over a hundred wars in that period, virtually all of them in the Third World. They have cost some twenty million dead, they have made refugees of almost that many, and they have uprooted many more. They have also destroyed the bases for economic and social development, both of which are impossible in theatres of war.

There are many very different kinds of conflicts in the world. A major type stems from the tensions between the nuclear superpowers. Another involves the conflicts arising in the Third World—which, as I have said, have dominated for some time. A third type, which is increasingly worrying, involves conflicts between North and South.

That conflicts in the developing countries have been so important was not entirely unexpected. The greatest changes of the world political map in the last forty years have stemmed from the disintegration of the old colonial system. Today one often fails to realize how unexpectedly sudden that was. Even in the 1940s and 1950s it was often confidently asserted that independence in Africa was a matter for the 1990s. Instead, it came about, both in Africa and in Asia, in a few years around 1960. The United Nations, which had about fifty founding members, suddenly became an organization of 150. Today it has 159 members.

What is the United Nations doing to meet the problems of peace, disarmament and development in the world of today? There has been no lack of attention to these problems. The first resolution of the United Nations—in 1946, forty years ago—was devoted to disarmament, and the United Nations has a long history of establishing committees and conferences on this theme. The 1981 Thorsson report on disarmament and development was particularly important. It established the extent to which armaments have drained the resources of the world, especially in scientific research, and it remains a classic document. So there has been a lot of talk in the United Nations about peace, disarmament, and their links to development. If words could solve the problem of peace, there would be nothing to worry about. But the arms race has not been stemmed, and peace seems perhaps more endangered than ever.

It is important to understand what the United Nations is and what it is not. It is not, and could never be, a world government, running the world in greater accordance with the principles of peace and progress outlined in its Charter than its member national governments are willing or able to do. It is an intergovernmental organization. It is precisely what its name suggests, that is, an organization which the nations of the world sometimes find useful to use in their diplomacy. At other times they may find it more fruitful, especially if they are powerful enough, to pursue their national interests directly through bilateral arrangements with other countries. The achievements of the United Nations have been spotty because governments have not always chosen to pursue their interests through multilateral diplomacy. But besides being a parliament of a

Göran Ohlin is the Assistant Secretary-General for Development Research and Policy Analysis in the United Nations, and he was assigned by the United Nations to be its official participant in the Vancouver Centennial Peace and Disarmament Symposium. Born in Sweden, and with a Ph.D. degree from Harvard University, Dr. Ohlin has had a long service with international organizations concerned with development issues. They have included the Organization for Economic Co-operation and Development, the Brandt Commission, the Pearson Commission, the World Bank and the United Nations Committee for Development Planning.

world torn by dissent, the United Nations is also a service organization that provides the world community with a lot of things that it desperately needs.

The reason that disarmament talks are so difficult, whether in the United Nations or elsewhere (as in the SALT negotiations) is of course a fundamental lack of trust among nations. There are tensions of many kinds, and I think one must give full attention to these tensions and their roots. Raymond Aron, a great French scholar in international relations, described the situation of our time as: peace impossible, war improbable. That formula sums up a situation of tension in which conflict is contained by an interest in survival. How could it be shifted in a direction in which peace would seem more possible and war impossible?

This is not an absurd question. The history of humankind is one long list of cases in which war once seemed a very real possibility but eventually became inconceivable. Canada and the United States is one example, Western Europe another. In Europe, Jean Monnet and Robert Schumann deliberately set out to create a continent in which the historical conflicts of France and Germany would no longer be able to lead them into war. What they had in mind was a strong economic integration, and there is no doubt that this is a very powerful force for pacification.

In this respect, the record of the United Nations is pretty impressive, but this is not sufficiently appreciated. There is hardly a channel of international relations that the United Nations has not facilitated and made more responsive to the needs of a shrinking world. The United Nations keeps track of world statistics and sees to it that all governments use the same standards in reporting information; guides navigation of the oceans and the air; regulates the use of telecommunication frequencies; directs the control of epidemics throughout the world; and, as best it can, provides for the care of political refugees. The United Nations is already supplying some of the services which a world government would need to provide just to keep things going.

In addition, the United Nations system operates a large program of development aid. We tend perhaps to think of development first of all as a way of directly raising the standard of living and of liberating people from abject poverty. But we should not overlook the fact that development will also link economies more and more closely. It is of special importance to promote trade and economic co-operation among neighbouring developing countries, which are so far much weaker than is the case with more distant industrialized countries. It was a stroke of genius when the Marshall Plan gave American aid for the reconstruction of Europe, on the condition that the Europeans could agree among themselves on its distribution. I wish we could have more of that in present-day aid programs, to promote regional integration, mutual trust, and eventually zones bound by regional peace treaties.

It is in this indirect approach to changing the world in a peaceful way and in a peaceful direction that I see the greatest hopes for a long-run contribution from the United Nations, rather than in direct attacks on the problem of disarmament—although it is certainly imperative that such talks continue.

I also believe that it is essential to create a stronger public desire for peace and development. There is a danger that—when meeting so many like-minded souls as at this symposium, or when we think of the impressive demonstrations for peace that take place in many countries of the world—we will assume that all reasonable people must see the reasons for putting human survival first and for shaping their policies accordingly. I am afraid this is far from the case—especially at a time when so many, even in industrial countries, suffer economic hardships and insecurities. People's minds turn toward their own worries and concerns and prevent them from taking a longer view of the madness of the arms race and of the intolerable differences in the human condition between the developed and the developing countries.

All of your efforts here express the spirit of the Charter of the United Nations. Groups like yours are its best comrades in arms in seeking to create a world in which not only is peace possible, but war impossible.

CHAPTER 16
Let There Be One World for All Humanity

DOM HELDER CAMARA

All human beings who are trying to help create a more human world know of Vancouver, the City of Peace. Other cities are commemorating centennials of war, centennials of victories, of killing enemies and destroying cities and countries. Vancouver is the City of the Century because its centennial celebration is the Centennial Peace and Disarmament Festival. My intention in proclaiming this truth is to remind us all that we are in exactly the right place to re-examine problems of war and peace. I don't have the ridiculous pretension of being here as a teacher, with lessons for you. I am here as a brother to think with you about complex problems of war and peace in our days.

The biggest evil in the arms race, and the biggest threat to peace, is a consequence of the number one problem that is crushing humankind: egoism. This is not unique to any one country, or any continent; nobody monopolizes it. Perhaps it has reached such absurd proportions to help open the eyes of persons of goodwill and, perhaps, to help the general growth of conscience of all human beings.

It is convenient to remember the events of yesterday for a better understanding of human problems of today and tomorrow. At the end of the First World War, many, many persons were sure that the confrontation of the century would be between East and West, between communism and capitalism. But during the Second World War, in order to overcome the Nazis, the West asked the collaboration of the East. At the end of this terrible world war, marked by the discovery and use of nuclear weapons, the biggest surprise of all came. Around the same table, in Yalta, communism and capitalism (Churchill, Roosevelt and Stalin) divided the world into zones of influence. And now we know what, because of this

Dom Helder Camara

injustice, the biggest confrontation of the century will be: the confrontation between North and South which is already rapidly growing.

When President Eisenhower was leaving the White House for the second time, he judged that as a duty of conscience he must denounce the alliance between military power and economic power. Today, behind all important powers, economic power is present—incarnated, above all, in the great transnational corporations—helping and controlling all the big forces of our time.

Where do they get, every year, these mad amounts of money—at the moment, $800 billion—that go into the arms race? Economic power permits, and keeps attention focused on, the arms race. The big countries know how terrible modern war is—above all, with the menace of nuclear, chemical and biological weapons. But for economic power it is more important to: divert attention from the terrible injustices of the trade imbalance between the industrialized countries and the countries which produce raw materials; divert attention from the consequences of the arrival of the great multinational corporations in the so-called Third World; divert attention from the fact that nature is being crushed and deserts created, to serve a consumer society.

For economic power, it is more important to divert the world's attention from the explosion of egoism by denouncing the demographic explosion. By failing to provide enough food and work for them, economic power tries to prove the necessity and urgency of ridding the world of a billion human beings. We know that twenty percent of humanity owns and exploits eighty percent of nature's resources, and we know that the third industrial revolution—which has brought automation and robotization—keeps progress, as always, at the service of only small groups of

Dom Helder Camara is the Archbishop Emeritus of Olinda and Recife in Brazil. Born in Brazil, he was ordained a Roman Catholic priest in 1931, and he has worked tirelessly since then to improve the level of education in his country, and to support workers, the poor and youth. Dom Helder's commitment to improving social conditions has made him both loved by the poor and despised by the conservative opposition in Brazil. He has survived one assassination attempt and has had his life threatened many times. In 1955 he was elevated to archbishop, and in 1964 he became Archbishop of Olinda and Recife—the poorest and most underprivileged part of Brazil. Dom Helder Camara has received twenty-three honourary degrees and a number of important prizes for his work for peace and social development. Some of his books, which have been translated into English, are: Revolution Through Peace, Spiral of Violence, Race Against Time, *and* Charismatic Renewal and Social Action: A Dialogue.

the rich. Rather than solve this inequity, for economic power it is more important to denounce the Third World because of its terrible debts, while collecting huge interest payments under conditions of usury.

Then what should we do? We need, without forgetting the arms race, to have a clear vision that without justice and love a true peace will be impossible. We need to fight against our own injustices and the poverty of our love. We need to increase our fight against the injustices in our own cities and our own countries by ever more opening our eyes and hearts to the poor of each city and country; to unemployment, a source of poverty and misery; to the aborigines, the natives of our countries; to the exiled persons arriving in our midst; to the criminals, who are only attempting to escape hunger and death. Then, when we look at conditions on a world scale, the injustices are even more incredible: more than two thirds of humanity is presently submerged in a subhuman condition.

Vancouver, excuse me. I love you. I love your people. But Vancouver, City of Peace, don't forget: without justice and love, true peace is impossible! Be an example by making a general call against injustice. Tell all the people who live full lives, rich lives, even superhuman lives, that they have a special duty to the billions who live subhuman lives. Tell all believers in God, Creator and Father of all human beings, of all races, colours, all languages, all faiths, that we have the same Father. Tell them that we must really help all the children of God who are living under the condition of animals. It would be terrible for them to think that God is not the Father, but only a step-father. And above all, tell all Christians that in fourteen years the year 2000 will arrive. This is not only the arrival of a new millennium, it is two thousand years since the birth of Christ. What a wonderful challenge: to live fourteen years trying to help obtain the union of our broken world.

First World, Second World, Third World, Fourth World—One World! One family with God as the Father of all of us, and Christ as our Saviour and our Brother.

CHAPTER 17

What the Arms Race Is Doing to People in the Third World

THOMAS L. PERRY, M.D.

During the three days in which the Vancouver Centennial Peace and Disarmament Symposium took place, approximately 120,000 children throughout the world died from preventable diseases, and 150,000 more people died of starvation. A large proportion of the children's deaths could have been prevented by immunizations which are given routinely to most Canadian children; and those children and adults who died of hunger need not have, if abundant food were properly shared between rich and poor countries. It has been said that "statistics are people with the tears washed off (1)."* But statistics can help put into perspective the magnitude of the harm being done to people, especially in the developing countries, by the obscene wasting of the world's economic resources on preparations for war. This chapter has been prepared to supplement with facts in tabular form the presentations given in Session III of the symposium by Joanna Miller, Reverend Lois M. Wilson, Bishop Thomas Gumbleton, Dom Helder Camara, and Göran Ohlin, all of them dealing with the problems of how the arms race harms the health, social and economic conditions of people in the Third World.

International Physicians for the Prevention of Nuclear War (IPPNW), the group which won the 1985 Nobel Peace Prize, concluded at its fourth Congress in Helsinki, Finland, in June 1984 that: "Physicians have a moral duty to persuade their governments to use resources to make the world a better place for all humankind." Further, the delegates in Helsinki concluded that besides their responsibility to educate themselves, their patients, and government leaders on the medical consequences of

---

* These numbers refer to references found at the end of the chapter. —ED.

nuclear war, physicians also have a responsibility: 1) to educate these groups on the socioeconomic effects of the arms race; 2) to conduct and foster research on the economic effects of the arms race on the quality of life in their own countries; and 3) to help find ways to promote a fair redistribution of resources from military expenditures to the health budgets of their own and other countries.

As a physician, I should like in particular to emphasize ways in which the huge sums now being spent preparing for war could usefully be diverted to improving the health of people in developing countries. Current expenditures by all countries for military purposes have been estimated by Ruth Leger Sivard as at least U.S. $800 billion (2), and in chapter 2 of this book, Rear Admiral Eugene Carroll reports that 1986 military spending worldwide will reach U.S. $900 billion.

Living in a rich country like Canada, we often fail to understand what life is really like for most people on the earth. How do they live? Table 1 gives some sobering estimates on what life was like in 1985 for many human beings. These statistics have been compiled from material in Ruth Leger Sivard's latest publication, *World Military and Social Expenditures 1985* (2).

TABLE 1

STATE OF THE WORLD'S PEOPLE—UNMET HUMAN NEEDS

Total population (1985)		4800 million
Living in severe poverty	>	1000 million
People unemployed, or underemployed	>	600 million
People starving or seriously malnourished	>	500 million
(*deaths from starvation = 50,000 per day*)		
Illiterate adults	>	600 million
School age children not enrolled in school		700 million

Table 2 illustrates the tremendous development gap between the richest and poorest countries of the world. Figures are for 1980 (3), but the difference would be comparable today. Indeed, by 1983 the annual gross national product (GNP) per capita in North America had risen to $13,310, compared to $250 a year in all of South Asia, and to $830 a year in Africa as a whole.

In 1982, there were two teachers per one thousand school-age children in the poorest developing countries, but sixty-seven per one thousand in the richest developed countries. The poorest countries had two hospital beds per 10,000 people, while the richest had 167. Bangladesh had in

TABLE 2

DEVELOPMENT GAP: 1980

WORLD POPULATION:	RICHEST 20%	POOREST 20%
GNP per capita	$9469	$206
Population with safe water	96%	39%
Life expectancy at birth	74 years	53 years
Infant mortality	20	120
(deaths per 1000 births)		
Adult literacy	97%	42%

1982 one physician for every 78,000 inhabitants, while Canada had one physician for every 570 persons (2). About 140 times as much money per capita is spent on health in developed countries as in the least developed countries (1).

The unmet needs of the world's children are especially distressing, as shown in Table 3. These figures, gathered from several reliable sources (1,2,4), show how badly we are squandering the future of humankind while we spend our wealth on so-called defence.

TABLE 3

UNMET NEEDS OF WORLD'S CHILDREN

Of 4.8 billion inhabitants, 1.9 billion (40%) are less than 15 years old.
   In the developing countries:
   300 million children are chronically hungry.
   100 million children are severely malnourished.
   300 million children, aged 6 to 11, do not attend school.
   Only 25% of entrants finish elementary school.
   Less than 10% of children are immunized against measles, diphtheria, tetanus, pertussis, poliomyelitis, tuberculosis.
   15 million children die annually (4 million due to lack of immunizations and 4 million from diarrhea).

Table 4 summarizes some public expenditures in preparation for war. These amount in 1986 to somewhere between U.S. $1.5 million and U.S. $1.7 million per minute. The United States is the world's heaviest spender for military purposes, and planned expenditures for deployment of the Strategic Defense Initiative ("Star Wars") will enormously increase American military spending over the next few years. Although

Canada's "defence" spending looks modest by comparison, it is worth considering what almost $10 billion Canadian could do for socially useful purposes both in Canada and in the Third World.

TABLE 4

PUBLIC EXPENDITURES IN PREPARATION FOR WAR

Entire World	1986	U.S. $800 to $900 billion/year (U.S. $1.5 to $1.7 million/minute)
United States**	fiscal 1987	U.S. $320 billion
	Star Wars initial research	U.S $30 billion
	Estimated Star Wars deployment	U.S. $1000 billion
Canada***	fiscal 1986–1987	Can. $9.9 billion

** President Reagan's proposed budget (*New York Times,* May 16, 1986).
*** 1986–1987 spending estimates, House of Commons (March 27, 1986).

Commonly cited examples of the relatively small fractions of world military expenditures which have either financed, or could in future finance very important health improvement projects are the World Health Organization's (WHO) successful campaign to eradicate smallpox worldwide, and the WHO's proposed campaign to eradicate malaria (Table 5).

TABLE 5

HEALTH COSTS OF THE ARMS RACE: I

WHO	10-year campaign to eradicate smallpox	= U.S. $100 million, or one hour of 1985 world arms expenditure
WHO	5-year projected campaign to control malaria	= U.S. $8 billion, or four days of 1985 world arms expenditure
	(*Malaria currently threatens 1 billion people in 66 countries, with 100 million new cases per year, and more than 1 million deaths per year.*)	

Larger scale proposed expenditures of money by the WHO would achieve much greater savings for the people of the developing countries in terms of suffering, ill health and premature death. These are illustrated in Table 6. If all the money wasted in military spending by all countries over a period of six months were instead invested in providing a *permanent* sanitary water supply for the two billion people who presently have no access to safe water, 80% of the illnesses suffered by these people could be prevented.

TABLE 6

HEALTH COSTS OF THE ARMS RACE: II

---

2 billion people (44%) of world population drink disease-contaminated water, estimated to cause 80% of all illnesses among these people.

WHO projected campaign to provide permanent safe water supply for these 2 billion people would cost the equivalent of 18 days of current military spending, each year, for 10 years.

WHO 20-year program to provide essential food and health in all developing countries would cost total of U.S. $400 billion (6 months of current military spending).

The WHO estimates that wise expenditure of about the same amount of money over a twenty-year period could provide a permanent, adequate food supply and health care system for all of the developing countries. The United Nations in a special session devoted to the problems of starvation in Africa recently concluded (June 1986) that expenditure of approximately U.S. $80 billion (which is about the amount the world spends on war preparations every six weeks) could stop desertification, construct necessary irrigation facilities, and introduce suitable agricultural practices which would completely prevent *everywhere in Africa* the dreadful suffering from famine that the people of the world recently witnessed on their television screens, as it was actually taking place in the Sudan and Ethiopia.

Table 7 shows some calculations of the years of useful life that are wasted by deaths in developing countries from infantile respiratory infections, which are relatively inexpensive to prevent, as compared to the years of life that are lost in rich countries by deaths from atherosclerotic heart disease, which is far more costly and complicated to prevent. The mortality rate for infants from respiratory infections is ten times greater in the Third World than in the wealthy countries, which are often the leading promoters of the nuclear arms race.

Tables 8 and 9 give two further examples of major public health problems which would be relatively easy to solve in developing countries: measles, which is a highly fatal disease for infants and young children in developing countries; and iodine deficiency, which in some countries is a major cause of stunted physical growth and of mental deficiency. Included are rough estimates of the costs of *permanent* eradication of measles, and of effective prevention of future ill effects from iodine deficiency. In each case, less than one day's world military expenditures could solve the problem.

TABLE 7

HEALTH COSTS OF THE ARMS RACE: III

Acute respiratory infections cause 2.2 million deaths per year in infants aged less than 1 year. Together with diarrheal diseases, they are the world's most important preventable causes of death.

COUNTRIES	INFANTS	CHILDREN 1–4 YEARS
	(DEATHS PER 100,000 LIVE BIRTHS)	
U.S.A. and Canada	146	8
Central America	1459	149
Israel and Japan	131	10
Africa	1454	467

Lost years of life (assuming that maximum life span = 90 years, with heart disease killing 15 years earlier):

DISEASE	MORTALITY PER 100,000	YEARS LOST PER 100,000
Heart disease (developed countries)	$500 \times 15 =$	7,500
Infantile respiratory infections	$1450 \times 89 =$	129,000

Source of data for these calculations(5).

Many further examples of the enormous savings in life, disease and human suffering which could be made by redirection of public funding from preparations for war to the funding of human needs undoubtedly could be described. Schistosomiasis, a parasitic worm infestation, affects 200 to 300 million people in Africa, Latin America, China and Southeast Asia, and causes chronic ill health which lasts many years. Recent scientific research suggests that developing a vaccine might be feasible, and use of the new anti-schistosomiasis drug, praziquantel (costing U.S. $2 per person treated), together with development of proper sewage systems, makes wiping out this great disease problem immediately practical (9). Expenditure of sizeable funds on medical research, instead of on enlarging nuclear arsenals, might also achieve the development of a vaccine against malaria, an increasingly urgent problem for many Third World countries where *Plasmodium falciparum* infections are becoming

TABLE 8

GLOBAL MEASLES ERADICATION vs. MILITARY SPENDING

Measles causes 900,000 deaths annually in developing countries. Case fatality rate 10% to 20%, children 1–4 years, in Africa and Asia. Measles also increases mortality from malnutrition and diarrheal diseases.

Prospects for complete eradication are good, as for smallpox, because:

No animal reservoir for measles virus

No chronic carrier state

Live vaccine now cheap and relatively heat-stable

Requirements for eradication: vaccinate 90% of children (12–15 months).

Eradicated in Gambia; 90% of counties in United States were measles-free in 1981.

Probable cost of global eradication:

U.S. $400 million, or five hours of 1985 world arms spending.

Source of information for this estimate(6).

TABLE 9

IODINE DEFICIENCY DISORDERS

Affected:	400 million people in Asia; also in Papua-New Guinea, Andes, Zaire
Cause:	Insufficient iodine in soil and diet (less than 20 microgram/day). (Normal diet should provide 80 to 150 microgram/day).
Effects:	Stillbirths, congenital malformations, and/or impaired growth and mental function in children and adults.
Prevention:	Add iodized salt to diet, or administer iodized oil by mouth or injection (once every 3–5 years).
Likely cost of prevention:	One oil injection for 400 million persons costs U.S. $2 billion or 22 hours of 1985 world arms expenditures.

Sources of information (7,8).

increasingly resistant to most of the usually effective anti-malarial drugs (10).

The cost of building a dyke across the Gulf of Bengal, sufficiently high and strong to prevent the disastrous cyclones which repeatedly drown many thousands of people in the low-lying Ganges delta of Bangladesh, was recently estimated to be about U.S. $1 billion. That is less than four percent of what the United States plans to spend on Star Wars research in the next five years, and less than 0.1 percent of what it is estimated that deployment of the Strategic Defense Initiative will cost the United States. One wonders how small a fraction of either superpower's annual military budgets would be required to reforest, irrigate, and redesign agriculture in drought-stricken areas of Africa, and to prevent the appalling famines that have caused such suffering recently in Ethiopia and the Sudan. Physicians and others interested in peace need to work out further practical details of how military expenditures could be diverted to solving major health problems for a majority of the world's peoples.

Figure 1 and Table 10 show the enormous growth of military expenditures by the developed countries over the last two decades, while the foreign economic aid these countries give has remained almost stagnant, and is now even less than their arms exports. For the developed countries as a group, foreign economic aid extended in 1983 was only 5.5 percent of what these countries spent on their own preparations for war. The United Nations has called on all developed countries to devote, by the year 1995, at least 0.7 percent of their annual GNP to aid to Third World countries. Reverend Lois Wilson in chapter 13 of this book urges that the deadline for attaining this goal be advanced to 1990. At present, only Norway, Sweden, Denmark, and the Netherlands have met this modest humanitarian goal. In 1982, the latest year for which figures are available (2), Canada spent a measly 0.43 percent of its GNP on aid to developing countries, and much of that was "tied" aid which compelled recipient countries to purchase Canadian goods, often to their own disadvantage.

I propose that people who are concerned with preventing nuclear war and who are shocked at the impoverishment and suffering of nearly two billion of our brothers and sisters, now urge the governments of *all* nations to make an immediate twenty percent cutback in military expenditures. It is inconceivable that such a modest decrease in military expenditures would constitute a threat to the defence of any nation. Indeed, such a cutback in expenditures by the two superpowers would increase their own and everyone else's security, as is argued persuasively elsewhere in this book by Admiral Eugene Carroll, Paul Warnke, Kosta Tsipis, Michael Pentz and Vitaly Zhurkin.

FIGURE 1

FOREIGN ECONOMIC AID AND MILITARY EXPENDITURES
BY DEVELOPED COUNTRIES

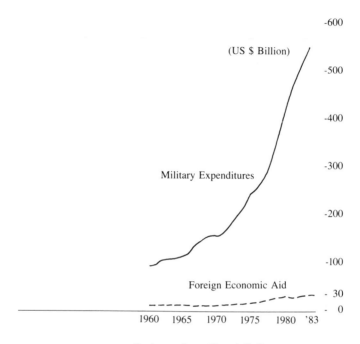

Redrawn from Sivard (2,3)

TABLE 10

FOREIGN ECONOMIC AID vs. MILITARY EXPENDITURES: 1983
DEVELOPED COUNTRIES*

GNP	U.S. $ 10,120 billion
Military operations	547 billion (5.4% of GNP)
Arms exports	34 billion
Foreign economic aid	30 billion (0.3% of GNP)

Source of data (2).

* Developed countries include the United States, Canada, most of Europe, the Soviet Union, Australia, New Zealand, Israel, and Japan.

I propose that for the developed nations one half of their twenty percent reduction in military expenditures should be redirected to meeting health and other social needs within the nation making that redirection. This redirection of funds to social needs in the home country could help to correct deficiencies in health care, education, and social services which are already painfully evident in rich countries such as Canada and the United States. The remaining half of the money saved, amounting to ten percent of previous military expenditures, should be allocated for foreign economic aid, and should be used, under WHO or Food and Agriculture Organization supervision, for meeting major health and nutrition problems in Third World countries. It can be seen from Table 10 that such a redirection of even ten percent of present military expenditures would almost triple foreign economic aid. Were Canada to cut its $9.9 billion military expenditures this year (Table 4) by twenty percent and devote half of that savings to economic aid to developing countries, it would immediately achieve the United Nation's recommended goal of 0.7 percent of GNP devoted to foreign economic aid.

Dr. Bernard Lown, in accepting the 1985 Nobel Peace Prize on behalf of International Physicians for the Prevention of Nuclear War, said in part:

> If science and technology have catapulted us to the brink of extinction, the same ingenuity has brought humankind to the boundary of an age of abundance. Never before was it possible to feed all the hungry. Never before was it possible to shelter all the homeless. Never before was it possible to teach all the illiterate. Never before were we able to heal so many afflictions. For the first time, science and medicine can diminish drudgery and pain. Only those who see the invisible can do the impossible.(11)

In my view, it is high time that peace-minded people learned to see the invisible!

Success in improving health and the quality of life anywhere on this planet could whet the appetite of all peoples to achieve the same goals for themselves. Success reinforcing success is likely to be infectious, and should once and for all convince us of the futility of wasting our resources in preparing to slaughter our neighbours.

References and Notes

1. V. W. Sidel, ''Destruction Before Detonation: the Impact of the Arms Race on Health and Health Care'' in *Lancet,* 2 (1985): 1287– 1289.

2. Ruth Leger Sivard, *World Military and Social Expenditures 1985.* (Washington, D.C.: World Priorities, Box 25140, 1985).

3. Ruth Leger Sivard, *World Military and Social Expenditures 1983.* (Washington, D.C.: World Priorities, Box 25140, 1983).

4. B. J. Schmidt, "Current Outlook for Children Around the World" in *Pediatrics,* 74 (1984): 294–295.

5. J. Chretien, W. Holland, P. Mackem, J. Murray, and A. Woolcock, "Acute Respiratory Infections in Children: A Global Public-Health Problem" in *New England Journal of Medicine,* 310 (1984): 982–984.

6. D. R. Hopkins, J. P. Koplan, A. R. Hinman, and J. M. Lane, "The Case for Global Measles Eradication" in *Lancet,* 1 (1982): 1396–1398.

7. B. S. Hetzel, "Iodine Deficiency Disorders (IDD) and Their Eradication" in *Lancet,* 2 (1983): 1126–1129.

8. Anonymous, "Control of Iodine Deficiency in Asia" in *Lancet,* 2 (1983): 1244.

9. G. Kolata, "Avoiding the Schistosome's Tricks" in *Science,* 227 (1985): 285–287.

10. G. Kolata, "The Search for a Malaria Vaccine" in *Science,* 226 (1984): 679–682.

11. B. Lown, "Nobel Peace Prize Lecture: A Prescription for Hope" in *New England Journal of Medicine,* 314 (1986): 985–987.

CHAPTER 18

Panel Discussion: Session III*

JOANNA MILLER, LOIS M. WILSON, AND GÖRAN OHLIN

Joanna Miller (session chairperson):
One particular question is being asked over and over again. What do we actually do about these problems? We see the problems, we understand the urgency—but what do we do? Can we have comments from the panel as to specific proposals which will move the process along?

Lois Wilson:
It is important that the proposals that come out of this symposium address not only the world scene, but also what we as Canadians commit ourselves to do. Otherwise the proposals are only going to be generalities. I outlined some suggestions in terms of our policies in development assistance, which are well within our reach if we are able to mobilize enough people to pressure the government to take action. I'd like to see some of these suggestions in the Vancouver Proposals for Peace. Otherwise people won't have tools to use; they'll have nothing to go on.

It seems to me an enormous sign of hope that vocational groups have come together, such as Physicians for Social Responsibility, Lawyers for Social Responsibility and Engineers for Social Responsibility. I would really like to see some Bricklayers for Social Responsibility, some Bus Drivers for Social Responsibility, some Hairdressers for Social Responsibility.

---

*Bishop Thomas Gumbleton and Ambassador Douglas Roche had to leave Vancouver before Session III ended and were unable to participate in the panel discussion. —ED.

Göran Ohlin:
We who work in the United Nations get enormous inspiration from the people who are so obviously committed to these causes and who volunteer to work for them. Though I haven't yet heard of Bricklayers for Social Responsibility.

Wilson:
They don't exist yet, that's why.

Ohlin:
I wouldn't be so sure. I have been absolutely flabbergasted by the number of such organizations and by the work they do. Consider for instance, the designing of bridges in the Third World. It turns out that our technical assistance people get volunteer contributions from retired designers and engineers. There are endless opportunities for doing the right thing. And I think you people are more ingenious than I in finding them out.

I would say that, not only in Canada but in all democratic countries, there is obviously a tremendously important kind of lobbying and political pressure that pays off—there is no doubt about that—in the human rights field and in the environment field. Ambassador Roche reminded us all of how the climate has changed. When I started in development in the early sixties, things were very different from now. The early intellectual climate has been reversed. Things which were almost inconceivable then are now taken for granted.

Miller:
Just by acting and spreading the word among friends, the atmosphere does change. Perceptions do change. Another question that has come up is what is the role of the United Nations, and whether you see any changes that could occur in the structure of the United Nations that could make it more effective. Perhaps some reference to the amount of the United Nations' effort that goes into its development work would be interesting to the audience. I think that's a very large operation.

Ohlin:
Let me just try to summarize what I think the critical issues are. The United Nations is under fire. It is under siege at the moment. This comes from two sources. It comes from those who object to it because it doesn't serve their purposes, and it comes from those who are indifferent to it because it seems to them that it has failed them. They are disenchanted with the United Nations because the United Nations has not delivered peace, and it hasn't delivered prosperity. I think that one must remember that if the governments of the world look at the United Nations and don't like

180

what they see, it is because the United Nations is a mirror which reflects the intentions of its members.

It is more difficult to know what to tell people who feel that there was, in the United Nations, the hope of world government, but that hope has not been met. I believe that the United Nations is now in a crisis. The question now is whether we will be able to rescue the important parts of the United Nations and make these more effective and at the same time get rid of an awful lot of bureaucratic wastage. This wastage accumulates in all bureaucracies and it is particularly difficult to get rid of in an international organization. If we can do both these things, perhaps there is hope for the idea of an international civil service: one which is beholden to no nation and no government, but to humanity as a whole and to the ideas and principles of the United Nations charter. If the idea of an international civil service can be resurrected and endowed with dignity, I think then the world would be better off.

Wilson:
Canadians ought to be writing to our Minister of External Affairs to the effect that we do *not* want to follow the Americans in their withdrawal from UNICEF, and their whole critique of some of the agencies of the United Nations. That doesn't mean to say that these agencies are not in need of some drastic reform, as has been mentioned. But let's not withdraw. If they were abolished, we would have to reinvent them.

Miller:
I think we should all remember one fact: that people basically, at least in a democracy, get the government they deserve. If we elect a government, and then spend the next four or five years railing against it and feeling dissatisfied, but we don't actively get into the political process—whether it is working with our member of Parliament, getting into a political party or changing the opinions of the people we meet—it is very hard for us to criticize effectively. If we are to make the changes that we have to, we must be much more active, all of us, in our various arenas. Many of the questions received this morning do reflect considerable anger against our present government and some of its actions. I know this anger is widely shared on certain things that the Canadian government is doing. But we have to translate that anger into positive action. If we don't like what they are doing, we should tell them so. And then tell them positively what they should be doing, or indicate the alternatives which we think would help put Canada on a better foundation in the policies that are followed.

We need to recognize that we are tremendously privileged to live in a country where we can speak freely, and can act without fear of assassination and so on—*but we have to do our part.*

PART IV

What Can Individuals Do for Peace?

James P. Anderton

CHAPTER 19

Nuclear Freedom in One Country—How and Why: A Case Study of the Development of a Nuclear-Free Policy in New Zealand

JAMES P. ANDERTON

INTRODUCTION

I bring you greetings from the people of New Zealand—from the *Pakeha* (white New Zealanders of European descent) and from the *Tangata Whenua* (the people of the land), the Maori people who named New Zealand *Aotearoa*—the land of the long white cloud. They were the great navigators of the South Pacific, who discovered our country and whose culture and heritage we *Pakeha* New Zealanders so proudly share. The long white cloud covering the land which you see as you approach New Zealand by sea or air is both a cloak of protection and a sign of the clean mist and rain which so often wash our land, keeping it green and keeping our environment the healthiest on earth. I bring you greetings from a nuclear-free New Zealand, and that is how we intend to keep it!

At a recent meeting of the Foreign Affairs Labour Parliamentary Caucus Committee, Baroness Young, the British Minister of State for Foreign and Commonwealth Affairs, told committee members that since

James P. Anderton is the Member of Parliament for Sydenham in New Zealand. He has been a member of the Labour Party for over twenty years, and was its president from 1979 to 1984. As a member of the present Labour government in New Zealand, he is active in the Select Committee on Foreign Affairs and Defence, and in the Select Committee on Planning and Development. Mr. Anderton has worked as a teacher and social worker, and is a managing director of an industrial design and manufacturing engineering company. He was one of the chief architects of New Zealand's policy of denying naval vessels armed with nuclear weapons permission to enter New Zealand harbours.

the Second World War the nuclear deterrent has prevented the Western Alliance from having to engage in wars. She was asked to explain the twenty-one million people who have died in wars since 1945. The Western Allies fought in some of these wars, such as the ones in Korea and Vietnam. She answered that these wars had not occurred in Western Alliance countries. This seemed to imply that it was all right for Western nations to engage in wars outside their own borders but not inside them—a strange kind of morality. I reminded her that the Vietnam war had taken place under the Southeast Asia Treaty Organization (SEATO) treaty, to which Britain was a signatory, and asked her where Britain had been during that war. The British ambassador answered that the British government had chosen to miss that war—and I advised her that the New Zealand government and people were choosing to miss the next one! I find that the closer one comes to the heart of the nuclear weapons issue, the more difficult it is to speak in other than very plain language, and to give very simple speeches.

Nuclear weapons and nuclear war have been discussed at both community and national levels in New Zealand, in a way that I believe is unprecedented in any other country in the world. There are many reasons for this. One is the small size of both the country and the population: three million people live on two relatively small islands (which, I hasten to add proudly, manage to include most, if not all, of the marvellous features of the Canadian landscape I have seen). Other reasons are that New Zealand has a cohesive and homogeneous social structure, as well as good systems for education and communication.

The bottom line for my country and its people has been the conclusion that we could not countenance, nor do we wish to be defended by, nuclear weapons. Having come to that decision, we naturally concluded that it would be illogical and wrong to encourage or participate in the proliferation of nuclear weapons, or to be part of a defensive or offensive strategy which included their potential or implied use. Nuclear war, to our minds, no longer has any place on humanity's agenda for the future. It attempts to solve human problems in an inhuman way; we have got to have better means of settling conflict.

The world has been living under the threat of nuclear war ever since the United States exploded the first atomic bomb on Hiroshima forty-one years ago. Since then, many people have claimed that nuclear weapons keep the peace—but they can do so only if human beings accept living in perpetual fear. This is *not* an acceptable basis for maintaining a lasting peace. In fact, the balance of fear, by generating a never-ending spiral of suspicion and anxiety about one's opponent's intentions, has resulted in a giddy arms race based on threat and counter-threat. It has been responsible for attempts to gain first-strike advantage and for efforts to respond to that capability.

The nuclear strategists contemplate what ought to be unthinkable preemptive attacks—and former hawks such as one-time American Secretary of Defense Robert McNamara state loudly and clearly at every opportunity that the risk of accidental nuclear war from human or technological error has never been greater. To cap it all, Professor Carl Sagan and a large number of other internationally renowned scientists now believe that the long-term consequences of any nuclear war would be global climatic catastrophe.

BACKGROUND TO PRESENT MOOD

New Zealand is a small country, far from world power centres. Yet, as a member of the Western Alliance, it is part of a privileged group of nations which jointly and separately has a major say in world affairs. Any disagreements New Zealand may have with other members of the Western Alliance can cause international reverberations.

New Zealand has refused to allow American nuclear warships entry to its ports. This is a matter of great concern to New Zealand's ANZUS Treaty partners (Australia and the United States), to New Zealand's other military allies (Britain, Malaysia and Singapore), to the allies of the United States, and to Pacific and Asian region countries generally. New Zealand has taken a stand which has international implications, a stand which is widely supported but still controversial at home, and very controversial abroad. What sort of country is New Zealand, and how did it come to take such a stand?

The people. New Zealand is a small country in the Southwest Pacific (104,000 square miles). It was first populated around A.D. 500 by Polynesian people, who took the name Maori upon contact with the British colonizers who claimed the country for Britain in the early nineteenth century. The current population is 3,230,000, of which ten percent are Maori, eighty-four percent of European descent, and six percent of other races. Anglo-Saxon culture, either local or imported from Britain and the United States, predominates, but there are vital Maori and Pacific Island minority cultural traditions which contribute uniquely to New Zealand society.

The economy. New Zealand has a temperate climate, ideally suited for growing grass and raising sheep and cows. A tourist industry, based on spectacular and unpolluted scenery, is also a major earner of foreign exchange, as are rapidly diversifying manufacturing industries. Most New Zealanders enjoy a high standard of living, with a comprehensive welfare system providing free public schools, high-quality hospitals, and benefits for those unable to work. This standard of living depends on maintaining and increasing exports to good customers, such as the United States.

Politics. New Zealand is a Westminster-style democracy. Its electoral system ensures that two parties dominate the political scene. There is one House of Representatives, seating ninety-five members of Parliament, who are elected triennially. The Parliamentary leader of the majority party becomes the prime minister. The two major parties currently in Parliament are Labour (the current government) and National. National is a conservative party, representing the interests of business, farms and conservative professionals. Labour is a more liberal party, with support from wage workers and liberal professionals. Labour has been in power for twenty-two of the last fifty-one years since 1935, but for only eight of the last thirty-seven years.

NEW ZEALAND AND THE UNITED STATES

New Zealand has been in practically every war available to it in this century—in South Africa, in World Wars I and II, in Korea, Malaya and Vietnam. In September 1951, the ANZUS Treaty was signed. This treaty is the symbolic cornerstone of New Zealand's subsequent military and political relationship with the United States. To New Zealand at the time, it represented security against possible Japanese or Chinese military resurgence. To the United States it was the first of a series of treaties planned to extend its influence in the region.

In 1954, New Zealand joined the United States and other nations in SEATO. SEATO involvement led New Zealand into providing military assistance to the United States in Thailand (1962–65) and in Vietnam (1965–73). In the 1960s, New Zealand opened its doors to American military bases: Project Longbank monitored French nuclear tests; the Antarctic research headquarters at Harewood Airport in Christchurch hosted an American Military Airlift Command and Naval Communications Unit; and a satellite tracking station at Mt. John sent encoded information directly to NORAD.

In 1968, however, an unprecedented public outcry prevented an Omega navigation system (for nuclear submarine guidance) from being sited in New Zealand. More visible and contentious than the bases, however, were the visits of American nuclear warships, which began in 1976 (following a tradition of non-nuclear ship visits). These ships were met by growing water-borne and land-based protests. It is in this context that the present Labour government has taken a firm stand against the entry of nuclear warships into New Zealand ports. Since it is official American policy neither to confirm nor deny the presence of nuclear arms on American warships, the United States will not guarantee that the ships are not nuclear-armed, and therefore our government will not let them enter New Zealand ports. New Zealand says that this stand, which is one small, practical step towards the creation of a nuclear-weapons-free South Pacific, is not intended to jeopardize the spirit or the letter of the ANZUS alliance, and that it does not do so. The United States maintains that it does, and has already reduced military and intelligence co-operation with New Zealand.

The annual ANZUS Council meeting, which was to be held in Canberra in mid-1985 was cancelled. Trade sanctions against New Zealand have been debated in the United States, and there are fears in New Zealand that the government may be "destabilized," as other governments opposing the United States have been. The relationship between the New Zealand and Australian governments has been strained over this issue, but so far has survived basically intact.

The third Labour government (1972–75) withdrew New Zealand troops from Vietnam. It also took France to the World Court, seeking an injunction against nuclear testing at Mururoa. When France went ahead, in defiance of a temporary ban, the government sent a New Zealand frigate to the testing zone, as a protest and to monitor the tests. A recent review of the peace movement in New Zealand by one of our better quality newspapers, the *New Zealand Times,* said: "When the United States tackled New Zealand's Labour government head-on over the nuclear ship ban, it made a fundamental mistake. The Reagan administration completely misjudged the depth of feeling on the issue in New Zealand."

A QUIET REVOLUTION

A quiet revolution has taken place in my country. Over the last three years especially, a huge number of peace-oriented groups have sprung up across New Zealand. They range from single issue groups, such as the Coalition Against Nuclear Warships (CANWAR) to the much broader-based Foundation for Peace Studies. Some represent only a handful, others many hundreds, such as the Auckland branch of CND (Campaign for Nuclear Disarmament). Some have been around for many years, others are, literally, days old. In terms of the world peace movement, they are uniquely independent, deciding their own priorities, setting their own goals.

This is the New Zealand movement's strength. There is no formal hierarchical structure, such as exists in the movements of countries like Australia and Britain. Each New Zealand group sets its own agenda, which has led to a vitality surprising even to members of the movement. There appears to be no orchestration and no ideological basis.

It is almost impossible to estimate precisely the total number of peace activists or sympathizers in New Zealand, though the very number of formal groups (350 at least) and their mailing lists (700 for CND in Auckland alone) suggest substantial numbers. Though no formal structure exists, many different groups in the peace movement have formed effective links with each other, normally on an informal basis. Sensitive defence material obtained by one group is quickly passed around via a network that must rival the rumour circuit of Parliament! The linkages in New Zealand are so good, and sympathy on nuclear issues in the community at large is so strong, that in January of 1985 CND in Auckland was able to get ten thousand protestors onto the streets within two days' notice of a possible visit by the nuclear-capable warship, the *USS Buchanan*.

Why has New Zealand done so well, comparatively, on the anti-nuclear front? New Zealand has a good historical base for struggling for justice. Many New Zealanders are determined to make this a better place than the old world. The Irish streak in us plays a big part. Add to this the ideal of racial justice, which many of us believed in when we were young, and which many of us still strive to realize.

We are a small country where small victories have been achievable in both the political and industrial fields. So protesting has a great tradition. You can actually *achieve* things. Peace marches—for example, Hiroshima Day marches—come quite naturally to us. Looking back over the years, dozens of Labour politicians have taken part in protest marches. Some of these politicians, of course, during the Vietnam war, would peep around the corner to see how many people had turned up, before deciding whether to go home or go and stand up front.

Then there is the Peace Squadron, an idea that followed on naturally from land-based marches. Auckland has one of the finest harbours in the world, and you don't have to be rich to own some sort of craft. The Squadron was an idea that captured the imagination. It was at the sharp edge of nuclear protest, or, as one headline said, "Protestors Board a Yellow Submarine." The hundreds of yacht and boat owners who sailed out with their crews and families to confront the nuclear warships on each visit are heroes to us, both for doing it at all, and for putting their precious boats at risk.

The Labour government's policy was definitely an idea that had found its time. In fact, many of us in the Labour party had already joined the peace movement. The "Nuclear-Weapons-Free Register" showed this. We knew on election day in 1984 that a majority of the new Labour government caucus was solidly against visits of nuclear-armed ships. A spontaneous, grassroots community response, with its mushrooming of small neighbourhood and special interest groups, has been the basis of the New Zealand peace movement. Although there are individuals whose names have become well known, the movement has not been the work of an effective few, but rather of many hundreds joining together in groups

James P. Anderton

Protest vessels surround United States submarine Pintado *in Auckland harbour*

Small boats blockade United States frigate Waikato *in Auckland harbour, New Zealand*

and giving what time and talents they could. From this energy came the mushrooming of many small suburban neighbourhood groups. In 1983 these turned out in force to support the Peace Squadron protest against the American nuclear warship *Texas,* which imprudently arrived on Hiroshima Day! In the next few months, two American nuclear submarines, and the British *Invincible* which had taken its nuclear depth charges to the Falklands war, came to our country. This apparent attempt to tire out the peace movement and accustom the public to the presence of nuclear ships was counterproductive, tending rather to radicalize people and provide a focus for protest. With nine such visits in as many years, usually in the middle of the Labour Party's annual conferences, New Zealanders are learning that they too are involved in the preparations for nuclear war.

Part of the difficulty and also part of the strength of the peace movement has been its very diversity—diversity of interest and of political understanding. But with this diversity, we are constantly learning from each other, and working with and learning from people whose ideas are different from our own. Ideas as well as skills are developed in the process. Professional groups have been very important in the movement, particularly the New Zealand branch of International Physicians for the Prevention of Nuclear War (IPPNW), and Scientists Against Nuclear Arms (SANA), who have been able to lend the weight of their professional status to the activities of other groups and supply them with well-researched and factual information.

Artists and musicians have developed peace themes and lent their skills to the movement, particularly in helping to give a positive, hopeful approach to issues which people sometimes find too depressing to face. This is something to which the peace movement has had to devote considerable thought over the past two years. Many people fear a nuclear confrontation and even see World War III—whether accidentally or deliberately started—as inevitable. They feel so powerless and despairing that their response is to block it out of their minds; they become angry if the subject is even raised. Sometimes, the more you learn, the worse it feels. This is why we try to emphasize the positive aspects of change—developing hope and building a better, more peaceful world. Peaceful relationships, not competition and aggression, must be learned and taught at an individual level as well as at the level of nations. This is an area of particular interest to educators in New Zealand, who are enthusiastic about incorporating such ideas into school curricula.

Concern about the dangers of nuclear-powered ships in our central city harbours led to fears about the weapons on board and New Zealand's involvement in naval exercises involving nuclear arms. This led in turn to the moral considerations of whether this involvement gave tacit support to nuclear war preparations by the superpowers. There has been a steady outward movement in focus: we began with local nuclear-free zones, grew to making New Zealand a nuclear-free zone, and now are seeing New Zealand as a Pacific nation, and focusing on the interests of the whole Pacific community. Without a single nuclear-free area ten years ago, New Zealand has now established 101 nuclear-free zones, in which sixty-five percent of our people live.

It has been possible to see a clear learning path for individuals: from concern with anti-nuclear issues and their relationship to our children's future, to nuclear testing and waste dumping in the Pacific. We have proceeded from an understanding of the importance of self-determination for small island nations and their fundamental right to be able to control their own foreign and defence policies, to an understanding of colonization and economic dependence. Then we have turned back to New Zealand with a greater understanding of our own position in the economic world and a greater sympathy and understanding for Maori political concerns, history and land rights.

Although the peace movement has involved many politically aware people, it has also included many others who were not previously politically active. For many people it has been an encouraging, empowering process to see how something as simple and symbolic as putting an anti-nuclear sticker on your own car or front door can grow, when everybody does it, into nuclear-free agreements for the whole South Pacific. We have insisted that nuclear-free-zone declarations are the business of local government, since local government would be involved in clearing up the mess of accident or war. We have insisted that small nations must take a stand for peace themselves, if they hope to influence big nations.

That the problem is so big is the very reason we must each do something. To quote Mahatma Gandhi, probably incorrectly: "What you do may not be all that important, but it is terribly important that you do it."

PUBLIC RESPONSE

Public opinion polls held just after the New Zealand election in 1984 showed that the new Labour government had overwhelming support for its "No Nuclear Weapons" policy. Seventy-seven percent of all New Zealanders were opposed to allowing nuclear weapons to enter our country. Ninety-three percent of Labour supporters were in favour of the ban, while fifty-five percent of opposition National Party supporters were also in favour of the Labour government's policy. Sixty-six percent of New Zealanders believe that they would not survive a nuclear war between the major powers, while nearly a quarter of them believe that there will be a major nuclear war within the next fifteen years.

This is a remarkable turnaround from 1976 when the first poll was taken on this issue in New Zealand. The result then was almost the exact reverse—fifty-three percent *in favour* of nuclear warship visits and thirty-eight percent *against*. Needless to say, there was a conservative government in office which reflected that mood.

POLITICAL RETURNS

I am on the Parliamentary Foreign Affairs and Defence Select Committee which is currently hearing submissions on the New Zealand Nuclear-Free Zone, Disarmament and Arms Control Bill. This bill will make it illegal to bring any nuclear explosive device into New Zealand waters or air-space or onto our soil. We have received over twelve hundred submissions from individuals and groups, and it is my very firm expectation that well over ninety percent of those will be in support of the bill. New Zealand is also a signatory of the South Pacific Nuclear-Free Zone treaty adopted at a South Pacific Forum meeting in the Cook Islands in August 1985.

CONCLUSION

No New Zealander who has contact with the international community could doubt the widespread admiration and respect the stand of our nation against the proliferation of nuclear weapons has won for us. Around the world we are seen as a country of courage and integrity. There is tremendous goodwill toward us, and a strong desire to see us hold out against all the pressures which have and will be brought against us to conform.

While I was in Vancouver last year there were "lamb and kiwi-fruit" parties being advertised, special New Zealand fruit sales and neighbour-hood "Kiwi Cultural Evenings"—each in its own way an attempt to give material as well as moral support to us.

I wish I could adequately convey the thanks and pride I feel, as a New Zealander, at being part of a worldwide movement against the insanity of nuclear arms—a movement which, at least in some quarters, we are seen to be leading. On my final day in Canada in April 1985, after the End the Arms Race rally at which I had the privilege to be a keynote speaker, I visited the small community of Cowichan, the name of the Canadian Indian tribe, some of whom still live there. The editor of the *Cowichan News*, in his report of the speech I gave to the local peace group (under the heading "Kiwis Lay it on the Line Against Nukes"), wrote:

> I'd like to send two of Jim Anderton's quotes to Prime Minister Brian Mulroney, who seems intent on hitching Canada's economic recovery wagon to Ronald Reagan's Star Wars dream . . . or nightmare.

"It isn't an easy road we've chosen, but there will be no selling of New Zealand's political soul for any economic gain," said Anderton.

"I feel proud to be a New Zealander. We are doing this because we believe it is right. I hope in the not too distant future that other nations will stand with us, but we would take this stand if we thought we were the only people on earth who believed it was right."

The editor concluded the report by saying: "If only we could import this kind of political courage like we can their lamb, wool and produce."

These are encouraging words from Canada, our Commonwealth partner and friend. It just goes to show that small can be beautiful—and influential. We can hold our head up as a nation. It's still a big world, but we, and you, do matter after all.

Joan Ruddock

CHAPTER 20
Unilateral Initiatives: Theory and Practice

JOAN RUDDOCK

Eleven days ago I would have come to this rostrum with a deep sense of shame—shame at being British, and thus, by citizenship, complicity in the American bombing of Libya.* Yet today I come with a sense of some small dignity born of the overwhelming rejection voiced by the British people of our government's action.

That outpouring of revulsion and anger at the use of American bases in Britain expressed the feelings of millions of individuals; individuals whose views have, I believe, been gradually but fundamentally influ-

Joan Ruddock is one of Great Britain's outstanding peace activists. She was elected chairperson of the Campaign for Nuclear Disarmament (CND) in 1981, 1982, and 1983. Founded in 1958 by Lord Bertrand Russell and Canon John Collins, CND is one of the world's oldest and most influential disarmament groups. Currently it has over 400,000 active supporters. Joan Ruddock founded, on the day the British government announced that it would deploy ninety-six cruise missiles at Greenham Common, the Newbury Campaign Against Cruise Missiles, and she still spends time regularly in the women's protest camps at Greenham Common. Ms. Ruddock has also worked for various British nonprofit organizations, helping the unemployed, the homeless, and the poor.

* On April 15, 1986, a large force of American war planes carried out a night bombing raid on Tripoli and Benghazi in Libya on orders of President Reagan to punish Colonel Gadhafi for suspected involvement in terrorism. Prime Minister Margaret Thatcher had permitted use of American bases in Britain for bombers participating in the raid. —ED.

enced by the message of the peace movement. Over the past six years, we in the Campaign for Nuclear Disarmament (CND) have tried to alert our country to the dangers of trying to settle international disputes with violence. We have tried to alert our country to the connections between the superpowers' nuclear arms race and regional conflicts, such as those in the Middle East. And we have tried to alert British citizens to the American presence in our country, and the subservience of British foreign policy to American global interests.

Last week people who had remained unconvinced by our message, or simply unconcerned, were jamming our switchboard asking for information, offering help and wanting to join CND. The post brought in the equivalent of $50,000 in spontaneous contributions. And people living next to American military bases were admitting to shock and fear. Most had become inured to reality, seeing and hearing frequent bomber exercises in simulated nuclear alerts. Suddenly, they were (literally) awakened to the fact that this time the planes had flown for real.

In publicizing the threat and nature of nuclear war, the peace movement has all too often been accused of trading in fear. That is not our purpose—we ask only for a recognition of the reality of our times. That reality properly engenders fear.

Let me now try to relate that reality, and CND's campaign, to the subject of today's seminar—how individuals can work most effectively to prevent nuclear war and promote multilateral disarmament. Work which individuals *can* do is easy to describe. In my experience the peace movement is so extraordinarily diverse and creative that there is no lack of *doing*. But the most effective structure for harnessing all this activity is another matter altogether.

I don't pretend to have definitive answers; while self-criticism on the part of the peace movement is essential, I think it is premature to make final judgments about the effectiveness of our actions. We have, after all, lived through forty years of interparty and interstate consensus on nuclear weapons, compared with a mere six years of contemporary anti-nuclear campaigning. Yet, while individuals can act on conscience and take a moral perspective regardless of outcome, mass movements and organized campaigns will be judged both on their aims and on the results of their tactics and strategies.

Our recent British experience dates back to the late seventies, when the Campaign for Nuclear Disarmament (set up in 1958, but quiescent since the Partial Test Ban Treaty) began to acquire new members. We were not "kissed back to life by the Kremlin" as reported by *Reader's Digest,* but rather reactivated by news of the neutron bomb. Subsequently, in 1979, dozens of new organizations sprang up in response to the announcement of NATO's so-called modernization plan. Within a year almost all of these groups had become part of CND. Today we are a mass movement with a local and national membership in excess of one-quarter million. And we, like our friends in Germany, have also found new ways of working and have incorporated feminism, Green thinking, anti-racism and concern for the Third World into our campaigns.

CND's aim is to have Britain unilaterally abandon nuclear weapons, nuclear bases and nuclear alliances. This is a prerequisite for a British foreign policy which has the *worldwide* abolition of weapons of mass destruction as its prime objective.

In North America, as indeed in continental Europe, this can look uncomfortably nationalistic—the Brits wanting to ''go it alone,'' disregarding bilateral and multilateral disarmament. That tendency exists, but it does not represent the philosophy of the peace movement as a whole. Unilateral disarmament as a goal is a response to the unique British position: our country both plays power politics with its own so-called independent deterrent and also eagerly hosts American nuclear weapons. It is also a response to the fact that multilateral measures have failed to remove a single nuclear weapon. In the current stalemate, we believe that the logjam can best be broken by unilateral initiatives.

Additionally, many members of our movement believe deeply that the possession and threatened use of nuclear weapons is immoral. Within the British context, there are no political or defence considerations to temper that immorality. Thus, on this single issue, in a society less certain than ever before about most things material and moral, millions of British people have become fundamentalists.

Our unilateralism is both a philosophy for action by individuals and a strategy for disarmament by governments. To us it is a positive contribution to nuclear disarmament worldwide, to be taken independently and unconditionally. To the present Conservative government it is ''one-sided appeasement'' or, in the libellous parlance of their supporters, CND equals ''communists, neutralists and defeatists!''

As individuals, our unilateralism begins with ourselves, with extricating our brains and spirits from mindless acceptance of the status quo and with accepting responsibility for forming an objective opinion and then acting upon it. As one of our activist clerics said: '' I can disarm the world by at least one person: myself. My action is important. The sort of world we have results from the sum total of the acts of individuals.''

Yet with rare exceptions, individuals can be most effective by acting together, both nationally and internationally. This point has not been lost in Britain where individuals have formed over one thousand local groups, and where CND, END (Europeans for Nuclear Disarmament) and Greenpeace participate in several international networks.

While activities are legion and specialist groups and interests numer-

ous, I think our overall strategy could be described as follows:
1. To resist, nonviolently, any military development in the nuclear field.
2. To question publicly and defeat the arguments supporting nuclear weapons, nuclear strategy and civil defence preparations for nuclear war.
3. To develop a public constituency of support (irrespective of party political allegiance) for nuclear disarmament, and in particular unilateral nuclear disarmament by Britain.
4. To promote our aims throughout the institutions and to set a new political agenda.
5. To emphasize the links between the manufacture, testing and deployment of nuclear weapons, and the direct and indirect human suffering they cause throughout the world.

Under pressure from the government we have had to add a new element to this list:
6. To defend our civil liberties and the right to dissent and protest in a democratic state.

Demonstrating resistance to military developments is the lifeblood of any peace movement. In common with resisters everywhere, we demonstrate at military bases to draw attention to their presence and purpose, to protest the same, and periodically to try to frustrate construction work or the deployment of weapons. Revealing the facts of the nuclear infrastructure is essential to any effective campaign, and despite generally hostile media, we have been greatly assisted by courageous journalists. Some of the facts may surprise you.

By demonstrating at the sites, for example, we were able to reveal that there were 135 American nuclear bases and facilities in Britain, at a time when the British defence ministry was admitting, under pressure in the House of Commons, that there were only fifty-four. Our list includes America's most important communications and intelligence centre, authorized to tap all our international phone calls; an oceanographic research centre whose real purpose is underwater sound surveillance for plotting submarine and surface-vessel water movements; and fourteen contingency military hospitals, some with fully equipped, mothballed and idle operating theatres.

We have also demonstrated, contrary to public opinion, that the British bomb is not something that simply exists in storage facilities. There is a production line at a major factory, which is still officially designated as an artificial limb factory! The location of this factory was recently removed from the ordnance survey map! Even more obviously threatening is the fact that it has recently been revealed that childhood leukemias in the local community are ten times the national average.

Furthermore, we are fulfilling the pledge we made when American cruise missiles were first deployed in Britain. Through a program called

Cruise-watch, convoys are tracked so that no matter what time of day or night the United States moves its weapons (normally 2:00 or 3:00 a.m.), cruise launchers cannot "melt into the countryside" as their owners intended. And now, after two years of remarkable effort, such a strong international network exists that last week, during the Libya crisis, we were not only able to announce a red alert deployment of cruise missiles from Greenham but also from Comiso, in Italy.

Through peaceful resistance we have become a force to be reckoned with, demonstrating the power of individuals who are prepared to act. The authorities have found it more prudent to halt work at bases affected by one-day protests than to undertake mass arrests. However, many acts of civil disobedience, undertaken on a smaller scale, have brought their penalties. More than ten thousand people have been arrested in the past four and a half years.

Resistance in Britain is, of course, best exemplified by the Greenham women, and no review of peace activities could fail to pay tribute to the extraordinary courage and example of the thousands of women who are part of the Greenham sisterhood. Small camps still exist there, though their occupants are subjected to daily harassment and sometimes deliberate violence. Testimony to this situation was contained in an end of year congratulatory message to the 501st Security Police Group operating at Greenham. The United States Air Force commander's list of their outstanding achievements included the following: "The Greenham by-laws went into effect, the superfence was constructed, and we hit one peace-woman with a vehicle." In the light of that remark, you can imagine how much support from North America is appreciated. So if any of you are looking for something an individual can do, just write a letter of support to the Women's Peace Camp, Greenham Common, Newbury, Berkshire, England.

Our resistance takes many forms: from the individuals who refuse to pay taxes for weapons, to the trade unionists who refused contracts to work on Trident, to the foreign office clerk who, finding that the British Parliament was not to be told in advance of the arrival of cruise missiles, passed a secret memo to the press and received a six-month prison sentence for her act of conscience.

Such overreaction by government constantly produced new recruits for the peace movement. This occurred most notably when we were planning a constant rota of blockaders to frustrate construction of the new cruise missile base at Molesworth. Our challenge and the presence of one hundred protestors on the Ministry of Defence land led to a full scale military assault on the camp in the dead of night. Over 1500 soldiers, supported by 700 police, erected a steel fence at a cost of 3 million pounds—or

$6.5 million—in a country that professes to be unable to provide dialysis machines for kidney patients.

To be effective, however, our actions need to be matched by arguments. In CND, we set out to expose the myths of nuclear deterrence, myths common in all our countries. They said "balance," we said "overkill." They said "deterrence," we said "war-fighting strategies and capabilities." We argue, using the many facts supplied by our peace movement friends in the United States, that the West seeks to regain nuclear superiority. We publicize risks, accidents, the threat of nuclear winter, and certain suicide should deterrence fail. On cruise missiles, we can quote our own government's glossy brochure which tried to sell us on these weapons: "The aim of using them would be to persuade the Russian leadership—even at the eleventh hour—to draw back." On Trident, we point to its obscene cost—more than our total education or housing budgets. We ask what is Polaris (the existing British submarine system) balanced with, and why, if its sixty-four-target capability has been a deterrent to date, should we need to be able to hit 896 targets with a future Trident force? We carefully examine the Soviet Union, criticizing it frequently. But we say, without the slightest endorsement of their system, that we do not accept that there is any evidence they have military intentions toward Western Europe. We believe that war itself is the deterrent on our continent. In short, we consider that nuclear weapons play no part in Britain's security and that the presence of American nuclear bases in Britain is a real danger, both to ourselves and to the peace of the world.

In consequence, we have been obliged to look again at our aims and at our international relations and to ask ourselves whether unilateral action is the best response to the threat we face. For a while, prior to cruise and Pershing II deployment, a multilateral freeze had obvious attractions. Today, with the nuclear arms race raised a few more notches, waiting for a multilateral freeze seems to many of us to offer too little, too late, though a British Freeze campaign is trying to get off the ground. But we are far from being isolationists. We place our unilateralism in an international context. We believe it is possible to achieve a new political consensus in Europe—East and West—around the idea of common security. We do not seek to inflame anti-American feeling, but to see that any influence Britain may have is used in a positive way for peace and superpower restraint. We constantly seek allies, and we know that we have them here in Canada. Your struggle to prevent cruise testing and against involvement in SDI is well known in Europe.

The title of our session asks for the promotion of multilateral disarmament. We believe that unilateral initiatives are not only relevant to the nuclear (or indeed conventional) arms race worldwide, but that they are probably the most potent key to beginning the disarmament process. I will quote to you from the United Nation's secretary-general's 1984 report entitled "Unilateral Nuclear Disarmament Measures." It says that "there is no either/or choice between unilateral and negotiated measures of disarmament," and that unilateral initiatives "may serve to improve the political climate by sending a clear signal to the other side." I recommend that you read this report if you have not done so already.

The CND promotes both unilateral and multilateral measures, but we believe that history suggests that the independent step, particularly if unconditional for some time at least, is most likely to provide the breakthrough. This was the route to the Partial Test-Ban Treaty. To quote our London-based International Institute for Strategic Studies (1963): "Historically, most arms races have not ended by multilateral agreements. They have either ended in war, or they have died away as the result of unilateral acts of prudence or restraint."

We believe that both superpowers could make major unilateral cuts in their nuclear arsenals without any loss of military security, as judged by their own nuclear deterrence theory. We have pressed repeatedly for Soviet concessions in intermediate-range weapons, in an attempt to strengthen West European demands for the removal of cruise and Pershing II missiles. Our ideas, always rejected in Washington, found no favour in Moscow either, until the advent of General Secretary Gorbachev. Now we are conscious of a new Soviet willingness to take unilateral initiatives, such as the test moratorium.

We greatly applaud this strategy, but disagree with its time-scale. Their unilateral initiative invites reciprocation. This can only come about through the force of Western opinion. This process requires more time. The Soviet initiatives are certainly becoming an embarrassment to the British government, which had previously concluded that the only obstacle to a Comprehensive Test Ban Treaty was verification. It is also worth noting that any combination of opposition parties in Britain would, if in government, have joined the USSR's moratorium.

As part of the peace movement, CND supports any genuine measure designed to halt the nuclear arms race and/or bring about real nuclear disarmament. I wish therefore that I could say something positive about proposals from the West. But I can't. President Reagan offers us the Strategic Defense Initiative which, while usefully recognizing the suicidal stupidity of Mutual Assured Destruction, only seeks to replace MAD with an enhancement of war-fighting capability. And as for Mrs. Thatcher—well, she has pronounced herself *unable* to envisage a world without nuclear weapons!

Our strategy, then, remains to achieve a majority in favour of the unilateral abandonment of all nuclear weapons and the elimination of all American military bases in Britain. How successful has that strategy been? Implied in everything I have said is the goal of changing public opinion and setting a new political agenda. You may judge therefore that the re-election of Margaret Thatcher's government was certain proof of failure. Primarily, the failure was on the part of the opposition parties, but there were lessons for us too. For while the majority supported the removal of cruise missiles and the cancelling of Trident, only one-fourth to one-third of the population backed total unilateralism. A strong sense of British Gaullism surrounds the possession of our aging Polaris, and we failed to anticipate what an impact the fear of defencelessness could have on the British people. Not surprisingly we are asked why we still persist, when the majority supports the most dangerous elements of British involvement in the nuclear arms race. Our answer is simple. As long as Britain reserves for itself the right to maintain a so-called independent nuclear deterrent, it must acknowledge the right of every other nation to do the same, and thus there is no future hope for the non-proliferation treaty. While Britain remains a nuclear power, there is likely to be a demand for nuclear weapons testing, and Polaris will eventually be replaced by some other system. And while Britain remains nuclear, foreign policy considerations will always be subjugated to a special relationship with the United States. Achieving majority support for the abandonment of all nuclear weapons remains our prime objective, and I want to use my remaining time to assess the state of our movement and the prospects for the future.

Firstly and most importantly, we, in common with our friends in the Federal Republic of Germany and the Netherlands, have broken the political consensus about nuclear weapons. The British Labour Party has adopted a non-nuclear defence policy and a commitment to try to move NATO in that direction, beginning with a declaration of no first use. The Social Democratic Alliance opposes Trident, and the Liberal partners of the Alliance oppose cruise. However, it appears to us that no party likely to gain power has a comprehensive strategy for nuclear disarmament linked with a new approach to foreign policy. An enormous amount remains to be done.

Even so, we have gained significant support from trade unions active in party politics, including those with many workers in the nuclear industry. There are eight million British trade union members affiliated to CND at this time. We have a positive program of arms conversion and a thriving network of people working for nuclear-weapons-free zones. We have a committed and active Christian community, young people, ex-servicemen and women, actors, writers and friends throughout the world.

We ought to succeed, but can we? The backlash from government has been unprecedented. We have been smeared and abused in the press. Some of these abuses have been orchestrated by government ministers. On the sworn testimony of an ex-MI5 agent, we know that we have been subjected to surveillance and illegal phone-taps (our case against the government will be heard in the High Court in July). By-laws are constantly being enacted without democratic debate, using the Military Land Acts of 1892. A further assault on civil liberties is being prepared under a public order bill currently in Parliament. We are determined not to be intimidated and find that as usual every struggle has its own reward.

But we have to admit that we are tired. It has taken considerable effort to overcome the setbacks of 1983–84 and to come to terms with the new era of Star Wars. Public opinion may have changed, but we do not yet have political power. We have to ask whether it is possible to elect an anti-nuclear government in Britain, the Netherlands or the Federal Republic of Germany. Would the civil service and the military frustrate its program anyway? Would the United States refuse to co-operate? Would the party leaders follow the example of New Zealand's David Lange or Australia's Bob Hawke?[†] For the present, these questions remain unanswered; as a peace movement our task must be to influence their outcome positively. This means that we must apply a greater effort, and this must be done more systematically and effectively. In CND we have spent the past year rethinking our strategy along these lines.

Our priority now is a series of integrated public information campaigns planned to last for eighteen months. Through research, we have identified a market of around nine million people who, while not hostile to us, remain uncertain about our arguments and sceptical of the possibility or effectiveness of change. We are appealing to this constituency with positive arguments and the positive results of becoming non-nuclear, rather than by sticking to the oppositional, anti-weapons grounds which characterized so much of our earlier campaigning.

Whether we can sustain the effort; whether we can maintain our numbers on the ground, while many of us are increasingly drawn into activities involving such issues as nuclear power and apartheid; whether party politicians can be made to campaign on the issue of nuclear arms when they have much softer options and a general election is in the offing—

[†] Joan Ruddock was referring to the present Labour Party prime ministers of Australia and New Zealand, both of whom campaigned in recent general elections on anti-nuclear weapons platforms. The Lange government in New Zealand stuck to pre-election promises and has banned visits of nuclear-armed warships to its harbours, whereas Australia's Bob Hawke has become a strong supporter of President Reagan's policies.—E D.

these are further imponderables. I only know that we are trying to become effective as never before.

I have talked in depth about the British experience because obviously that is where my own expertise lies, and because CND is anxious that our strategy be known abroad. Also, I hope that it may serve as a warning to Canadians and their peace movement.

In conclusion, however, I would like to offer some general thoughts. On policy, for all of us the bottom line is surely the campaign for a comprehensive test ban and for a non-proliferation treaty, and to oppose SDI. On being effective for peace, I offer the following:

1. If we want to promote peace, we have to find it in ourselves. This means rejecting militarism, racism, sexism, nationalism and elitism among leaders. It means working nonviolently and co-operatively.

2. We must make clear the links between the arms race, which is led and marketed by the developed world, and the poverty and starvation which prevail in the underdeveloped world.

3. We must take the trouble to maintain international links, providing crucial communication channels within the peace movement.‡

4. We must never hesitate to act because our action seems too small. We must never put aside anger and emotion, but instead channel them wisely.

The nuclear arms race is the greatest conspiracy of all time—a conspiracy through which five nations have forced the developed world to live in a shadow of doom, and the underdeveloped world to experience that doom through hunger and starvation. In such circumstances it seems to me nothing short of a miracle that so many individuals, East and West, North and South, are organizing for peace. It is a privilege and a joy to join you in this symposium in your beautiful city. May we all be strengthened by the experience, rededicated to our struggle for peace and mindful of the fact that ''We do not inherit the earth from our parents, but borrow it from our children.''

---

‡ An example of communication is that last week in Britain we could tell our press that demonstrations against the bombing of Libya *were* taking place in the United States as well as in Europe.

CHAPTER 21

New Forms of Power: The Green Feminist View

PETRA K. KELLY

THE PATRIARCHAL SYSTEM

I would like to use this occasion to speak about the hopes of Green women all over the world—hopes for new forms of power, grassroots power, and the possibilities for nonviolent change!

In the past, men have left home to go to war. Now women all over the world are leaving home for peace and social justice. A Canadian woman physicist, Ursula Franklin, once stated: "War has always been a decision of the few, for which the many paid. When women got into the peace business it was in the first place because of their experience of mopping up the leftovers of decisions in which they had no part." Many women in the Green movement, not only in the Federal Republic of Germany, but in all parts of Europe and in all parts of the world, are searching for a path toward peace by engaging in grassroots, nonviolent and very courageous work.

It has become clear to so many of us within the Green movement that resistance to war and to the use of nuclear weapons and nuclear energy is impossible without resistance to sexism, to racism, to imperialism and to violence as an everyday pervasive reality. There is a very profound relationship between the fact that many women and children are commonly attacked, beaten up, and raped and that a nuclear war, as well as an ecological catastrophe, threatens this entire planet earth, which has no emergency exit.

We women in the Green movement do not seek to have equality by virtuously copying male values and male privileges. We seek, quite simply, half the earth and half the sky for our very own, in accordance with self-determined values. We seek never to state that women are better than

Petra Kelly

PHOTO: WERNER SCHüRING

men—we seek to restore a balance, a harmony of the feminine and masculine values which are contained in every one of us, men and women. As for myself, a feminist and a believer in nonviolence as the means and as the end of politics, I believe that the world we know is not as it should be, and that this can be changed. When we are trying to rid the world of things as oppressive as chemical and biological weapons, conventional weapons and interventionary politics, or poverty, sexism and racism, it can help us to look at their structural underpinning—a system of patriarchy—and to see the state and military power as a basic and linked aspect of that system, both in East and West.

Many people have been arguing about which came first, and which should be confronted first. But we are more concerned with trying to understand the interconnectedness of patriarchy, military power, the economic and political systems in both East and West, the state, and how all of these affect our society. Patriarchy is and remains a system of male domination, prevalent in both capitalist and socialist countries. It is oppressive to women and restrictive to men. Patriarchy is a hierarchical system in which men all over the world have more value, more economic, social and political power, and under which women suffer from oppressive structures and from individual men. We can see this clearly in all areas of our life, affecting our political and economic structures, our work, our personal relationships, our family life, and our homes. Men are the centre of a patriarchal world in East, West, South and North— whether they want to be, or not.

There are many structures of domination, such as that of nation over nation, economic class over economic class, race over race. But the domination of women by men remains a constant feature within every other aspect of oppression. It is so basic to our world that it is seen by most men and women as part of "human nature," and therefore something

Petra K. Kelly is a founder of the Green Party in the Federal Republic of Germany. She is well-known as one of Europe's leading proponents of nuclear disarmament. Educated in Germany, the United States, and the Netherlands, Petra Kelly holds degrees from the School of International Service at the American University and the University of Amsterdam. Since 1970, she has actively supported the anti-nuclear, ecological and feminist movements. In 1979, she joined the Green Party and served as its chairperson from 1980 to 1982. In 1983, she was elected to the Bundestag, *the German Parliament, and has served both as a spokesperson for the Green Party Parliamentary delegation, and a member of the Foreign Relations Committee. A sought-after speaker, she has been invited to address audiences in Europe, the United States, Australia and Japan.*

that cannot be changed. But I believe that norms of human behaviour can and do change over the centuries, and that these aspects of domination can be changed as well. No pattern of domination is necessarily part of human nature, whether it be individual acts of rape or total war and annihilation.

When speaking with my sisters in the Third World, they tell me this quite clearly: across the cultural divide, sexism is the only thing all countries have in common. It is a man's Third World. It's the one thing a black man and a white man can shake hands on, if nothing else. This was also the opinion of Jane Goldsmith, who has made a study on international aid which was reported in the *Guardian* (November 5th, 1984). One can clearly register this fact: where the power is, that is where women are *not!* There are, of course, some exceptions, like Prime Minister Margaret Thatcher. But Thatcher is a better man than most because she has adapted herself so loyally to male values and to patriarchal values in politics, industry, and in the decision-making hierarchical process.

Women produce two-thirds of the world's food, and yet they comprise two-thirds of the world's illiterate population. We perpetuate sexism through our systems for providing international aid to the Third World. Our aid in fact stabilizes male power-bases and has very little to do with truly improving the economic and social conditions of women in Third World countries. In Africa, Asia and in other parts of the world, women work sixteen hours a day, placing their own health in jeopardy, and usually they lead three lives: a life for their husbands, a life for their children, and a life for the household and family.

Present technology within the patriarchal systems has made it possible to create first-strike missiles such as the Pershing II, which can reach the Soviet Union within six minutes. Yet those very same patriarchal societies have *not* been able to solve the problems of meeting the most basic human needs in many parts of the world. Women in Asia, Africa and Latin America still must fetch up to twenty kilos of water at a time from places far from their homes. This can take up to five hours a day, as it does, for example, for the Masai women of Kenya's Rift Valley. Gathering wood for cooking may also be a two-to three-hour job each day, and may take even longer in areas of extensive deforestation. Women work as a full unit of economic production all over the world, and yet they do all the unpaid housework and child care on top of that.

Men must give up their privileges and special rights if we are to succeed in creating a more loving and equal society. Women are not only half of the present human race, but they also are the principal nurturers of all the coming generations. We cannot continue to watch women in the Third World being systematically dispossessed. We must not only help women reclaim their earth in the Third World; we must also learn to reclaim our earth right here in Canada and in Europe.

I began with those examples of the *little war* being waged against women everyday, because it is strongly interconnected with the *big war* waged against humankind and the planet earth. Recently, I had visitors from the arctic area of Canada's Northwest Territories. There, Inuit, Inuvialuit, Dene and Métis women attempt to maintain a fine balance between their traditional lifestyles and the modern wage economy. I began realizing once again how little we in Europe understand about the native way of life, about wildlife resources, about the ecological relationships in that part of the world, about true peace with nature and with ourselves.

For too long, many women in the European peace, women's and ecological movements have been preoccupied with their own problems of emancipation and with the deployment of American and Soviet missiles. But we need to look at the nonviolent struggle of women all over the world: whether it be in the Pacific region, where so much nuclearization and militarization is going on; or in Chile, Brazil and Nicaragua; or in Turkish Kurdistan; or in Poland; or in South Africa; or in the Philippines where women are now struggling for a democratic way of life. We women all over the world must not only mourn over the past and present discrimination and violence brought against us. We must also be in a rage and defy all those structures which oppress us on a global scale. As the women of the Pentagon Action wrote in 1980:

> While we work, study and love, the colonels and generals who are planning our annihilation, calmly walk in and out the doors of their so-called defence ministries in East and West. They have accumulated thousands and thousands of nuclear, chemical and conventional weapons and are presently planning biological weapons. All of this at the rate of three to six bombs a day!

Women are defending the forests in India, they are demanding nuclear-free constitutions in the Pacific Islands, they are campaigning against the chemical and nuclear civilian industry, and against the unending build-up of weapons of mass destruction in all parts of the world.

Women are struggling also for nonviolent conflict resolution, so desperately needed today, and I would like to mention here also the courageous women of Canada's Northwest Territories, who are struggling for preservation of native lifestyles and cultures. And I want to praise women in Canada fighting against cruise missile testing, against German armament factories on Cape Breton,* and against American and German

* Thyssen Aktiengesellschaft in the Federal Republic of Germany has recently proposed investing $100 million to build a factory on Cape Breton Island to manufacture tanks and armoured cars for export to various militaristic Arab countries. German laws currently

military training activities in Goose Bay, Labrador.[†]

We can no longer separate ourselves from the suffering and wisdom of our sisters in Asia, Australia, Africa, South and North America, and in our own country. There can be no true peace, there can be no respect for human rights and justice while one race dominates another, while one people, one nation, one sex despises another. Women at the Pentagon, women at the cruise missile and Pershing II bases, indigenous women in Canada and Australia, women in Manila, women supporting Winnie Mandela in South Africa, women joining hands and lighting candles on the Alexanderplatz in East Berlin, women within the human rights movements and within the independent peace groups in Eastern Europe — they are here today in great numbers, but will return in *hundreds of thousands* in the months and years to come.

NEW FORMS OF POWER: NONVIOLENCE AND FEMINISM

When we talk about new forms of power, it is not about power over others in order to dominate or to terrorize or oppress. When we speak about nonviolence and civil disobedience, it is rather about abolishing power, as we have known power, and redefining it as something common to all, to be used by all, and for all. Patriarchal power is to be replaced by *shared power,* by the discovery of our own strength, as opposed to a passive receiving of power exercised by others, often in our name.

Often women who work in the peace and ecological movements for true disarmament and for a demilitarized society are portrayed (misleadingly so) as expressing their so-called true nature, since women are said to be the guardians of life on earth. But we are working in these movements, *not* because we are meek or weak. We work in these movements because we have become very angry, angry on our own behalf, angry for our sisters, angry on behalf of our children and the entire planet earth. We are motivated not only to guard our lives but to begin to guard the lives of all people.

Many of us have been inspired by the works of nonviolent men like

---

prohibit such exports directly from the Federal Republic. Nevertheless, the federal government in Ottawa initially supported this investment as a good way to combat unemployment in Nova Scotia! See also the end of Petra Kelly's chapter. — ED.

[†]Military aircraft from the United States and the Federal Republic of Germany conduct low-level supersonic flights over forested areas west of Goose Bay, Labrador, seriously disrupting caribou migration routes and many other aspects of life for native peoples living in the region. Petra Kelly refers to this in greater detail near the end of this chapter. — ED.

Gandhi, Martin Luther King, Caesar Chavez, and many of us have been inspired by what we have read about Thoreau, who spent a night in jail for refusing to pay taxes to support the Mexican-American war. On the other hand, many of us know very little about the many courageous women who have practiced nonviolence, but who have not received the same attention as the men I have just mentioned: women like Dorothy Day, women like Winnie Mandela, the women of Greenham Common, women of the Bolivian mineworkers, women in Eastern Europe, in Africa, in Asia, and in the Pacific. When we look at the idea of nonviolent resistance and at the idea of accepting suffering while practicing nonviolence and civil disobedience, then we must realize that when Gandhi and other men spoke about voluntary suffering, they also talked about the value of its impact: suffering on a voluntary basis, resulting in an *extra shocking* invisible impact. Yet many women all over the world who have taken on voluntary suffering receive less visibility and moral credit than the men who do it.

I am reminded of the participation of the women at Greenham Common. The male media concentrated on the family left at home to cope, while playing down the hardships of the women who camped out during one of England's harshest winters. Any commitment to nonviolence, which is real and authentic, must also begin with a recognition of the forms and degrees of violence which are perpetrated against women by men. This means to me that we must call upon women to form a chain around the world and to resist not only those who say that war and violence are inevitable, but also to love only those men who are willing to speak up against violence. We invite all men who oppose violence to join us in our cause for peace. We urge them to break out of their *rigid* patriarchal institutions and out of their own conditioning!

I was very much touched by an appeal that was issued during the nonviolent blockade of the five nuclear nations' missions to the United Nations on June 14th, 1982. The blockade, entitled "Blockade the Bomb-Makers," was intended to disrupt nuclear diplomacy for a short moment. Those participating in the blockade expressed their view of civil disobedience in the following way: "We are aware that the probability of nuclear war increases minute by minute with each new warhead put in place on each new submarine or missile. We are afraid for ourselves, for the trees and animals and plants and especially for our children who, cut down uncomprehending in the moment of their growth, will be the real victims of a possible nuclear war." In many ways we learn the tactics of civil disobedience from our young children, who are born knowing how to go limp and stubborn when they will not be moved, and who, though seemingly helpless in a world of adults, exert a very real power which forces us either to break their wills or to take their needs and desires into account. "The will of the people acting together to achieve what they believe to be possible and true—a world in peace and full of social justice, where the needs and desires of all are met in freedom—this will is very hard to break."

And so we must all, women and men of a peaceful nature across the world, begin moving together toward the doors of the nuclear laboratories and weapons factories, toward the gates of the nuclear and chemical bases, toward the doors of military alliances like NATO and the Warsaw Pact, toward the doors of those who tread upon human rights, toward the doors of those who oppress and discriminate. As we sit then and blockade those doors, we must also begin our silent meditations and our hopeful songs and our conversations among ourselves so that we can feel energized and strong and not alone. Then, the distance between our convictions and the limits of our daily lives ceases to exist. When we bring ourselves this far, nonviolently blocking the doors of those who plan our annihilation—who co-operate with those who destroy the health of our children and the planet earth—then we can also help inspire others to come with us. What else is there to do other than practice civil disobedience and nonviolence at a time when $1.3 million are spent every minute on the arms race? We have never before been so endangered. We must call upon people to renew their efforts in a nonviolent campaign of resistance and civil disobedience. These forces must be stronger and more far-reaching than anything that history and the world have experienced before. We must convince the old established authorities of a new enlightened authority: the power of reason, of love, of communal awareness, of moral conscience. Never again can people say: "We did not know."

We must never forget that the immense sums spent on researching, manufacturing, storing and deploying weapons of *all kinds* constitutes a genuine case of embezzlement by the leaders of the nations involved in the arms race. There is a clear-cut contradiction between the insane overproduction of weapons (which wastes precious raw materials and the brain-power of people around the world), and the total number of unsatisfied needs in the lives of those who live in the developing countries or among the poor of our affluent society. These are the real victims of the arms race today. Over seven million children under the age of five died last year. That is comparable to the World War II holocaust happening over and over again every four and a half months. Something has to be *dead* within us, if we allow these injustices to go on!

A close friend of mine, Professor Ichiro Moritaki of the Japanese antinuclear movement (*Gensuikin*) stated: "What befell Hiroshima can happen to all of us. The whole world is a Hiroshima which the bomb has not yet hit. The decision lies with all of us, whether humanity must die together or whether it can live together.'' If we succeed in preventing the ultimate epidemic, the Third World War, then it will be only because we, the people at the grassroots level, finally rely on our own strength, without depending on experts, narrow arms-control diplomacy and negotiations.

When I think of the lessons I learned in Germany as well as in American schools, then I realize how contradictory our situation has become. At the end of World War II, and after the liberation of the European continent from German fascism, many people, including many American policy makers, hoped that Germans would never again take up a gun or turn toward re-arming. Now, forty years later, there are so many young and courageous people in the Federal Republic of Germany refusing to do military service, refusing to pay war taxes, attempting to be recognized as total conscientious objectors and joining many social movements for true disarmament and demilitarization—and now they are considered wrong! And these very same people, working in grassroots peace movements, in Third World and women's movements, and working within the Green Party, have been denounced so many times, over and over again, as being naïve, as being dependent on the Soviet line of thinking.

Unfortunately, some members of the Canadian Press like Ilya Gerol and Mike Tytherleigh of the *Province* continue to discriminate against us in a most unfair and untrue way. Mike Tytherleigh wrote in his column on April 25th, 1986: "One thing, it's ironic that the fear of nuclear war has been hyped up by the professional peaceniks to such a degree that blinds us from the basic global issue and that, surely, is freedom.''

And furthermore Mike Tytherleigh stated—and this really shocked me: ''If I'd bothered to look at the artifacts from the 1945 Hiroshima explosion in Hiroshima, displayed at the Orpheum, I'd think about how we heard the city had been bombed and cheered because it might hasten an end to the barbarism of a Japan gone mad.''

The German Press—even on the right—does not write like this any more! Those claims are all so very absurd, and they are also tragic.

What would happen if the Green Utopias of today became the realities of tomorrow? Drastic reduction of our military budget; calculated and unilateral steps out of our military alliance; acknowledgment of the right to total conscientious objection; withdrawal of all foreign troops; implementation of an authentic and honest human rights policy in every part of the world; an end to all weapons exports and all civilian and military nuclear exports; the development of forms of social and civilian-based defence; a change from the production of arms to the production of socially useful and ecologically safe products; movement toward a just, peaceful and nonexploitative Europe of autonomous regions (which also includes our neighbours across the Iron Curtain); and a stop to wishing the other side were dead. Can these Green Utopias become the realities of tomorrow? Can new forms of power emerge from below?

We in the Federal Republic of Germany still have a very long way to go and much to learn on the way to becoming a truly democratic society, for we do not have any traditions of nonviolence or civil disobedience. We know that pitting ourselves nonviolently against all forms of repression and militarization can be painful, can inflict much suffering on ourselves, and brings many risks. And yet it is the *only way* to have control over our lives. I should like to cite here an appeal published by women from five European countries where deployment of American and Soviet missiles has taken place:

> We are women in five European countries where the deployment of new American and Soviet weapons has begun. We are women from different cultures, from Eastern and Western, Northern and Southern Europe, some of us involved in the church, others not, some of us feminists, pacifists and members of many other human rights and environmental movements.
>
> Despite our differences, we are united by the will for self-determination, to struggle against the culture of militarism in the world, against uniforms and violence, against our children being educated as soldiers and against the senseless waste of resources. We demand the right of self-determination for all individuals and peoples. We want to make a specific cultural contribution to changing existing social structures. That is why we also challenge conventional gender roles and why we ask men to do the same.
>
> The freedom to determine one's own fate also means freedom from exploitation and violence: in our thoughts and actions, at our places of work, in our relationship with nature and the relationship between men and women, between generations, between states, between East and West and between North and South in global terms.
>
> Together we want to break this circle of violence and the anxieties created in us by this violence: anxiety about nuclear weapons, fearing the death of humanity and the end of the earth, fears about the rape of our bodies and souls. Together we wish to confront these anxieties and be able to overcome them, no longer illegally, but with the right of free expression of opinion for everyone, especially in those places where the right is denied on a daily basis. There can be no realistic peace perspective without respect for human rights.

The deployment of new nuclear weapons in our countries has limited our freedom and increased our fears. Our obligation to break the circle of violence has grown because of our potential shared responsibility for a possible catastrophe. We are conscious of being both perpetrators and victims of systems of violence. In both roles, we are not the ones who have made the decisions. We reject both roles. Nor are we reassured by the fact that representatives of both superpowers are about to negotiate over our heads again in Geneva. Once again we are expected to pin our hopes on their seeing reason and voluntarily renouncing the production and use of weapons of mass destruction. Once again talks on how to hold talks are supposed to make us believe that it is possible to solve the problems from above.

Instead of this, we choose the way of self-determined initiatives from below. This road does not go via the militarization of society, which is why we reject any involvement in the preparation of war—nor does it traverse missile ramps or the destruction of nature and interpersonal relationships.

We do not want a peace which oppresses us, nor a war which will annihilate us.

Forty years after Auschwitz and Hiroshima, forty years after the bloc confrontation began, we want at least now, to begin collectively getting to know and understand each other better and meeting one another beyond the wall which divides not merely the borders of our countries but all too often our hearts and minds as well.

We have begun détente from below: join us!

The changes in the Philippines have made me hopeful about the possibilities of nonviolent change. It was good to read in the *International Herald Tribune* on February 26th, 1986, that American Secretary of State George P. Shultz stated that the main factor in the departure of Mr. Marcos was not pressure from the United States but ''what the Philippino people had to say.'' And it was evident in the streets of Manila. ''The new government has been produced by one of the most stirring and courageous examples of the democratic process in modern history,'' Mr. Shultz said. At least those who are governing us are slowly beginning to recognize the strength and the power in grassroots change. On the other hand, it is quite a contradiction that Mr. Marcos and his entire staff and family have been offered safe haven in Hawaii, and it is still unclear how the United States will handle the corruption and the economic war which Marcos and his family had waged against the Philippino people. Mr. Shultz, when asked why Mrs. Aquino has been calling for reconciliation in the Philippines, stated: ''I think out of this comes the sense of the importance of nonviolence and perhaps compassion.'' These are quite unusual statements coming from the representative of an administration which is waging war against Nicaragua, which is calling the Contras ''freedom-fighters'' and is comparing the criminal and corrupt Contras with the ''founding fathers'' of the United States.

THE WAR ZONE CALLED EARTH
Superpower politics is becoming more and more cynical. We had great hopes that at one point the United States would join the nuclear testing moratorium of Soviet Secretary General Gorbachev. But the United States declined to join the moratorium and held its most recent nuclear test not long ago. An American official explained in the *International Herald Tribune* on March 19th, 1986: ''They [the Soviet Union] know we won't stop testing. They want testing to go on and to pin the blame on us.'' What kind of perverse logic is this? The facts remain very simple: both superpowers must stop testing altogether if we are to believe one word they say about disarmament.

But cynicism in politics continues: the Western side claims to have defensive, deterrent, peace-keeping nuclear weapons, while they, the Soviet Union, are said to have aggressive, expansionist, first-strike bombs. By considering the enemy the sole aggressor, we avoid looking at the threat we ourselves pose. I know that military personnel in charge of nuclear warheads are deliberately *not* told where they are aimed. One such soldier had no difficulty in visualizing his own family and city being destroyed by a Soviet attack. When he was then asked to imagine the effects which his weapons would have on his opponents in the Soviet Union he demurred, saying that this was unthinkable—that it would undermine his whole job if he were to begin to consider it.

The present state of the world is so absurd and near mass-suicide that we must, on an individual and collective basis, do everything possible within the realm of nonviolent and civil disobedience. For example, Dr. Benjamin Spock has said that the U.S. Postal Service has prepared a three hundred page strategy for continuing ''normal'' first-class mail delivery to nuclear survivors. This document contains the startling revelation that Nuclear Emergency Change-of-Address forms are already stocked in post offices around the nation!

Both sides have massively built up their nuclear arsenals. Both have deployed first-strike nuclear weapons, the United States in Western Europe, and the Soviet Union in the German Democratic Republic (East Germany) and Czechoslovakia. The United States has failed to engage in really serious arms control discussions with the Soviet Union, and has failed to stop its nuclear testing. At the same time, European statesmen, including François Mitterand, Helmut Kohl, Franz Josef Strauss, and even some parts of the German Social Democrats, are looking toward a stronger, united Western Europe, in the military and technological sense. They are supporting a strong European army, a future European nuclear *force de frappe,* and in the future the Federal Republic of Germany may possibly even become part of a so-called European nuclear superpower. The head of the German police in Munich, Helmut Kollert, recently suggested that the Federal Republic of Germany build its own nuclear weapons, since prohibiting Germany from owning them was discrimination! We reject this European militarization, for it leads Europe on the road to becoming a third military and nuclear superpower. The past agreement, which the German government has signed with the United States concerning the Strategic Defense Initiative (SDI), is an agreement which makes a Euro-SDI possible. And we reject categorically such a Euro-SDI, for it will encourage a massive build-up of nuclear weapons on the other side, and it will accelerate the arms race even more.

We are living in a war zone called earth! There is war in Afghanistan, an atrocious war which so many of us within the worldwide peace movement have ignored; there is war and military conflict in Angola, with the constant threat of invasion from South Africa. There is the forgotten war in East Timor. East Timor became independent from Portugal in November 1975, but Indonesian troops invaded the island ten days later. Since then, two hundred thousand people (one-third of the population) have died or disappeared as the result of Indonesian military offensives, torture and executions. These figures and facts are endorsed by Amnesty International. There is the very tense situation in Egypt in its relations with Libya. There are the very tense relations between the United States, Europe and Libya. In El Salvador, in Chad, in Honduras, in Guatemala the "disappearances" of people are continuing. In Chile, General Pinochet renewed emergency powers on the eve of the anniversary of his seizure of power and the murder of Salvador Allende in 1973. In Colombia, the thirty year guerrilla war reached new intensity during 1985. The Iran-Iraq war, after more than five years, remains in a stalemate. Iran is reported to have more than one million men under arms, including many children. And then there is Kampuchea. The crimes committed by the Khmer Rouge of Pol Pot have been all too quickly forgotten. And there is the fierce fighting within Kurdish areas. Lebanon continues to be torn apart by warring militia groups and by Israeli and Syrian rivalry. And there is dying in Mozambique. South Africa continues to control Namibia with four motorized brigades and fifteen battalions of twenty thousand men. There is unrest and dissatisfaction with an undemocratic political system in Nepal. There are violent clashes in New Caledonia. There has been no improvement in the situation of Northern Ireland. In Newry alone, fourteen policemen have been killed in the past twelve months. In Peru many people have disappeared, and human rights violations have grown. In South Africa, in the first nine months of 1985, over six thousand opponents of apartheid were arrested or held without charge, and over one thousand people were killed in the sixteen months ending in December 1985.

One brave young woman working in an Irish supermarket chain began, all on her own, refusing to register South African fruits and vegetables into her cash register, until eventually many other colleagues joined her. Grassroots power starts with each and every one of us! We must change ourselves first—in order to convince others. Gert Bastian and I and a group of Green Parliamentarians and friends occupied the German embassy in Pretoria, South Africa, in September 1985. We occupied the embassy nonviolently for forty-eight hours to show that we could not agree with the policies of our government, of German firms and businesses in South Africa. But our own interior minister, Friedrich Zimmerman, closes his eyes when colleagues of the *Bundeskriminalamt* arrange vacation trips to South Africa for German policemen, as recently happened.

And there are the violent confrontations between the Sri Lankan government and the minority Tamil community. In Sudan there were widespread riots and demonstrations followed by a military coup. There has been fierce fighting along the Thai-Kampuchean border. And in the Western Sahara, there has been a war of attrition for the ten years since Spain left the territory. Morocco has built a great defensive wall of sand, one thousand miles long, lined with mine fields and electronic surveillance equipment, which is effective against the Polisarios. King Hassan of Morocco plans to spend $1 billion on arms over the next five years to equip his forces for a long struggle against the Western Saharan people. And the list of military conflicts in the war zone called planet earth goes on and on.

There is hope for the Philippines, hope for New Zealand. If enough countries would follow the example of New Zealand, it would greatly reduce the risk of nuclear wars. A very close East German peace friend of mine, Barbel Bohley, once quoted a short poem written by a Swiss pastor:

> Where would we get to
> If everyone said,
> Where would we get to,
> And no one went,
> To have a look,
> Where we'd get to,
> If we went.

Nonviolent men and women together must begin to focus their attention on the ultimate ends of disarmament. We must not seek merely to limit or abolish weapons. We need to reorganize and restructure the world. As the world spends over U.S. $2 billion every day on arms, a reduction of any kind has ramifications which will affect many, many aspects of our lives. Peace is not only the absence of war or conflict, but also the absence of structural violence.

In the end, I believe in doing away with armies, with secret police, with secret services like the CIA, the KGB or the German BND. And I believe in social or civilian-based defence, in making the souls and hearts of the people strong and using the democratic spirit as a form of defending one's democratic values. There are many creative and powerful tools for social defence. These include general strikes, total nonco-operation with the so-called opponent should there be a threat from without or within, and paralyzing one's own industrial plants and resources in case an opponent should want to take them over in times of conflict or aggression.

Here in Vancouver, in 1983, the World Council of Churches decided that the production and deployment of nuclear weapons is a crime against humanity. That is the first step of our path toward peace, naming those things by their right name. At the same time we cannot keep human rights in a pending file. This is *not* a two-stage program: first must come disarmament and then, when there is a period of détente, will come some democratization. Both our struggle against the arms race, and our struggle for human rights in all parts of the world must be fought simultaneously. Our friends in Eastern Europe, the Czechs in Charter 77, the Polish workers in *Solidarnosc,* our friends in the Helsinki Watch Committees in the Soviet Union and our friends in the churches and in the ecological and Ploughshares movement in the German Democratic Republic cannot wait and watch until we give them a signal for that second stage, the so-called human rights lift-off. There have been so many eloquent pleas for peace and for human rights coming from Eastern Europe and Latin America. It is wrong to say that human rights must be a condition for disarmament; and it is wrong to say that human rights will be the consequence of disarmament. *Both must take place together, as part of a single process,* the making of a democratic peace—*a peace that will not be oppressive.*

NATIVE RIGHTS AND MILITARY POWER
And this brings me to my final point, a point which I hope you will allow me to state here as your guest. Canada, I believe, is or could be in the same position as New Zealand. Canada could, as an active *nonaligned* country, be struggling on the front line of peace. It could put forth new

nuclear-free and chemical-free initiatives, it could begin a Canadian nuclear- and chemical- and conventional-weapons-free zone! I know how strong the Vancouver peace movement is, and I am glad to have the opportunity to get to know our many friends here better.

When we speak of the growing militarization of Canada, as Bishop De Roo has done so eloquently, then I must also point a finger at my own government. In December 1983, the Federal Republic of Germany renewed, for three years, an agreement with the government of Canada for low-level fighter-bomber flight training in Labrador. There are Phantoms, Alpha Jets and also German Tornadoes training out of Goose Bay. The territory affected has been under dispute between Canada and the indigenous Inuit people, because it is being settled and mined without any form of agreement or compensation. Low-altitude (under thirty metres or one hundred feet) supersonic flight has been shown to disrupt the migration and calving of caribou, the species upon which the Inuit chiefly depend for food. The history of Labrador is complex. Perhaps Article 1 of the International Covenant on Civil and Political Rights, to which Canada is a party, should be applied. This principle, rooted in Article 1 of the Charter of the United Nations and in the preamble, calls on all states to respect the right of all peoples to self-determination, the free use of their own land and resources, and to subsistence. While it is far from settled whether the Arctic Indians or Inuit can claim to be the people in this sense, thankfully the issue has been raised in the United Nations Commission on Human Rights.

We in the German Green Party are following those developments very closely. The United Nations Special Committee on De-Colonization also is competent to investigate instances of improper military use of non-self-governing territories and, in fact, has criticized the United States military use of bases in the Virgin Islands. The committee could, on petition from the Inuit people, convene meetings in order to investigate the West German use of Labrador. It is clear that German military authorities were well aware of the objections of the Inuit to their presence, yet the German government renewed their agreement with Canada. I believe that the Inuit people's fundamental rights are being compromised by German military exercises in Labrador. In a recent parliamentary inquiry which we put to the German government about low-level flying in Labrador, we received, unfortunately, all the cynical answers we expected. A reply by Herr Wurzbach of the Ministry of Defence dated February 4th, 1985, stated that the representatives of the people of the Goose Bay region have been participating in a decision-making process concerning the low-level flights, and are in constant contact with the representatives of the German air force at a local level. Furthermore, the letter cited Minister

Joseph Goudie as stating that there has been no proof for the criticism concerning the low-level flights and their effects on people's health and the environment.

The Green Party demanded an immediate stop to all low-level flights in Labrador. But the German Parliament voted against our request. All parties, including the CDU/CSU, FDP and SPD,[‡] voted against our formal parliamentary motion. Parliament even rejected our recommendation that a group of Parliamentarians from the Defence Committee be sent to Labrador to speak with the local people about their problems with low-level flights.

We are worried, because the Canadian government has invited NATO to establish an immense $800 million NATO Tactical Fighter and Weapons Training Centre at Goose Bay, Labrador. If approved, the NATO base would bring to Labrador air-to-air and air-to-sea manoeuvres, expanded low-level flying, three to four bombing ranges and Instrumented Air Combat Manoeuvring Ranges. It would become impossible for the military to avoid the camps and the hunting and gathering parties of the Inuit people, when the training activities reached their full operational level. I am told that NATO will make a final decision about this base sometime in 1986. Therefore, we must do all that we can now to raise consciousness about military training activities in that area. Military training activities and the various Euro-Canadian economic initiatives which are now on the drawing board, cannot be allowed to take place without the permission of the Inuit people. Also, the kinds of training activities that are occurring at the moment, and which will be expanded if the NATO base is built in Labrador, are part of a NATO war-fighting strategy known as "Deep Strike." This strategy is very destabilizing and will lower the threshold for a nuclear war.

We are demanding of our German government that it not support the construction of the NATO Tactical Fighter Weapons Training Centre, and that it stop all low-level training. But we must also hope that there is just as much pressure here in Canada against such plans. "Luftwaffe over Labrador" makes me feel ashamed and embarrassed. Are all northern territories and untreatied native homelands now open for German and NATO military groups to rent? The use of aboriginal territory for military purposes must be stopped immediately if native people are to believe that the Canadian government is seriously considering the concepts of Indian nationhood, aboriginal rights and title. But we in Germany have an even greater responsibility never to misuse the land of aboriginal people for military or economic purposes.

[‡]These are the acronyms for the Christian Democratic Union / Christian Social Union, Free Democratic Party, and the Social Democratic Party. —ED.

I am equally embarrassed by the plans of Thysssen AG of Duisburg, Germany, to build a weapons or tank factory on the east Canadian island of Cape Breton. I realize there has been much opposition by peace and religious organizations to this factory, in which Thyssen will invest $100 million. We have been informed that Thyssen would like to have a licence for the export of tanks and other vehicles produced in Cape Breton, to Saudi Arabia, Kuwait, Bahrain, Pakistan and Algiers. In response to an inquiry I put to the German Parliament about the Thyssen plans, I was simply informed that Thyssen would not increase its production of "defensive goods."

Furthermore, there is no such thing as peaceful uranium mining, *not* in any part of the world, and *not* in Canada! We are grateful for all the nonviolent activities and for the civil disobedience which Canadians are employing to put an end to the militarization of Canada, and to put an end to the abuse of your land and your indigenous peoples. It is we who must learn from the lifestyle and from the philosophy of the indigenous peoples. They are truly friends of the earth.

Unlike our friend, Professor Kosta Tsipis, *I do not believe* that there is a *safe* civilian nuclear industry.° The civilian and military uses of nuclear energy are Siamese twins, and both are highly dangerous, including in times of peace. Both contribute to proliferation, and present an intolerable risk of nuclear build-up. We must also see the many grave health risks which both military and civilian uses of nuclear energy pose to society.

One of my dearest "sisters," Dr. Rosalie Bertell, now director of research at the International Institute of Concern for Public Health in Toronto, has written a very valuable book: *No Immediate Danger? Prognosis for a Radioactive Earth*. Rosalie Bertell writes:

> Honest coping and the healing of a dying earth must eventually demand total human attention, loving gentleness and care, drastic changes in lifestyles and priorities, and a permanent change in human attitudes and values. . . . Women are conspicuously involved globally in assisting people through these stages of comprehension and psychic growth. We have no other way out of our dilemma than to find new nonviolent solutions. This means we must also develop our personal inner resources and gain a broader view of our relationships. We must become

---

°Kosta Tsipis did not say, either in his lecture (chapter 3), or in answer to questions (chapter 5), that the civilian nuclear industry is safe. He did not discuss the merits and dangers of nuclear power generation. He did say in chapter 5 that in his view nuclear wastes could be disposed of relatively safely. —ED.

planetary citizens, able to listen to the powerless, able to imagine a world not organized around the rule of the fist.

We must imagine a world without violence and without war preparations.

PHOTO: DAN KEETON

Mayor Takeshi Araki

CHAPTER 22

The Spirit of Hiroshima

MAYOR TAKESHI ARAKI

At 8:15 a.m. on August 6, 1945, an atomic bomb was detonated at an altitude of some 580 metres (1900 feet) over the city of Hiroshima. The city—a major one in Japan with 350 years of rich history and culture, and with a population of 350,000—immediately lay devastated in the midst of the bomb's flash. The destructive power of this atomic bomb was equivalent to the energy generated by the explosion of the total payload of about 2,600 B-29 heavy bombers each loaded with five tons of TNT bombs. Intense thermal rays flashed across the city. With a terrific explosion, a huge pillar of flame rose right up into the sky, flattening buildings and claiming an enormous number of casualties. It was, in fact, a hell on earth. At the time of the bombing, I was working at the office of a factory located 3.5 kilometres (2.2 miles) from ground zero. I was barely able to

Takeshi Araki is the mayor of Hiroshima, Japan. He is a Hibakusha—a survivor of the atom bomb dropped on Hiroshima on August 6, 1945. After graduating in law from Tokyo Imperial University in 1940, Mayor Araki worked in Nagasaki and later in Hiroshima. He has had a long and distinguished career in public service, including service as president of the Atomic Bomb Casualty Council of Hiroshima and president of the Hiroshima A-Bomb Victims Association. In 1975, he became mayor of Hiroshima, and has been re-elected mayor three times since then. Mayor Araki and the mayor of Nagasaki, Hitoshi Motoshima, organized the First World Conference of Mayors for Peace Through Intercity Solidarity. This conference has developed into a permanent international organization of mayors and councillors working for the abolition of nuclear weapons and for world peace.

escape uninjured from the demolished office. The vomiting of blood, which I suffered twenty days later, forced me to recuperate away from Hiroshima.

Since this unprecedented devastation to our city happened in an instant, accurate data on the magnitude of the disaster is still hard to obtain. Research undertaken so far has made clear the following points: in Hiroshima, 350,000 citizens were exposed to atomic radiation; more than 140,000 died instantly or during the following four months; and the city area of thirteen square kilometres (five square miles) was reduced to ashes.

The instant and widespread mass destruction caused by the explosion of the atomic bomb was amplified by the combined effects of heat rays, blast and radiation. This indiscriminate massacre was perpetrated against people, including non-combatants, without distinctions as to age and sex. The heat rays emitted by the detonation and the fire ball attained a temperature of several million degrees centigrade. The thermal impact was so intense that everything combustible within a five-hundred metre (1640-foot) radius from ground zero was consumed. Not a single fragment of human bone could be discovered in that area. In terms of blast, the Hiroshima bomb produced an extremely high pressure of one hundred thousand millibars at ground zero. The surrounding air expanded enormously creating a blast front which advanced as an extremely high-pressure shock wave, and destroyed all buildings within a 1.8-kilometre (1.1-mile) radius of ground zero.

In terms of radiation, gamma rays and neutrons were released from the fireball at the instant of explosion. Most of those who were within a one-kilometre (0.6-mile) radius received a lethal body dose of over four hundred rads. Those who were barely able to survive at that time suffered from the after-effects of radiation and either died later, or still suffer today. Irradiation by the atomic bomb destroyed human cells and produced acute symptoms such as high fever, diarrhea, hematemesis, and hematuria. Longer-term physical problems included keloids, cataracts, leukemia, and breast and lung cancer. In addition, medical reports indicated cases of microcephaly caused by *in utero* exposure. The genetic effects of radiation as a result of chromosomal damage are also matters of deep human concern.

The atomic bomb caused other forms of damage besides disease and physical destruction. The bombing completely destroyed civic and family life, and indeed the community itself. As of March 31, 1985, there were 113,885 *Hibakusha* (atom-bomb survivors) in Hiroshima and 73,587 in Nagasaki. The total number of *Hibakusha* in Japan is 367,344. The citizens of Hiroshima who endured such an inhumane nuclear holocaust know that nuclear weapons should never be used again, whatever the reason may be. Such lethal and devastating weapons portend the end of human history. Mankind must not allow this tragic but real possibility to occur. And this is why we are so strongly opposed to the use of nuclear weapons.

Forty-one years have now passed since an atomic bomb was dropped on a city for the first time in human history. Despite our calling for the total abolition of nuclear arsenals, these horrendous weapons have been continuously developed. Today, stockpiled nuclear weapons are equivalent to some one million Hiroshima-type atomic bombs.

The question posed by nuclear weapons goes far beyond the damage of war. It poses the most crucial problem regarding the existence of mankind: we now have the ability to exterminate all living things, eliminate human society and perhaps destroy the earth's entire ecosystem. Destruction of this magnitude threatens human survival. Today humankind is confronted with the most serious danger in human history. We are at an important crossroad: one path leads to survival, and the other to death and destruction. Standing at this very crucial crossroad, we must remember the tragedy of Hiroshima.

In Hiroshima, the Peace Memorial Park is built near ground zero. It contains six hundred exhibits related to the atomic bombing of Hiroshima, selected from among more than 6,800 collected artifacts. The purposes of these historical exhibits are to disseminate information about Hiroshima's atomic bomb experience: to let visitors see the actual nature of the bombing, and to confront humans with the cruelty of nuclear weapons. Last year 1,440,000 people visited the museum. Forty percent of them (570,000) were junior high and high school students on "peace study" assignments. These young people must now pass on the spirit of Hiroshima to the next generation. As they assume major responsibilities in society, they will carry the torch of hope and peace into the twenty-first century.

The Memorial Monument for Hiroshima, City of Peace (the atomic bomb memorial cenotaph) stands near the centre of Hiroshima Peace Park. On this monument is an epitaph which reads: "Let all the souls here rest in peace; for we shall not repeat the evil." This epitaph is a living pledge for peace: everyone who stands in front of the monument reads these words on behalf of every other human in the world. It is the spirit of Hiroshima itself, based on humanism in its most fundamental sense. By enduring grief and overcoming past hatred, the spirit of Hiroshima means that we pledge ourselves to the coexistence and prosperity of all humankind. To quote from the UNESCO Charter: "Since wars begin in the minds of men, it is in the minds of men that the defence of peace must be constructed." One torch ignites another, in unending succession, and still the first torch keeps burning. The flame of

Hiroshima should be lit from one person to another and handed down to posterity.

The number of distinguished guests who visit Hiroshima continues to grow. It may be because our continuous efforts toward peace have made the spirit of Hiroshima permeate the world little by little, and also because leaders and people of the world increasingly recognize the meaning of Hiroshima. The local newspaper *Chugoku Shimbun* reported on January 21, 1986 that among Japan's municipalities, Hiroshima City received the largest number of visits by distinguished guests from abroad. I was impressed to hear the actual number. We received 524 guests from thirty-one countries for the period of April through September of 1985, the year that marked the fortieth anniversary of the atomic bombing. Over the last five years, we had the honour of welcoming Pope John Paul II, the late Olof Palme, former prime minister of Sweden, President Sandro Pertini of Italy, Secretary-General Javier Perez de Cuellar of the United Nations, Mr. Jimmy Carter, former president of the United States, and President San Yu of Burma.

During his pastoral visit to Hiroshima on February 25, 1981, His Holiness Pope John Paul II delivered an appeal for peace at the Hiroshima Peace Memorial Park. Standing in falling snow, he declared: "War is the work of man. War is destruction of human life. War is death. To remember the past is to commit oneself to the future. To remember Hiroshima is to abhor nuclear war." No words express better the spirit of Hiroshima than those of Pope John Paul II.

Now I would like to have the honour of quoting from a speech by the late Olof Palme,* which the former prime minister of Sweden delivered at the Workshop of the Independent Commission on Disarmament and International Security Issues held in Hiroshima on December 18, 1981. Dr. Palme pointed out the futility of war by saying:

> There was one picture in the museum which showed, as it read, a human shadow imprinted on a stone step. The granite-hard stone remained, but presumably there had been one person sitting there on the stone steps, and not even the ashes of that person remained, because he had been hit by a five thousand degree

---

* At an earlier session of the Vancouver Centennial Peace and Disarmament Symposium, the audience of seventeen hundred persons rose for a minute of silence to honour Olof Palme, who was assassinated on February 28, 1986. Prime Minister Palme was one of the six heads of state who signed the important Five Continent Appeal of May 1984. He had given active and sympathetic consideration to participation in this symposium, but due to the pressures of governmental affairs in Sweden, reluctantly declined an invitation to be a speaker. On a motion by Ambassador Sean MacBride, the symposium participants and the audience endorsed a statement of condolence which was sent to the Swedish government. —ED.

centigrade heat wave. And one wonders whether this will be the fate of the entire human race if this madness of the arms race continues: to be no more than a human shadow imprinted on stone steps.

Many people were horrified to see the displays in the Peace Memorial Museum. People of the world, especially the leaders of nations, should visit Hiroshima so that they might realize the true nature of atomic bombing.

In today's nuclear age, we must disseminate information about the atomic experience and cultivate an international public opinion to call for lasting peace and the total abolition of nuclear weapons. As citizens of a city that experienced the devastation of the atomic bomb, we in Hiroshima believe that it is our mission to do so. An appeal for peace at the United Nations is especially important because the United Nations serves as a symbol of peace-keeping in the world. In December 1976, one year after my inauguration as the mayor of Hiroshima, I met with former United Nations Secretary-General Kurt Waldheim and called for the elimination of nuclear arsenals and for comprehensive arms reduction. In May of 1978, an exhibition entitled "Hiroshima and Nagasaki—a Photographic Record of an Historical Event," coincided with the First Special Session of the United Nations General Assembly on Disarmament. Because it was the first photographic exhibit of atomic bombings held at the United Nations headquarters, we tried to display as many photographs as possible. Despite some objections that a few of the photographs depicted excessive and graphic cruelty, our strenuous insistence overcame those objections, and the first exhibition materialized intact. Since 1978, the "Hiroshima Atomic-Bomb Photographic Exhibition" has been held in sixty-three cities of nineteen countries.

In June 1982, I addressed the Second Special Session of the United Nations General Assembly on Disarmament. In my statement I called for an immediate and complete ban on nuclear tests, and a freeze on, and ultimate elimination of, all nuclear weapons stocks. I also called on the heads of nuclear powers and those in leading positions in the countries of the world, and especially on their young people, representing the next generation, to come to Hiroshima to see and understand better the awesome damage of an atomic bomb. I proposed that cities throughout the world unite to pave a road, transcending national boundaries and races, that will lead to the abolition of nuclear weapons. We have been calling for this intercity solidarity since January of 1983. Today we proudly report that 131 cities from thirty-three countries have joined in our intercity solidarity program, and that this network of cities is still expanding globally.

In order to give this approach a solid foundation, the First World Conference of Mayors for Peace Through Intercity Solidarity was held in August of 1985, in commemoration of the fortieth anniversary of the atomic bombings. Representing sixty-seven cities in twenty-two countries including the United States, the Soviet Union, and nonaligned nations of Asia and Africa—and transcending political boundaries, ideologies and creeds—139 mayors and councillors gathered in Hiroshima and Nagasaki. I quote from the "Hiroshima Appeal" adopted by the participants:

> The first atomic bomb ever used in history against humanity devastated the city of Hiroshima in an instant and deprived many people of their precious lives. It still imposes the suffering of its after-effects on the A-bomb survivors. Through a careful observation of the true nature of A-bombing, we have realized that the nuclear catastrophe is unimaginably overwhelming. We have acutely felt that the tragedy shall never be repeated. We take the experience of Hiroshima as our own and consider it not as a mere incident of the past but as a warning to the future of humankind. We have pledged ourselves to exert our utmost efforts toward the total abolition of nuclear weapons and the attainment of lasting world peace. We have pledged to unite ourselves by establishing firm bonds of friendship and solidarity, transcending national boundaries, ideologies, and creeds in order to secure the lives and prosperities of our people and bequeath to future generations the history and culture of our cities, which took thousands of years to develop.

As an essential precondition for the total abolition of nuclear arsenals, the most crucial and urgent task we face is to ban nuclear testing immediately and comprehensively. Every time nuclear tests are conducted, the City of Hiroshima sends a telegram of protest to the nation concerned. The number of telegrams stands today at 375. We strongly opposed the underground nuclear tests conducted by the United States on March 22 and April 10, 1986 and urged President Ronald Reagan to work for an immediate and comprehensive ban on nuclear tests and the total abolition of nuclear weapons. We also requested Soviet leader Mikhail Gorbachev to continue the Soviet moratorium on nuclear testing and to work for the elimination of nuclear arsenals.

I urge the leaders of the United States and the Soviet Union to reduce nuclear arms, ban nuclear testing and ban the development and production of any nuclear weapons. These two nations bear a special responsibility for maintaining world peace, as confirmed in their joint communiqué issued on the occasion of the summit talks held in the fall of last year. This document provided some new opportunities for progress toward arms control and nuclear disarmament. I keenly feel the necessity to cultivate intercity and interpeople solidarity against the arms race. This solidarity can serve to discourage the two superpowers from abusing summit talks for national propaganda purposes, and to encourage them to seize these new and precious opportunities for peace.

Nineteen eighty-six is the "International Year of Peace" designated by the United Nations to secure and promote world peace and security. On this occasion, Hiroshima City plans to invite laureates of the Nobel Peace Prize to hold an international peace summit and concert. An exhibition of peace posters by school children in Japan and abroad will be given as well. A symposium and a lecture on peace will be given as well and the presidents of IPPNW (International Physicians for the Prevention of Nuclear War) will attend.[†] We will take these opportunities to confirm the preciousness of peace and the dignity of life. It is our aim to foster international public opinion so as to establish a solid foundation for the total abolition of nuclear weapons and the realization of lasting world peace. In order to prevent the tragedy from being repeated, we have to form an intercity and interpeople solidarity that transcends national boundaries, ideologies and creeds—a solidarity that overcomes distrust and hatred.

It is obvious that if a nuclear war broke out, there would be neither winners nor losers: the earth would be destroyed. As citizens and potential victims of war, we should take the initiative to promote an international movement against nuclear war and a movement for the elimination of nuclear arms. Hiroshima is not merely a witness to history. Hiroshima is an endless warning for the future of humankind. If Hiroshima is forgotten, the mistake will be repeated and human history may be brought to an end. In order to prevent the tragedy of Hiroshima from being repeated, I ask you to join in our efforts to form a global solidarity.

[†]The two co-presidents of IPPNW, Dr. Bernard Lown of the United States, and Dr. Evgeni Chazov of the Soviet Union, received the 1985 Nobel Peace Prize on behalf of the International Physicians for the Prevention of Nuclear War in Oslo, Norway on December 11, 1985. IPPNW has over 154,000 physician members from forty-eight countries working actively to prevent nuclear war.—ED.

Alderwoman Libby Davies

CHAPTER 23

The Special Role of Municipalities in Working for Peace

ALDERWOMAN LIBBY DAVIES and GARY MARCHANT

In the past few years, the peace movement in Canada has grown remarkably. Civic governments, by increasingly supporting disarmament initiatives, have encouraged this growth. The special role played by municipalities in publicly opposing the arms race results from the close relationship between civic governments and the public. Civic governments are often more accessible and accountable to the community. They permit, and even encourage, local organizations and individuals to have a say in policy-making. Most councillors are approachable and willing to listen, and city council meetings frequently include presentations from the public. For these reasons, municipal governments are often quicker to respond to changes in public perceptions than is the federal government.

Peace groups in particular have found civic governments to be accessible and responsive. Cities and towns are a natural organizing base for the peace movement. Individual peace groups have joined to form city

Alderwoman Libby Davies has been a member of the Vancouver City Council since 1982, and now serves as the chairperson of the Council's Special Committee on Peace. Born in England, she has lived in British Columbia since 1969, and has a long record of active public service in Vancouver on behalf of underprivileged residents in the downtown eastside, women, and senior citizens. She represents the Committee of Progressive Electors (COPE) in Vancouver City Council, and played a major part in council's decision to declare the City of Vancouver a nuclear-weapons-free zone. She is an expert on the responsibility of municipal governments to protect city residents from death and destruction in a nuclear war.

Gary Marchant

coalitions in most larger centres, and smaller municipalities usually have their own peace group. A close working relationship has often developed between the local peace group or coalition and sympathetic members of city councils. Because the federal government is particularly inaccessible and less sensitive to public opinion on nuclear weapons policy, peace groups find city councils to be valuable and powerful allies in pressuring the federal government to alter its policies.

Another reason for the special role civic governments play in working for peace is that cities and towns would be the primary targets in a nuclear war. The only nuclear bombs ever used in war were dropped on cities. In a recent letter, the mayors of Hiroshima and Nagasaki urged cities to become actively involved in the search for peace: "When we consider that in war, especially nuclear war, people of the cities suffer most, it becomes obvious that cities, scientific research institutes, press agencies, civilian organizations, and also each individual must work diligently in the search for peace."

JURISDICTION AND LEGAL ASPECTS

Those opposed to civic governments taking positions on peace and disarmament issues often argue that peace is not a civic matter. They argue that peace is beyond the jurisdiction of cities, and that it may even be illegal for municipalities to deal with such issues. However, there are strong arguments for the position that municipalities do have a legal and a moral right to be involved in peace issues. In 1982, a resident from Oak Bay, British Columbia, went to court to argue that it is illegal for cities to spend money on disarmament referenda, since such questions are not within the jurisdiction of municipalities. The Municipal Act of British Columbia states that a local referendum can be held in British Columbia on "any question which affects the municipality and with which the council has the power to deal." The implication of this wording was the key point in contention during the Oak Bay case. On November 17th, 1982, British Columbia Supreme Court Justice Patricia Proudfoot decreed that questions about nuclear disarmament on municipal ballots were legal, because nuclear arms proliferation affected "not only the municipality but the entire universe." This ruling firmly established that

Gary Marchant has been a student activist for peace at the University of British Columbia, and was a founder of Students for Peace and Mutual Disarmament at that institution. He is vice-president of the Vancouver peace coalition, End the Arms Race, and is a member of the Vancouver City Council Special Committee on Peace. Recently awarded his Ph.D. degree in genetics, he now plans a career in law and public affairs relating to science.

municipalities in British Columbia have the legal right not only to speak on peace issues, but also to spend time and money on them.

The federal government has also implicitly recognized the right of municipal governments to be active in promoting disarmament. A pamphlet published by Emergency Planning Canada in 1980 stated that "under constitutional arrangements, initial responsibility for handling most emergencies lies with the municipal, provincial and territorial governments. Each is responsible for its own emergency program. Most emergencies are dealt with by the municipalities in which they occur." The pamphlet defines emergencies as "everything from floods to nuclear war." Since it is widely recognized that the only solution to nuclear war is prevention, this federal government pamphlet implies that municipal governments have the "initial responsibility" for preventing nuclear war by promoting disarmament.

As well as the legal right, municipal governments also have the moral responsibility and duty to work for peace and disarmament. Ending the arms race and preventing nuclear war is not just one of the many issues we face in this complex world. It is the *one single issue* at which we must succeed if any other issue, or thing, or person is to matter. Preventing nuclear war is not just the responsibility of one group of people, or one level of government, or one political philosophy—it is the responsibility of everyone. Because the very existence of the human species is at stake, there is no place, organization or chamber where discussion and action on this issue is out of place or inappropriate.

Albert Einstein once said that "mere praise of peace is easy, but ineffective. What is needed is active participation in the fight against war and everything that leads towards it." The time is past when any person, institution, or level of government could leave the threat of nuclear war to be solved by others.

WHAT CITIES HAVE DONE FOR PEACE

In recent years, municipal governments in Canada have compiled an impressive list of achievements in advocating and working for peace and disarmament. Perhaps the most important measure undertaken by municipalities has been the declaration of particular towns and cities as nuclear-weapons-free zones (NWFZs). By prohibiting the deployment, production, transit or storage of nuclear weapons or their components in a particular region or municipality, NWFZs help to restrict the spread and expansion of the nuclear arms race. As well, by declaring itself to be a NWFZ, a town or city symbolically conveys to the leaders of the world the active opposition of its citizens to the continuation of the nuclear arms race. The United Nations General Assembly endorsed the concept of NWFZs on June 30, 1978, in a resolution that states: "The process of establishing such zones in different parts of the world should be to encourage, with the ultimate objective of achieving a world entirely free of nuclear weapons.'' Already over 2800 towns and cities from 17 countries have declared themselves to be NWFZs. In New Zealand, the federal government declared the whole nation to be a NWFZ as a direct outcome of earlier NWFZ declarations by the vast majority of that country's towns and cities*. As of January 1986, there are over eighty nuclear-weapons-free zones in Canada, including major cities such as Toronto, Vancouver, Hamilton and Regina as well as the entire province of Manitoba. In British Columbia local governments have declared thirty-five towns and cities to be NWFZs. Over half of British Columbia's population now lives in nuclear-weapons-free zones.

In 1982 and 1983, approximately two hundred Canadian municipalities conducted public referenda on general disarmament. In every case, the public voted in support of disarmament, with an average voter support of 76.2 percent. Another important action that civic governments have frequently taken is the adoption of resolutions urging the federal government to change its position on particular disarmament issues. For example, ninety-one Canadian municipal councils passed motions endorsing a mutual and verifiable nuclear weapons freeze. Many councils are also on record as opposing cruise missile testing in Canada. Civic governments have undertaken a wide variety of other disarmament measures across the country, including co-sponsoring peace marches, organizing public education events and activities, dedicating a peace garden, establishing a special council committee on peace and forming sister-city attachments with towns and cities in the Soviet Union and other countries.

FIRST WORLD CONFERENCE OF MAYORS FOR PEACE
The First World Conference of Mayors for Peace Through Intercity Solidarity, held in Japan in August 1985, gave cities even further momentum in promoting peace. The mayors of ninety-eight cities from twenty-three countries attended the conference, which was hosted by the mayors of Hiroshima and Nagasaki. In his declaration to the conference on August 6, 1985, marking the fortieth anniversary of the atomic bombing of his city, Hiroshima Mayor Takeshi Araki said:

> Hiroshima, an A-bombed city, has been devoting itself to
> building a city dedicated to peace — a living symbol of the ideal
> of lasting world peace. It is in this spirit that we are hosting the
> First World Conference of Mayors for Peace Through Intercity

* For more details of the actions taken in New Zealand, see chapter 19 in this book, by James Anderton. —ED.

> Solidarity this year, for it is our hope that all the cities of the world aspiring to lasting peace will be able to develop intercity solidarity transcending national boundaries, ideologies and creeds, and will impart momentum to the international quest for peace.

Mayor Hitoshi Motoshima of Nagasaki appealed to cities to become actively involved in the search for peace: ''A large portion of the world's population is concentrated in cities, and if a nuclear war breaks out, it is obvious that cities and their inhabitants will be the first in line for destruction and death. The protection of citizens from nuclear war is a vital duty of all city mayors.''

The mayors from the ninety-eight cities at the conference unanimously agreed that cities must be involved in the disarmament issue. They agreed to make the conference an ongoing, permanent organization. Each mayor pledged to communicate the results and carry on the work of the conference in his or her own country. At the conclusion of the conference, the mayors issued the ''Hiroshima Appeal,'' which said in part:

> We take the experience of Hiroshima as our own and consider it not as a mere incident of the past, but as a warning to the future of humankind. We have pledged ourselves to exert our utmost efforts towards the total abolition of nuclear arsenals and the attainment of lasting world peace. We have pledged to unite ourselves by establishing firm bonds of friendship and solidarity, transcending national boundaries, ideologies, and creeds in order to secure the lives and properties of our people and bequeath to future generations the history and culture of our cities, which took thousands of years to develop. . . . We must lay a well-established foundation for lasting world peace through intercity and interpeople solidarity.

THE CITY OF VANCOUVER AND PEACE

The city of Vancouver has been at the forefront of the cities for peace movement. The following sections describe some of the peace initiatives undertaken by the city, the mayor and the council of Vancouver.

Nuclear-weapons-free zone. On April 19, 1983, Vancouver City Council passed a motion that declared Vancouver to be a nuclear-weapons-free zone. The motion stated ''that any manufacture, storage, transportation or distribution of such weapons or their components be banned within our boundaries.'' The motion also called for the city council to ''strike a committee to put specific content into the nuclear-weapons-free zone declaration for Vancouver.''

Following the recommendations of this committee, Vancouver City

Council amended the City Bylaws to give legal force to the NWFZ declaration. Council amended the Zoning and Development Bylaw (#3575) to include: "No person shall use or occupy land and no development permit shall be issued for the manufacture, distribution or storage of a nuclear weapon or any component thereof."

Similarly, it amended the Fire Bylaw (#2193) to include: "Notwithstanding any other provision of this bylaw, it shall be unlawful for any person to store or transport a nuclear weapon or any component thereof within the City."

Other measures taken by city council to give substance to the NWFZ declaration included putting fifteen NWFZ signs around the perimeter of the city, a postal meter stamp and a historic plaque. As well, Council passed a motion urging the federal government to declare the Port of Vancouver a NWFZ. City council has no jurisdiction over the port, which is operated by the Canada Ports Corporation on behalf of the federal government. The Minister of Transport has so far refused to act on council's request to have the Port of Vancouver also declared a NWFZ.

Municipal Referenda. Vancouver City Council has approved and conducted two municipal referenda on peace issues during civic elections. In the November 1982, municipal election, voters were asked the following question: "Do you support the goal of general disarmament and mandate the federal government to negotiate and implement, with other governments, the balanced steps that will lead to the earliest possible achievement of this goal?"

A resounding eighty percent of Vancouver voters approved this resolution, and city council sent the results to the Canadian government, the United Nations and the governments of the United States and the Soviet Union.

On November 17, 1984, Vancouver voters had a second opportunity to vote in a disarmament referendum during a civic election. This second plebiscite dealt specifically with cruise missile testing in Canada, and was worded as follows: "Are you in favour of Vancouver City Council asking the federal government to exercise its option under the bilateral agreement with the United States government, to cancel any further testing of the cruise missile in this country?" Fifty-seven percent of decided voters supported this resolution.

Co-sponsorship of annual peace walk. Each April, tens of thousands of Vancouverites take to the street and participate in the annual Walk for Peace, to protest against the continuing nuclear arms race. Since 1984, Vancouver City Council has co-sponsored this important event with the End the Arms Race peace coalition. The Vancouver Walk for Peace has become North America's largest annual peace event, with close to 100,000 people participating in each of the last few years. The success of this event, and city council's strong involvement in this and other peace activities, has given Vancouver the reputation as the ''Peace Capital of North America.'' As a co-sponsor of the Walk for Peace, the city absorbs all the costs for policing and traffic control during the event. As well, the mayor and members of city council lead the walk with the city banner; and the mayor brings greetings from the city to the participants of the rally at the conclusion of the Walk for Peace.

Special Council Committee on Peace. Through its co-sponsorship of the annual Walk for Peace and support of other disarmament initiatives, Vancouver City Council established and maintained a close informal relationship with the broadly-based peace organization in the city. To put this important relationship on a more official and permanent basis, city council established on March 12, 1985, a Special Council Committee on Peace. The committee includes representatives from city council and various peace organizations, and meets regularly to discuss initiatives the city can take to promote peace. The two primary functions of the committee are to act as a clearing house for various initiatives on peace presented to the mayor and councillors for consideration; and to initiate ideas and proposals for peace-related activities in co-operation with other Canadian municipalities.

One of the first tasks of the committee was to correspond with mayors and councils of member municipalities of the Federation of Canadian Municipalities requesting responses to the following questions:

1. Has your municipality been declared a nuclear-weapons-free zone?
2. Has your municipality conducted any referenda on peace?
3. What other motions regarding peace and disarmament has your council approved?
4. Do you anticipate any further initiatives in this area in the near future?

The responses received indicated that municipalities have become increasingly aware that peace is a valid municipal issue. In the coming months, the committee hopes to establish close links with other Canadian municipalities to consider what initiatives can be taken together to further the aim of reducing the possibility of nuclear conflict.

Vancouver Centennial Peace Festival. The Vancouver Centennial Peace Festival included a special session on municipal involvement in peace issues. The Vancouver Special Council Committee on Peace organized the session and Vancouver Mayor Michael Harcourt opened it. A highlight of the session was a presentation by Mayor Takeshi Araki of Hiroshima on the program for peace through intercity solidarity and the results of the first mayor's conference held in Hiroshima in August 1985. Approximately thirty municipally-elected officials from British Columbia and as far away as Toronto and Seattle participated in the session. Alderwoman Libby Davies, chairperson of the Vancouver Special Council Committee on Peace, described the actions and initiatives taken by Vancouver City Council in the past three years, and described the role of the Special Council Committee on Peace and its efforts to develop a network of Canadian municipalities working for peace. She circulated copies of a city peace leaflet which was distributed to every household in Vancouver just prior to the Vancouver Centennial Peace Festival, providing factual information on the current status of the arms race and the growing hope for peace. The leaflet asked the people of Vancouver to "accept your responsibility as a citizen of Vancouver—a city committed to nuclear disarmament and a nuclear-weapons-free zone—by actively working for peace." The leaflet urged citizens to:

> Write your member of Parliament and your prime minister. Ask the government of Canada to urge the United States to stop testing nuclear weapons and to urge the Soviet Union to maintain their halt on actual testing. Ask them to declare *all of Canada* a nuclear-weapons-free zone. Ask them to insure that the NORAD agreement does not get us involved in "Star Wars" or the militarization of space. Ask them to end testing of the air-launched cruise missile. Ask them to ban ships bearing nuclear arms from entering Canadian ports. Stand up and be counted!

Alderwoman Davies also distributed a resource kit developed by the Special Council Committee on Peace, giving detailed information for elected officials and peace groups who hope to convince their local city councils to support disarmament issues. Copies of the resource kit entitled "Cities and Disarmament," are available from the Special Council Committee on Peace, Vancouver City Hall, 453 West 12th Avenue, Vancouver, B.C. V5Y 1V4.

Councillor Jane Noland from Seattle City Council described Seattle's successful twinning with the Soviet city of Tashkent. The sister city relationship has included creative and positive citizen and official exchanges to promote better understanding between the two cities and their people.

Although it was only a brief part of the Vancouver Centennial Peace Festival, the session on municipal involvement in peace exemplified the many and diverse ways cities can work for peace, from holding referenda on peace, passing motions, establishing special civic peace committees, declaring themselves NWFZs, issuing municipal peace leaflets, to developing strong sister city relationships and supporting the courageous initiatives of the cities of Hiroshima and Nagasaki. Clearly there is an important and special role for municipalities to play.

The success of the Vancouver Centennial Peace Festival itself is a strong indication of what a city can do to involve its citizens actively in stopping the arms race and promoting peace. Now that the Peace Festival has concluded, the Special Council Committee on Peace has a major task to follow up on the Vancouver Proposals for Peace [following the introduction to this book—ED.] which were prepared by the experts participating in the Vancouver Centennial Peace and Disarmament Symposium. They have been referred by Vancouver City Council to the Peace Committee for consideration and implementation. There are many other legacies flowing from the Vancouver Centennial Peace Festival, and it is significant that there is an ongoing established council-appointed committee to carry on the momentum sparked by the Peace Festival.

The 1985 Walk for Peace crossing the Burrard Street Bridge in Vancouver

Part of the 1986 Walk for Peace approaches B.C. Place Stadium for the rally

CHAPTER 24

Panel Discussion: Session IV

LIBBY DAVIES, JAMES P. ANDERTON,
JOAN RUDDOCK, PETRA K. KELLY,
AND TAKESHI ARAKI

Libby Davies (session chairperson):
Mayor Araki, has President Reagan visited Hiroshima, and if so, what was his reaction?

Mayor Araki:
President Reagan has not been to Hiroshima. However, there is the summit meeting in Tokyo in early May, and we have invited President Reagan and all the leaders of the world who will be at the Tokyo summit to come to Hiroshima. We have also informed them that if, because of their very busy schedules, President Reagan and the others are not able to visit Hiroshima, the mayor of Nagasaki and I will gladly go to Tokyo. If President Reagan and some of the other leaders could spare us a few minutes that would be greatly appreciated. We have also requested that the exhibition of artifacts from the bombing of Hiroshima be on display in Tokyo.

Davies:
James Anderton, what is the very first thing one should do to prevent war?

James Anderton:
Live in New Zealand! I think one answer is that peace really starts with ourselves. We each have to settle our own differences within our own countries, and we have to learn how to deal with and to accommodate conflict there. Those who disagree have got to learn how to disagree in a peaceful way. Plenty of conservative people in New Zealand did not

245

agree at first with the Labour government's policy. But one way in which we converted them was to have the Americans try to hit us with a big stick, because then that actually raised the question of national sovereignty. So that kind of action—the pressure tactic—certainly coalesced New Zealand opinion. But fundamentally I think preventing war requires that the individuals and communities of every nation put themselves in the position of other people. We need to see that we shouldn't just seek equality, or democracy, or a higher quality of life for ourselves, we should seek these things for the whole world as one human family. And when we can do that we will have taken a big step forward for peace in the world.

Davies:
Petra Kelly, the Green Party emphasizes that they will co-operate with independent peace movements. How is this to be understood? Does this mean that the Green Party will not work with peace movements in countries like Sweden, Denmark and New Zealand, where the demands of the peace movement are supported by governments or Parliaments?

Petra Kelly:
We wish this to be understood in the following way: wherever governments are not in any way pursuing the type of peace policies that we Greens mean by peace, especially in countries where it is very difficult to have independent peace movements, we support these countries' peace movements. We believe that when we visit a country, we should consult the people at the grassroots level. So, if we go to Eastern Europe, we will give equal time to the government—we will listen to them—but we also go to the people. In Eastern Europe they have had a very hard time protesting for independent civil rights and peace. But of course we also support peace movements, such as those in Sweden or in Denmark, which work closely with their governments. Political leaders like Olof Palme and many others have given great support to the peace movements. So the Green Party really has a dual policy—support for both governmental and independent peace movements.

Davies:
Mayor Araki, this question is from the delegation from Kitimat, British Columbia. "For a year now we have been speaking to citizens of the Soviet Union via shortwave radio Moscow, as well as twinning with a Soviet and an American city. We visit their ships and host their crews when they dock in our city. What do you think about such contacts, especially over Radio Moscow?"

Araki:

We all know that there is only one race on the earth, and that is the human race. To this extent we must all live together and survive together. It is necessary to cross international boundaries, to leave aside political differences, and to communicate with one another. By doing this, distrust becomes trust, and confrontation becomes communication.

The city of Hiroshima already has formed sister city relationships with the city of Honolulu, the city of Hannover, and the city of Volgograd in the Soviet Union. We have found that by forming sister city relationships, we create strong contacts with the people of these cities. We highly encourage this type of communication: it is very important for the people of one city or country to meet the people of other regions.

Davies:

Joan Ruddock, how can we combat the magic phrase "job creation," which actually means work for destruction?

Joan Ruddock:

With difficulty! It is obviously a very powerful phenomenon, this need people have to retain their jobs, particularly when there is economic recession. The possibility of more work or a new job is clearly fundamentally attractive to ordinary people who want to work. I have never argued, and I think this is immensely important, that any individual should give up his or her job for *my* conscience. What we need to do is show workers the many job opportunities which could be available to them which do not involve military production. I know this is a major question for you in Canada. It is a major question for us in Britain. CND has been told that our program for disarmament would result in the loss of hundreds of thousands of jobs. To counter that we have actually undertaken, with the help of academics who are involved in the peace movement, in-depth research looking at where jobs currently are available, and where they could be made available. We have been looking at the skills and the resources of factories and plants included in military production, doing the costing and working out what forms of production could be undertaken as an alternative.

There is an immense amount of work that can be done on conversion from military to socially useful production. Conversion is feasible; it is practical. But in this present climate we have got to prove it. I believe this is a task which the peace movement has got to take on, in conjunction, as we are doing in Britain, with the whole of the trade union movement. We must get them to put their money into it, because the trade unions generally have a lot more money than the peace movement. I am

247

glad to say that they are working extremely well with us in Britain, and a lot more money is being spent to study arms conversion.

Davies:

In order to increase public participation in the struggle for peace with justice through disarmament, our news media must become more responsible. What can we as individuals do to get the media to address our concerns? How can we get disarmament on the front page and keep it there? Perhaps New Zealand might provide us with lessons on this.

Anderton:

The peace movement has to be creative; it has to create what the media call "media opportunities." If you can't beat them, you have got to join them. The media of our country could not resist taking a photograph of a young surfie stopping a Long Beach class cruiser in the middle of the channel. That was just irresistible, and I'm sure as hell glad that photo wasn't relegated to the back page. It was on the front page. In every way it can, the peace movement has to present itself as serious and concerned —but also as human.

Also, I think the appearance of many serious scientific and professional groups supporting the peace movement has been a very important development, because the media tend to be more attentive to someone with qualifications after their name than they are to the so-called ordinary peacenik. If you can produce a physicist or a scientist, that tends to dazzle the New Zealand media. They tend to believe what they are told by such experts.

So you have got to use every avenue open to you. It is no good bashing the media. One of the things I have noticed is the fact that the report of this symposium in your local newspaper is buried on page G12. That means not many people are going to see it. Well, I guess we have to ask ourselves why that is, and we have to do something to improve it, which means the responsibility lies as much with us as with the media. Media bashing doesn't get you very far either, because after all they own the means of communication.

Using the media effectively is not easy. It has exercised the minds of the New Zealand peace movement over many years. But the creativity of people knows no bounds. And I can tell you that after a while, if the majority of people actually support the peace movement, which is the situation in New Zealand, the media are *forced* to report peace news, because it is the news that the majority of the country actually wants to see. That's when you get on the front page and not on the back page.

Kelly:
Our German experience with the media is a very, very difficult one. In fact, the Green Party has sometimes nonviolently occupied the offices of television stations in order to hold long negotiations with the producers. We have had demonstrations where, if fewer than one hundred thousand people show up, there is not a line in the newspapers. When we made the huge human chain from Stuttgart to Ulm in Germany, it was news the first time we did it. But even when we ended up having Congressman Ron Dellums from California, and a Nobel Prize winner from Argentina, and Ramsay Clark, the former attorney general of the United States, the German press did not report one line.

I cite this experience because after all these years of hard work to make peace an issue in the media, we still have a very big battle ahead of us. For example, when the Parliamentary group of the Greens—twenty-eight members of Parliament—went to South Africa to occupy the German Embassy nonviolently, we ended up realizing that some of the reports on our actions were actually taken off the news at night. The people who control the media simply decided that these reports would not be aired. I say this with all sincerity. I don't want to bash the media, but we have an extremely difficult problem dealing with them. Because once five hundred thousand people appeared in a demonstration in Bonn, *anything* less than that has become no news at all. That is the type of problem we have had to confront.

Ruddock:
We have a similar problem in Britain. I think we have got to bear in mind that the media is fickle. New Zealand is an exception, where obviously the media has had to perceive peace issues differently. Our media, where we remain a minority interest, is going to do what it wants to; when it decides our time is over, it will go on to something else.

We have to recognize that if necessary we must publicize the issues ourselves. In Britain we have increased our own publications—our newspaper and our monthly magazine. We decided to work harder on these publications, and on encouraging people in every locality to go out on the streets with information to give out to people, to let them know on a regular basis that the peace movement is alive and active. It is not an adequate substitute. It would be better to get coverage in the national media, and it is essential that we continue to work at this. But we must not just sit back when a media blackout hits us. We have actually got to go out there and make sure that the information we want to publicize gets publicized. Frankly, some of the coverage we get in the media we could well do without anyway.

Araki:

In Hiroshima, the major newspaper is the *Chigogu Shimbun;* its daily readership is about 760,000. This newspaper has a very progressive approach to Hiroshima's situation. For instance, it plans to invite reporters and other media people from all over North America—and I believe that Canada is included this year—to visit Hiroshima and Nagasaki on August 6th and August 9th, the anniversaries of the days when the bombs were dropped on these cities. When these people return to their respective cities and towns they will, of course, write about what they saw and experienced firsthand. This is a very effective way of letting the people in other parts of the world know about what happened to Hiroshima. We are very pleased that the newspaper in Hiroshima has taken this approach.

Davies:

Petra Kelly, we are told that in the German Democratic Republic (GDR) and in the Soviet Union people are not allowed to demonstrate against nuclear arms. Do you know if a peace movement exists in these places? Does the Green Party demonstrate in the GDR?

Kelly:

First of all, we have quite a lot of contact with the Swords Into Ploughshares movement, with the Women for Peace in the GDR, with the Protestant and Catholic churches in the GDR, and with many individuals who are trying to resist the draft. We also have contact with the Helsinki Watch committees and many other people in the Soviet Union.

Because I am a member of Parliament, I have been able to contact these groups more easily than others could. It is a privilege that M.P.s have. However, sometimes this has led to very uncomfortable situations. In May 1983, when Gert Bastian, other Green Party members and I went to the square in the Alexanderplatz in East Berlin to demand, as we demand anywhere, unilateral steps toward disarmament, we were arrested. After demanding to see President Honecker (of the German Democratic Republic) in an open letter, it became quite an unusual situation; that open letter was published in an East German newspaper, as was his reply to us. Finally, we had a long discussion with him in November 1983. We have also tried to initiate spontaneous, joint nonviolent actions with East Germans. Because of this, the East German government has refused to allow some of us to return to the GDR for a year. I describe this kind of treatment wherever it happens: the Greens have been arrested in Turkey just as often. It doesn't make any difference where we demonstrate. We Greens were arrested in Ankara in Turkey—our NATO ally—and taken to prison for a longer time than in Germany.

250

This shows that all these governments have something in common: they praise the peace movements of the other side, but they ignore their own independent peace groups. Our German government *always* praises the peace movements on the other side, but never our own. The peace movements in all countries have to walk a tightrope between the major military blocs, and become more loyal to each other. The contact that we have had with other Eastern European human rights groups has shown me that we are really one people, and we are all striving for the same thing. The peace movement must exercise its right to speak with whomever it likes, regardless of ideology or walls or blocs.

Davies:
Would you comment on the idea of diverting a portion of one's taxes to peaceful rather than military uses, as Conscience Canada proposes with its peace tax fund? Is this an effective form of political pressure?

Anderton:
The New Zealand Labour government has a policy that it will increase the level of aid to the developing world over the very small amount that we actually give. This is something like $100 million. Even though we are a very small country, this is only about 0.25 percent of our gross national product. The aim, internationally, is 0.7 percent.* Now this would mean New Zealand's giving something like $300 to $400 million instead of $100 million. Our Foreign Affairs Select Committee proposed that appropriation to the minister of Finance. After he had been resuscitated from the medical emergency caused by this bold suggestion, we brought him around to consider moving it up to 0.5 percent per year so that at least we would make some forward progress.

I think that politicians underestimate the commitment to international justice by the majority of their citizens. I think they would find support for a more generous policy if they took the majority of citizens into their confidence—if they explained and communicated and used the power of the state to show them what conditions are like and what needs there are in the rest of the world to obtain a just economic order. We sometimes do see outpourings of public support, for example, in the aid for Ethiopia—but surely we don't have to see hundreds of millions of starving children in front of us on television before we act. I have more respect for the intelligence and the integrity of people on this planet than that, and I wish other politicians did too.

* The United Nations has called on all developed countries to contribute annually at least 0.7 percent of their gross national product as aid to the Third World. As of 1985, only Sweden, Norway, Denmark and the Netherlands had met this goal. —Ed.

Ruddock:

Our experience in Britain is the other way around: it is not what we are giving money to that is a question, it is what we are withholding money from. In Britain we have a peace tax campaign in which people decide for themselves how much of their taxes they think should actually go to armaments. Some people object to all armaments; some people object to nuclear weapons only. So each person works out what percentage of his or her taxes is going to pay for objectionable armaments, and then they refuse to pay that amount of money to the government.

If you have an employer it is very difficult to do this, because you have to persuade your employer to withhold it for you. If you are self-employed, and thankfully there are many people in the peace movement who do have that option, then it is possible to do this on your own. I am glad to say that this is a very considerable, growing movement. By with-holding taxes, people feel again that an individual can do something on the basis of conscience. The penalties, I'm afraid, are very strict. People who have gone on appealing and appealing against guilty sentences in the courts ultimately have lost their appeals; they have, because of their refusal to pay taxes, actually gone to prison. But it is another way to demonstrate your commitment and your conscience. I am delighted people are prepared to do that.

PART V

What Can Governments Do for Peace?

Paul Warnke

CHAPTER 25

What Governments Can Do To Prevent Nuclear War And Promote Multilateral Disarmament

PAUL C. WARNKE

Even in the most boisterous of democracies, like Canada and the United States, only the government can take formal action to lessen the risk of nuclear war. Citizens can protest or applaud, but government officials decide. We can, however, grade them on their performance. I intend to do so here. For purposes of this discussion, I will divide governments into three categories and suggest what they might do to remedy past failures and improve the prospects for nuclear sanity. First, I will deal with the performance of the nuclear superpowers; second, with the record of allied countries; and third, with the possibilities for effective action by nonaligned countries.

The history to date of the atomic age, in terms of controlling nuclear arms and lessening the risk of nuclear war, is one of wasted opportunities

Paul Warnke is the former director of the United States Arms Control and Disarmament Agency and was the Chief United States negotiator during the Strategic Arms Limitation Talks in 1977 and 1978. These negotiations led to the SALT II agreement which, although never ratified by the United States Senate, has so far been adhered to by both the Soviet Union and the United States. After practicing law from 1948 to 1966, Paul Warnke was appointed general counsel to the American Department of Defense and subsequently became assistant secretary of defense for International Security Affairs. In this position he voiced concern about American military involvement in Vietnam—an unpopular and unusual position for government officials to take at that time. Mr. Warnke is now a prominent lawyer with Clifford and Warnke Attorneys at Law in Washington, D.C.

and misapplied priorities. The two nuclear superpowers, the Soviet Union and the United States, have made bold statements about ridding the world of nuclear weapons. But at the same time they have built up strategic arsenals of over ten thousand warheads each. When the tactical battlefield nuclear weapons are added in, the number of nuclear weapons which both together possess is about sixty thousand; almost all have a destructive power greater than the atomic bomb which leveled Hiroshima, and many are in the megaton category.

Any sane analyst must recognize that these weapons have no genuine military utility. They cannot be used without courting national devastation and perhaps an end to all civilized human life. Yet, faced with this gravest of dangers, the avoidance of which should be an overriding common interest, neither the United States nor the Soviet Union has met its responsibility. Instead, their unthinking resort to military force in response to far less grievous threats has derailed progress in arms control at critical points.

The examples are tragically many. As a result of preliminary discussions between the United States and the Soviet Union, the stage was reached in early August 1968 when concurrent announcements were to be made in Moscow and Washington about the initiation of the Strategic Arms Limitation Treaty (SALT) talks later that year. On the very day of the planned announcements, however, Soviet tanks and troops moved against a government in Czechoslovakia that appeared to be departing from ideological orthodoxy.

As a result, the talks on limiting strategic arms were delayed for a year, and during that year deployment of MIRVed (multiple independently-targetable re-entry vehicles) missiles began. It is these missiles, each with the ability to direct three, six, ten or even fourteen warheads at separate targets, which have given rise to concern about preemptive strikes. The retaliatory deterrent on which both sides depend for security has thus been perceived as more vulnerable, and accordingly both the number and types of nuclear weapons have been increased. Also as a result, the Soviet Union is less secure today than if it had withheld its armed fist in August of 1968.

Again in 1979, the Soviet resort to military power to shore up the government of its choice in Afghanistan not only prevented ratification of the SALT II Treaty but delayed the resumption of talks until well into the first term of the Reagan administration. Between 1979 and 1982, both sides developed weapons of greater accuracy. Sea-launched cruise missiles, virtually impossible to count and limit numerically, were deployed.

Currently, the use of American bombers against Libya, in an ill-conceived response to international terrorism, has at least delayed preparations for a second summit meeting between President Reagan and General Secretary Gorbachev. In addition, the ill-advised furnishing of American and Soviet arms to regional combatants and contending sides in civil wars sours the dialogue and flattens the hopes for constructive negotiations. Military force continues to prove itself an inept instrument of foreign policy.

Just forty-one years ago, the United States and the Soviet Union had put aside their ideological and political differences to end what was then the greatest danger to human society—the threat of Hitler's Nazi Germany. The leaders of these two nations should be charged now with meeting their responsibility to humankind in dealing with the even graver risk of nuclear war. The present pattern of sparring for advantage by military intervention in the affairs of other nations must be broken and the common threat addressed as the paramount priority.

With regard to the countries aligned with the nuclear superpowers in their respective military pacts, I will leave it to my Soviet colleague to talk about the Warsaw Pact. From my standpoint, however, I must say that I don't believe our NATO partners are playing a particularly constructive role in dealing with the nuclear issue. Take, for example, the question of the so-called intermediate-range nuclear forces. In sharp contrast to the deep concern expressed in Western Europe about the 1983 deployment of the American Pershing II ballistic missiles and ground-launched cruise missiles, we now hear some European opposition to the idea of withdrawing these weapons, even if, as Mr. Gorbachev suggested in his January proposals, the Soviet Union eliminates its European-based SS-20s. What we find is a renewal of reliance on "extended deterrence," the footless and perilous strategy of threatening to convert any conventional military conflict in Europe into a nuclear exchange. Suggestions that NATO should move toward a policy of no first use are greeted with anguish rather than thoughtful consideration.

We and our allies should agree, once and for all, that nuclear weapons cannot be designed and used to fight, survive and win a nuclear war. Instead, as President Reagan himself observed in his State of the Union speech in February 1984: "The only purpose of either side's having nuclear weapons is to see to it that they are never used."

Also disappointing is the reaction of the French and British to the fact that Soviet elimination of the SS-20s directed against European targets would require that they not proceed with the planned major expansion of their nuclear forces. It is, I submit, unrealistic to insist that the United States can negotiate about Soviet weapons that can hit Western Europe but not the United States, and yet contend that the proposed quintupling of Western European missiles that can hit Soviet territory must be ignored.

Moreover, if we really believe that nuclear arms should be limited and reduced, then all countries should be discouraged from acquiring or increasing them. I am against any more nuclear weapons, whether they are Russian, American, French, British or Chinese. We are entitled, I believe, to count on our allies to co-operate with us in preventing nuclear war and promoting nuclear disarmament.

With regard to the third category of countries, I welcome the efforts that have been undertaken by the six world leaders—President Alfonsin of Argentina, Prime Minister Papandreou of Greece, Prime Minister Rajiv Gandhi of India, President de la Madrid of Mexico, President Nyerere of Tanzania and Prime Minister Palme of Sweden, tragically lost to the world by an assassin's bullet. Their Five Continent Peace Initiative marshalls the moral force of world opinion to appeal to the nuclear superpowers to downgrade their differences and give top priority to avoiding the nuclear cataclysm.

The answer to the nuclear dilemma is not the futile pursuit of nuclear supremacy. That's gone forever. Neither the United States nor the Soviet Union will be willing to trust its security to the indulgence of the other side. Accordingly, each country will do whatever is necessary to maintain its ability to deter the other side from using, or threatening to use, its nuclear forces.

The other countries of the world, however small, are populated by human beings who have a right to exist without the constant dread of nuclear obliteration. Such ventures as the Five Continent Peace Initiative and the Great Peace Journey, chaired by Inga Thorsson of Sweden, are imaginative efforts to bring the nuclear superpowers to their senses and to insure human survival.

What are some of the steps that could be readily and speedily taken? First, it is essential that the United States and the Soviet Union recognize that greater security against the nuclear threat can only be achieved by mutual measures of arms control. Both should recognize their mutual vulnerability. Not even their immense strength can save them from the ravages of a nuclear war. Neither communists nor capitalists are fireproof or blast-resistant.

American officials who are skeptical about arms control frequently contend that the Soviet leaders do not accept "the dogma of agreed vulnerability." They suggest that the concept of Mutual Assured Destruction is simply a theory that has been discredited, rather than an inescapable fact. This is the basic argument that undergirds the American Strategic Defense Initiative. Secretary of Defense Caspar Weinberger argues that this change in American strategy "stands alone as the right, and indeed, the only thing to do to remove the threat of mutual destruction, regardless of Soviet activities."

This is the counsel of folly. I know of no one who likes the fact that security today depends upon the threat of retaliation. But unappealing as this may be, it is the best protection against nuclear war until the time at which a new world order may permit the total eradication of all national nuclear forces. An effort to escape from this mutual hostage relationship, by unilateral build-up of either strategic offence or strategic defence, will mean only a world in which each side, at a time of crisis, will begin to wonder how long it dare wait before launching its weapons in panic and desperation.

The negotiation of a genuine, comprehensive arms-control treaty will take years. But there are certain interim steps that can be taken in the right direction. These must be based on the recognition that neither side will sacrifice its retaliatory deterrent, that neither side will co-operate in giving the other an invulnerability that it lacks itself.

Accordingly, as a precondition to major reductions in offensive arms, both the Soviet Union and the United States must undertake to limit their strategic defence efforts to basic laboratory research. They could then reach agreement to cut offensive forces by at least ten percent a year for the next several years, conducting these cuts in accordance with the ceilings and sub-ceilings negotiated in the SALT II Treaty. This would mean cuts in the overall total of MIRVed missiles, as well as in the numbers, allowed under a separate ceiling, of the most destabilizing of strategic weapons, the MIRVed silo-based ICBMs (intercontinental ballistic missiles).

With regard to intermediate-range nuclear missiles, the Soviet Union should agree to pull back from East Germany and Czechoslovakia those shorter-range nuclear missiles that it moved forward in response to deployment of American Pershing II and cruise missiles in Western Europe. This withdrawal should take place immediately, in response to the agreed withdrawal of the American intermediate-range nuclear forces and the Soviet SS-20s.

The United States cannot, of course, negotiate controls over British and French nuclear forces. It can, however, agree that the Soviet Union would be entitled to match in intermediate-range nuclear warheads any significant increase in those deployed by the British and French. Our Western European allies must recognize that, inasmuch as they are part of our side for purposes of Soviet nuclear weapons reductions, it is only reasonable for the Soviets to treat their nuclear forces as part of our side.

As called for by the six world leaders of the Five Continent Peace Initiative, negotiations for a comprehensive nuclear weapons test ban should be completed without delay. The only argument against a test ban is that it would block development of new nuclear weapons. This is also the best argument for it.

Additionally, the United States and the Soviet Union should agree to ban any further testing or development of anti-satellite weapons. Not only is it impossible to draw a clear line between anti-satellite and anti-missile capability, but satellites in fixed orbits can be destroyed far more easily than ballistic warheads. An attack on satellites at a time of tension would be tantamount to an act of war.

Finally, the threat of conventional hostilities that could escalate to a nuclear exchange can be significantly lessened by a prompt agreement that NATO and the Warsaw Pact will both adopt a purely defensive posture in Central Europe. This would mean decreasing the mobility of their forces and pulling back the heavy armoured divisions from the central front. The concern about surprise attack would thus be greatly lessened. Moreover, there would then be created a powerful inhibition against moving the armoured divisions back to the East-West dividing line. A decision to move them back could not be made lightly, and would be recognized as sure to trigger a strong defensive reaction.

I recognize that these proposals are not dramatic and will be less than satisfactory to those seeking far-reaching disarmament. They would, however, greatly lessen the risk and the consequences of military conflict; and they can be done now, with no reassessment of fundamental premises and no waiting for resolution of other differences.

The real issue of international security today is not whether there will be a Pax Americana or a Pax Sovietica. It is whether collective human folly will achieve the poet's vision of Caesar's Pax Romana—whether we will create a solitude, with no one left to call it peace.

CHAPTER 26
Problems of Preventing Nuclear War

PROFESSOR VITALY ZHURKIN

One who visits Vancouver is struck by the many faces of this extremely beautiful city. One sees that it combines old and new, traditions and innovation, independence of spirit and openness toward a larger outside world. Probably the reason for this is that since discovery of the site by Captain George Vancouver in the eighteenth century, and since it began to become a city exactly one hundred years ago, when the transcontinental railroad reached it, Vancouver was never self-centred. This is because it has been at the crossroads of trade, political, and cultural routes, and closely connected with the wider world.

In our days, in the present decade, this close interdependence between the city of Vancouver and the outside world has expressed itself in a distinctive contribution of the people of this city to the growing worldwide movement against the danger of nuclear war: the famous Vancouver Walks for Peace, which started in the 1980s.

Today, there is a closer relationship between contemporary and future worries than has ever existed before. The obvious reason for this fact is that the world is rapidly becoming smaller and more interdependent. It consists of many nations with their varied legitimate interests. The modern world is complicated, diverse and dynamic, and shot through with contending tendencies and contradictions. It is a world of the most troublesome alternatives, anxieties and hopes. Never before has our home on earth been exposed to such great political and physical stress. Never before has man exacted so great a tribute from nature, and never have people been so vulnerable to the forces they themselves have created.

Similar problems face even quite economically developed countries;

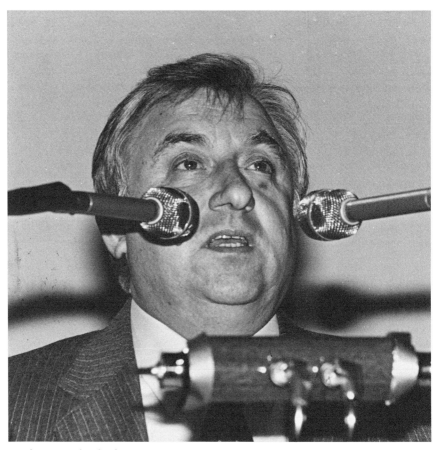

Professor Vitaly Zhurkin

while the Third World faces even greater difficulties—poverty, hunger, disease, and the gigantic debts the developing nations owe to major imperialist powers.

At the same time, the central point of the interdependence of contemporary humanity is clearly evident and widely recognized. The world must unite against the danger of self-destruction in the flames of nuclear war. The modern world has become much too small and fragile for wars and policies based on military strength. It cannot be saved and preserved if humankind continues to believe, as it has for centuries, that wars are permissible and acceptable. This idea must be shed once and for all, resolutely and irrevocably.

Throughout the world, people have grown to understand the immense dangers of nuclear war and a kind of rebellion has sprung up against nuclear weapons, a growing demand to prohibit their testing, production and deployment, and finally to get rid of them altogether. Today this demand unites more and more people. There are three main reasons for the growing desire for disarmament. The first and most obvious one is that as an understanding of the dangers of nuclear war grows, so does humanity's latent impulse for self-preservation. The second reason is that it has become increasingly clear that if the arms race continues, fuelled by the United States and its allies, terrible dangers lie ahead. Whatever new weapons we consider—the MX or Midgetman missile, Pershing II or cruise missile, or space weapons—each is more accurate, more deadly, more destabilizing and less controllable than its predecessor. The third reason for the growing desire to eliminate nuclear weapons comes from a concern about the consequences of further extremely dangerous and provocative actions by the United States, such as its attack against Libya. This was a clear-cut and blatant example of state terrorism directed against the population of an independent country, and a member of the United Nations.

More and more the question faces all of humanity: in what form shall we enter the next century, the next millennium? Will we still be in the process of ever increasing the arms race and the danger of war? Or by

Professor Vitaly Zhurkin is the deputy director of the United States and Canada Studies Institute of the USSR Academy of Sciences. He graduated from the Moscow Institute of International Relations, specializing in the study of international conflict, problems of military and political strategy, and arms control and disarmament. Professor Zhurkin is the author of numerous articles on these subjects, published both in the Soviet Union and internationally. Vitaly Zhurkin is the vice-president of the Soviet Association of Political Scientists, and a member of the Executive Committee of the Soviet United Nations Association.

concentrating our efforts, as the Soviet Union proposes, will we develop new approaches to the major problems facing humanity, above all the problem of war?

The Soviet Union recently developed new conceptual approaches to major world problems at the most important Soviet political forum, the Twenty-seventh Congress of the Communist Party of the Soviet Union. The Congress developed many novel ideas and new initiatives which represent the Soviet approach to these issues. These ideas are based on a growing realization that human thinking unfortunately can lag behind quickly changing realities. Therefore, we must rethink many customary attitudes to contemporary problems, including those in the political and military areas.

The Congress stressed that in the nuclear age no state can defend itself by military and technological means alone, even with the aid of the most up-to-date defences; security is increasingly becoming a political task, which can be resolved solely by political means. What is primarily required is the will to take the path of disarmament.

The principle of universal security was proclaimed as one of the important elements of Soviet foreign policy. This principle proceeds from the assumption that it is impossible today for one side to enjoy security at the expense of the other side.

The whole world watched during the four post-war decades while the United States drove ahead with plans to create its security at the other side's expense. This only provoked new and more dangerous spirals in the arms race. The United States was the first to create atom and hydrogen weapons; the first to deploy heavy intercontinental bombers; the first to deploy intercontinental ballistic missiles and submarine-launched cruise missiles; the first to start the process of MIRVing (MIRV: multiple independently targetable re-entry vehicle) their missiles; and the first to create and deploy cruise missiles. The Soviet Union was forced to react to all these attempts by the United States to gain military superiority. Today, the latest attempt to achieve military superiority is clearly embodied in the American Strategic Defense Initiative, the so-called Star Wars program.

These attempts to achieve superiority are doomed to failure. They only result in making life on our planet more dangerous. It is not possible to gain military superiority, to win an arms race, or a nuclear war for that matter, and attempts to do so cannot bring any kind of political gain.

It should be understood by everyone that security can only be reciprocal between the Soviet Union and the United States. And in international relations as a whole, security must be worldwide. The increasing dynamism of world development and the growing number of active participants in international politics have altered and complicated the world picture; but it is impossible to change this situation or set the clock back.

One must adapt oneself to reality. And that means learning to live in the present complex and controversial world, taking into account its realities and reckoning not only with one's own interests, but also with the interests of other countries and peoples in finding mutually acceptable solutions. At the Twenty-seventh Communist Party Congress, General Secretary Mikhail Gorbachev put it in these words: "Without shutting one's eyes to social, political and ideological contradictions, to master the science and art of behaving in international affairs with restraint and moderation, to live in a civilized manner, that is in the conditions of proper international communication and co-operation." Later, he said: "In the present situation there is no alternative to co-operation and interaction between all countries. Thus, the objective—I emphasize, objective—conditions have taken shape in which confrontation between capitalism and socialism can proceed *only and exclusively in forms of peaceful competition and peaceful contest.*" Realizing that the world we live in is becoming too small and too fragile for wars and power politics, for imperial ambitions, for a runaway arms race, or for ideological and political intolerance, the Soviet leadership appealed from the rostrum of the Congress to all countries and all peoples to co-operate in the name of peace and in the name of the future.

The Congress stressed that now, as never before, ways must be found for closer and more productive co-operation with governments, parties, and mass organizations and movements that are genuinely concerned about peace on earth and the destinies of all peoples. An all-embracing system of international security must be built which would include the military and political, as well as the economic and humanitarian spheres.

In the military arena, such a system would follow upon these fundamental steps:

1. The nuclear powers must renounce all plans for, or attempts at, nuclear or conventional war, either against each other or against third countries.

2. An arms race in space must be prevented, all nuclear weapons testing must cease, and all such weapons must be destroyed.

3. Chemical weapons development must be banned, existing chemical arsenals must be destroyed, and the development of all other means of mass destruction must be renounced.

4. The levels of all countries' military capabilities must be lowered to limits of reasonable adequacy.

5. Military alliances must be disbanded; as a step toward this, the enlargement and formation of new alliances must be renounced.

6. Military budgets must undergo balanced and proportionate reductions.

It is important to stress in this connection that the Soviet Union recognizes that the present level of both sides' nuclear arsenals is much too high. For the time being, these nuclear weapons ensure equal danger to each side—but only for the time being. If the nuclear arms race continues, the threat to both sides may become so great that even parity will cease to be a factor in preventing nuclear war. Consequently it is vital, in the first place, to make great reductions in the level of military arsenals. In our age, genuine equal security is guaranteed not by the highest possible, but by the *lowest possible level* of strategic parity. For genuine security, nuclear and other types of weapons of mass destruction must be totally excluded.

Nuclear disarmament is the key to strengthening both international and national security. The Soviet Union is the first state in the history of the nuclear age to propose an extensive and concrete program aimed at the complete and universal elimination of nuclear weapons within a precisely defined time frame. In the program presented by General Secretary Mikhail Gorbachev on January 15th, 1986, the Soviet Union proposed that a process of ridding the earth of nuclear weapons, while at the same time banning space-based weapons, should be implemented and completed within the next fifteen years—that is, by the year 2000.

Under this program, the Soviet Union has proposed that both the United States and the Soviet Union reduce by fifty percent those nuclear weapons which are capable of reaching each other's territory. The USSR considers this to be only a first stage, which would be followed by further reductions in Soviet and American arsenals, as well as in the arsenals of the other nuclear powers. Reliable verification, including on-site inspections, would also be established.

As is well known, the Soviet Union has for a long time been proposing to rid Europe of both medium-range and tactical nuclear weapons. As part of the first stage of this program, the Soviet Union believes that an agreement can be reached to eliminate completely both Soviet and American medium-range missiles in the European zone—including both ballistic and cruise missiles. By reaching such an agreement, the two powers would take a first step toward ridding the European continent of nuclear weapons. At the same time, the United States should not, of course, supply its strategic and medium-range missiles to other countries, and the United Kingdom and France should pledge not to build up their own nuclear arsenals. American and Soviet medium-range nuclear weapons would be completely eliminated in the further stages of the program.

The Soviet Union also proposes that in this century chemical weapons should be completely banned, and all existing stockpiles eliminated. The industrial base for their production should be made subject to strict control, including international on-site inspections. The Soviet Union proposes a ban on the development of non-nuclear weapons which, based on new physical principles, would be as destructive as nuclear weapons, or other weapons of mass destruction. To implement this program for reducing and eliminating nuclear arsenals, we must set in motion the entire existing system of negotiations, and ensure that disarmament is pursued as efficiently as possible.

Characteristically, the Soviet approach features a serious desire to consider opinions and realistic ideas proposed by the people and mass movements of the other side, as well as those proposed by official circles. A number of examples vividly illustrate this point.

For a long time, many in the West felt that the Soviet Union should give more detailed consideration to verification of future arms limitations and reductions. In the program presented on January 15th, 1986, as well as in a number of the latest Soviet disarmament proposals, a very detailed approach to all aspects of verification has been developed.

But ever since the Soviet Union declared a unilateral moratorium on nuclear weapons tests and appealed to the United States to join this moratorium, American official circles have exaggerated the problem of verification. They have refused to stop nuclear testing, under the pretext that a moratorium is "impossible" to verify without on-site inspection. The Soviet Union recently proposed to include on-site inspections in the inventory of verification measures. The United States nevertheless has continued testing, and acknowledged that the real reason for it is their desire to modernize their nuclear potential and pursue Star Wars research. It has thus been proven that their verification objections were simply a propagandistic diversion.

The West has repeatedly stated that the Soviet Union does not back up its nuclear disarmament program with proposals for reducing conventional arms. As is now known, the Soviet Union has made detailed and far-reaching proposals for substantially reducing conventional forces, as well as strategic and tactical nuclear forces, in Europe. In addition, the Soviet Union has proposed strengthening international security in the Far Eastern-Pacific area.

It is very important for me to explain the Soviet attitude to Star Wars, or the Strategic Defense Initiative—in other words, American plans to place weapons in outer space. These plans are sometimes presented as an alternative to deterrence. In reality, they are another attempt to develop first-strike nuclear capabilities.

The first element in the new large-scale American project which evokes Soviet concern, is that it sends the arms race spiralling into outer space, an arena that heretofore has been outside the limits of the arms race. If a country wants to do away with nuclear weapons, it logically follows a simple and clear path for their reduction and, finally, for their total elimination. Instead, the United States proposes that existing nuclear arsenals, with their tremendous overkill potential, should be augmented with space-based weapons whose new possibilities for mass destruction have not even been fully studied.

Fourteen years ago, during "the great debate," American, Soviet and other scientists and politicians came to a unanimous conclusion about any large-scale anti-ballistic missile system. It could "shield" the country possessing the system from a nuclear retaliation only if that country had already launched a first strike and weakened its opponent's retaliatory forces. In other words, a shield is the most important element for those who contemplate a nuclear attack.

The fact that weapons are intended now to become space-based does not change this view in the least. On the contrary, this fact makes it even more convincing. Space weapons are not defensive weapons. They are a direct extension of the most dangerous offensive strategic armaments—the first-strike weapons.

Star Wars plans would undermine the fundamentals of strategic stability. A situation would arise where major decisions with irreversible consequences would be made essentially by electronic machines. Human reason, political will and morality would have no part in the decision-making process. An error, a miscalculation, or a technical failure of highly complicated computer systems, could lead to catastrophe.

The Star Wars program is a large-scale plan for developing new weapons which threaten all humankind. The world community of nations was on a similar threshold forty years ago, when the nuclear age had just begun. The resulting arms race has led eventually to the stockpiling of immense nuclear arsenals which can terminate human history. From the beginning, attempts to thwart this most dangerous process were unsuccessful, even though as early as 1946 the Soviet Union proposed an international convention aimed at banning production and use of nuclear weapons, and has since then been a staunch supporter of nuclear disarmament.

Now, forty years later, the international community has a real chance to avoid repeating such a mistake: it can prevent the development of an arms race in space. Here again, the Soviet position is unambiguous: it puts forward a concept of "Star Peace" to counter the Star Wars plans.

The Soviet Union understands that concepts of international security have more aspects than just their military ones. The Soviet concept of an all-embracing international security system includes these political principles: a strict respect for the right of each people to choose independently the ways and forms of its own development; the just political settlement of international crises and regional conflicts; the development of measures to build confidence between states; the creation of effective guarantees against attack from without; the inviolability of each country's frontiers; and the development of effective ways to prevent international terrorism, including methods which would ensure the safety of international land, air, and sea communications. A system of international security also should include economic principles, including the establishment of a new world economic order guaranteeing equal economic security to all countries.

Humanity today faces a question of paramount importance. Is it possible to stop the downward spiral into nuclear war, and build a real system of collective security? There is only one answer to this question: Yes! To this unprecedented challenge, I believe that humanity is able to, and *will* present an unprecedented response. The danger of war should and will be eliminated!

Professor Michael Pentz

CHAPTER 27

To Prevent Nuclear War and Promote Nuclear Disarmament: It's Time for a New Look

PROFESSOR MICHAEL PENTZ

SOME BASIC QUESTIONS

As the title of this final session of the symposium, and the title of this paper imply, to prevent nuclear war we must first achieve nuclear disarmament. This in turn requires that we first stop the nuclear arms race. Therefore, we must begin by appraising the nuclear arms race itself.

Discussions about what governments (or individuals or peace movements) can do to end the nuclear arms race and move towards nuclear disarmament are often bedevilled by the many different definitions of arms-control terms. Those involved in discussions often seem to talk past, rather than to, each other. They use terms such as "nuclear deterrence," "the nuclear strategic balance," "countermeasures to restore the military balance," "disarmament measures based on equality and equal security," "the principle of parity and equal security," "balanced multi-

Professor Michael Pentz was born in South Africa and emigrated to the United Kingdom in 1947, where he taught physics and conducted research on nuclear fusion and microwave spectroscopy at the Imperial College of Science and Technology in London. He worked for eleven years at the European Organization for Nuclear Research (CERN) in Geneva. In 1969, he became the dean of the Faculty of Science at Britain's Open University, one of the world's leading distance-learning institutions for undergraduate and postgraduate education. He served in this position until his retirement in 1986. Professor Pentz was Vice Chairperson of the Campaign for Nuclear Disarmament (CND) in Britain from 1982 to 1984, and he was the founding chair from 1982 to 1985 of Scientists Against Nuclear Arms (SANA).

271

lateral nuclear disarmament," "unilateral nuclear disarmament"—all of which contain important hidden premises about the nature of nuclear weapons and the nuclear arms race. If those engaged in the discussion define these terms differently, then dialogue becomes fruitless.

Politicians and the press have asserted *ad nauseum* that nuclear weapons have kept the peace for *x* number of years (*x* is currently equal to about forty). They imply by this that if we just carry on stockpiling more and "better" nuclear weapons, our weapons will keep the peace for another *x* number of years. My first premise is that this assertion is not only unproven (and unprovable) but is also dangerously misleading. In reality, the nuclear arms race has already greatly decreased national and international security. The so-called strategic balance which is already fundamentally unstable, is becoming even more tenuous because of developments in nuclear weapon systems. Unless we stop and reverse the present trend, the outcome inevitably will be the ultimate catastrophe of nuclear war.

So before we can answer the question of what governments can do to prevent nuclear war—be they nuclear or non-nuclear states, or "great," "middle" or "small" powers—we need to take a closer look at the nuclear arms race and ask ourselves: what is this thing, what's happening with it, what drives it?

THE NUCLEAR ARMS RACE: A REAPPRAISAL

The nuclear junk-heap.   Essentially, the nuclear arms race is a competition between the Soviet Union and the United States, as a result of which they have now accumulated between them about fifty thousand nuclear weapons. Furthermore, the pace of the race is about to heat up once again; the total numbers of weapons will almost certainly increase quite sharply over the next decade or so, and the quality of these weapons and delivery systems will also change. Though there is occasional talk of superiority being the aim of the arms race, the more respectable explanation is that it is a matter of maintaining a thing called "strategic parity." Since each side's concept of parity involves matching the other side's nuclear arsenal somehow, and since each side misapplies worst case analysis when appraising the other side's capability and intentions (1, ch. 7),* the quest for parity by one side always looks to the other like a quest for superiority, whether it is such in reality or not. The process is therefore self-sustaining.

As a minor complication, three other countries (up to now) with pretensions to great-power status—the United Kingdom, France and China —play their own little games with nuclear weapons around the edges of

* See References and Notes at the end of this chapter.—ED.

the central contest. They claim that they do not really contribute to the nuclear arms race, but that, in a world where some countries have nuclear weapons (including some whose regimes are, unlike theirs, "nasty"), the only way to be secure is to have their own "independent nuclear deterrent." Other countries are, of course, discouraged from following this example; instead, they are urged to sign the Non-Proliferation Treaty.

If one looks at the numbers of nuclear warheads which the two major nuclear powers have stockpiled over the past twenty years or so, the progress of the race so far seems pretty clear. Counting only those warheads on long-range strategic missiles, an American advantage in 1965 of about 1,600 to the Soviet's 300 has been replaced by a Soviet advantage in 1985 of about 9,200 to the United State's 7,700. In fact, however, the United States compensates with a substantial advantage in nuclear warheads carried by long-range bombers (it has over 4,000; the Soviet Union about 800).

Since these numbers of warheads are very much larger than would be required for mutual deterrence, one must find some other measurement of parity or disparity, preferably one that relates somewhat to current targeting strategies. One such measurement is lethality. This is measured by the explosive yield of the warhead, and more critically by the accuracy with which the warhead can be delivered to the target (2, pp. 54–55; 3, pp. 58–69). Lethality is a measure of counterforce capability —the ability to destroy individual targets such as missile silos or command and control centres. Twenty years ago, the total lethality of American nuclear missiles was ten times greater than that of the Soviet Union. The Soviet Union closed this lethality gap when they caught up in 1979 and 1980. Now, however, the United States has opened wide the gap again by deploying cruise, Trident II and MX missiles—all of which are much more accurate than the previous generation of missiles. The gap will remain open until the Soviet Union, by improving the accuracy of its land and submarine-based missiles and possibly by deploying its own long-range cruise missiles, closes it once more.

Parallel with the deployment of more nuclear weapons with ever greater counterforce capability, there has been, at least in the United States, a spate of nuclear war-fighting theories to justify the abandonment of old-fashioned deterrence (in which one merely possesses nuclear weapons but has no intention of using them).

Nuclear deterrence is obviously an unstable system. Leaving aside the moral, legal and logical objections to the notion of nuclear deterrence based upon the threat of Mutually Assured Destruction, and assuming that such classical nuclear deterrence could, in principle, be effective, we need only ask: how many nuclear warheads on each side would suffice for the purpose? It is obvious that a few tens, or at most a few hundreds, each one capable of devastating a city would be enough. Yet there are now at least 35,000 American and Soviet nuclear warheads that can hit targets more than 500 kilometres (over 300 miles) away. Nearly 24,000 of these can hit targets more than 5,000 kilometres (3100 miles) away. If the system of deterrence is stabilizing, then why has the number of warheads grown to several hundred times greater than necessary, and why are the delivery systems so much more accurate than they need to be for deterrence?

If the present feeble constraints of SALT I and SALT II are broken—and it seems increasingly likely that they will be—the numbers of strategic nuclear warheads and the accuracy of their delivery systems will rapidly increase in the next decade or so. In other words, a more dramatic escalation in nuclear war-fighting capability will take place than has ever occurred before. Any significant deployment of anti-missile weapons (so-called strategic defence systems) will make such an escalation inevitable and limited only by economic resources.

The external appearances of the nuclear arms race are clear enough, and it is happening; it is even accelerating. And its final outcome will be catastrophic. Yet, when we examine more closely the characteristics of nuclear weapons, and the strategies for their use (1,3), we find a paradox: nuclear weapons "can serve no military purpose whatsoever... when both are properly understood, the nuclear weapon and security are seen to belong in different worlds (1, introduction)." Indeed, there are serious grounds for doubting, with George Kennan, "whether these devices are really weapons at all (3)." Robert S. McNamara, a former American secretary of defence, analyzed the military usefulness of nuclear weapons and concluded that "they are totally useless—except only to deter one's opponent from using them (4)." As I pointed out in Vancouver's 1984 symposium, *Nuclear War: the Search for Solutions:* "Even if one agrees —which I do not—that McNamara's exception is valid, one is confronted here with a weapon with the unprecedented characteristic that it is useful only if you do not use it. One can see why Kennan had his doubts about whether these things are really weapons at all (3)."

If nuclear weapons are really not weapons at all, then the term arms race is also misleading. Even the word race does not properly define the process through which these weapons are accumulated. In a race, one can rationally judge whether one side is ahead, or one behind, or whether they are roughly equal. But there is no way to judge which side is ahead in the nuclear arms race, for there are no rational strategies for the use of nuclear weapons. Is one side winning the race if it can devastate its opponent's cities thirty times over, while its opponent can only devastate the first side's cities twenty-five times over? In terms of counterforce strategy, the present Soviet missile force is (if one makes fairly optimistic assumptions) capable of destroying about fifty-seven percent of the American missile silos, whereas (making the same assumptions) the American missile force is capable of destroying only about fifty-one percent of the Soviet missile silos. Does this mean that the Soviet Union is ahead of the United States? To dispel this idea, one need only think about the retaliatory capacity of the American intercontinental ballistic missiles (ICBMs), not to mention the destructive power of the relatively invulnerable American nuclear submarines and long-range bombers.

It is a strange race indeed: when it ends there can be no final winners, only losers: and among the losers will be the spectators, as well as the participants.

So, "the nuclear arms race" is a double misnomer. Firstly, nuclear explosive devices are not "arms" because, completely ignoring their morality or legality, they cannot be used in conflicts or wars to achieve rational military, political or economic goals. Even their threatened use is irrational. Secondly, the process of stockpiling these devices is not a "race," because there is no way to judge who is ahead or who has won.

Suppose, for the sake of argument, we accept McNamara's view that nuclear weapons can have only one use — "to deter one's opponent from using them." It follows that somewhere between ninety-five and ninety-nine percent of the existing stockpiles have absolutely no utility at all. Coincidentally, nuclear winter may be triggered by the explosion of as little as one to five percent of the current nuclear stockpiles (5). The detonation over cities of as little as one hundred megatons (less than one percent of the total explosive yield of the American and Soviet stockpiles) might be sufficient to produce a climatic catastophe of the nuclear winter type (5).

When one looks closely at the nature of nuclear "weapons," the first conclusion one reaches is that ninety-five to ninety-nine percent of the present stockpile is militarily useless. Therefore, we must ask ourselves why so much money and effort is being spent on useless nuclear "weapons." Why are the nuclear powers piling even more nuclear junk on top of their already mountainous junk-heaps? Why do some officials even propose to spend many billions of dollars developing "strategic defence" systems with the avowed purpose of making these same useless nuclear weapons obsolete? Would it not be simpler, cheaper and more rational simply to scrap all, or nearly all, of them? Why is there so much fuss about even setting some sort of limit, or imposing even a temporary freeze, on the numbers of devices each side can have?

The doomsday machine.   The process of escalation by one side, countered by further escalations by the other side, is profoundly irrational. It has all the appearances of a doomsday machine, with its own internal momentum. Self-propelled and out of control, it careens crazily toward the final abyss. To understand the inner reality of the nuclear arms race, we have to try to discover the inner workings of this doomsday machine.

The driving force of the machine appears to be what has been called the military-industrial-bureaucratic-technical-scientific complex. The individual politicians, military men, scientists, engineers and businessmen who make up this complex seem to be imprisoned within it; they cannot control or escape from it. Every now and again an individual emerges from the machinery, usually through retirement, and gives us some insights into the way it works and into the utter irrationality of its behaviour. We usually discover that the individual concerned has been aware, perhaps for years, of the fundamental truth of Lord Mountbatten's declaration: "The nuclear arms race has no military purpose. Wars cannot be fought with nuclear weapons. Their existence only adds to our perils because of the illusions they have generated."

And when we ask why this individual did not speak out against this peril sooner, we obtain even more interesting insights into the web of perfectly ordinary, understandable mechanisms of entrapment within the complex.

Of course, the complexes of the Soviet Union and the United States operate very differently, especially because of the powerful arms industry lobby in the United States, which has no counterpart in the Soviet Union. It seems, however, that the military, bureaucratic, technological and scientific pressures within the Soviet doomsday machine function in broadly similar ways to their American counterparts.

The two countries fuel their machines similarly: they fear each other, mistrust each other's intentions, chronically misuse worst case analysis and overestimate each other's capabilities. Both countries (and indeed, the minor nuclear-weapons countries like Britain) lubricate the machinery with illusions, self-deceptions and rationalizations that might be collectively described as nukethink. This takes a variety of forms (I will discuss some examples later), but nukethink's basic failure is its inability to grasp the fact that nuclear weapons simply cannot be placed in the same category as battleships, tanks, artillery or infantry divisions, or any other real weapons.

WHAT CAN INDIVIDUALS DO?

The history of the nuclear arms race—or, in other words, the story of how the doomsday machine has taken shape, and the course it has followed over the past forty years—reveals that humanity is confronted with an unprecedented phenomenon. It is not only irrational and ultimately suicidal. It is also clearly outside the control of existing political decision-making systems. In spite of numerous declarations, such as those made by the United Nations General Assembly, that nuclear disarmament is the most urgent and important of all human needs, the nuclear-weapons powers have not agreed to a single nuclear disarmament measure. It is freely admitted that the nuclear arms race has increased the danger of war and decreased the security of the nuclear-weapons powers, and, indeed of the entire world. Yet the nuclear arms race continues, and governments seem incapable even of slowing it down, let alone stopping it.

I drew attention to this problem and its implications in my contribution to the 1984 Vancouver symposium:

> Whatever detailed practical measures might be considered as possible first steps back from the edge of the final abyss, such as a no first use treaty, a multilateral or unilateral freeze, a comprehensive nuclear test ban or independent nuclear disarmament measures, we must reckon with the fact that they will remain mere possibilities unless some completely new element, equally without precedent in our history, can be introduced, some new political force which is not imprisoned in the doomsday machine and which is strong enough to stop it and dismantle it.(3)

My point is that the situation calls for *external* intervention. This means that people must intervene—especially citizens of the nuclear-weapons states—and impose policy changes upon their governments. People can intervene in many ways, from large-scale campaigns organized by the peace movement to private lobbies and counselling sessions by individuals. The most appropriate forms vary from one country to another and from time to time. Because the nuclear-weapons states are the most deeply entrapped in the doomsday machinery, the governments of non-nuclear-weapons states must also intervene. Therefore, the people of countries without nuclear weapons must also pressure their own governments.

I concluded my contribution to the 1984 symposium with these words:

> I believe that such a new political force is beginning to emerge. It is the worldwide movement for nuclear disarmament and world peace. It is only just beginning to be aware of its own novelty and its own potential. The concept of massive democratic intervention in the processes of political decision-making—of no longer "leaving it to them"—is, I believe, a new one. It is true that history abounds with examples of political change brought about by popular pressures, expressed through the ballot box and through other forms of action, including armed struggle. The limited forms of democracy that exist, in the East and West,

were born of such popular struggles. What is needed now is more powerful and more universal. It is interventionist democracy at an altogether higher level than has ever before been achieved. If it is to succeed, in the limited time available, it will have to mobilize in effective action a majority of the peoples of at least the nuclear-weapons countries, with strong support from peoples and governments worldwide.(3)

Why is it proving so difficult to achieve this? I believe that the explanation lies in the pervasiveness of nukethink, in particular on the misconception that scrapping most of the nuclear arsenals (whether unilaterally or multilaterally) would be a disarmament measure. It is commonplace to hear people say: ''Yes, of course, nuclear weapons are terrible, and there are far too many of them. But without them we'd be defenceless! So we can't risk getting rid of any of our own nuclear weapons unless we are sure that *they* are doing the same. We must preserve the strategic balance, otherwise *they* will be tempted to attack us.''

It is not only the generals and the politicians who talk about ''parity'' or ''strategic superiority,'' and it is not only the arms manufacturers and the weapons technologists who lobby the generals and the politicians with projects for gaining a ''decisive advantage'' or restoring ''parity''as the case may be). Unfortunately, the illusions of nukethink have pervaded the attitudes of doves as well as of hawks—nukethink riddles arms control literature and the language of the peace movement. For three years I was an elected officer, and am now a vice-president, of one of the largest peace movement organizations, the British Campaign for Nuclear Disarmament (CND). I would have had a hard time, in meetings with CND members and supporters, explaining that nuclear disarmament is not an immediate campaigning goal!

The politicians, the military, *and* the general public mainly resist proposals to reduce the numbers of nuclear ''weapons'' through unilateral initiatives, and even resist proposals to refrain from increasing numbers when the other side increases theirs. They resist because of their deep-seated belief that nuclear weapons ''defend'' and ''deter.'' They feel, therefore, that they must not allow the enemy to obtain even a temporary advantage in numbers.

A striking example of this occurred when Leonid Brezhnev offered to reduce the number of SS-20 missiles deployed in Europe. He stated that he did not require NATO to reduce its missiles commensurately, even though at that time both sides had approximately the same number of intermediate-range nuclear weapons. He required only that the United States agree not to deploy Pershing II and cruise missiles. Ordinary Soviet citizens responded by flooding the Soviet Peace committee with letters. Their gist was clear: ''What can Comrade Brezhnev be thinking of? Has he forgotten the lessons of history? How can he offer a strategic advantage to the Americans! Our only hope of peace and security lies in the strength of our defences.''

Nowadays, when we call for nuclear disarmament, we invite just such a response. Independent initiatives, it seems, are out of the question: they might upset ''parity'' and the ''strategic balance.'' It has to be ''balanced, multilateral nuclear disarmament,'' based on a prenegotiated treaty and including proper verification at all stages. In other words, we have reached the same old dead end, and it serves only as a convenient reason to continue the nuclear arms race.

What we need now is not necessarily *complete* nuclear disarmament. We do need to dismantle and scrap at least 47,000 nuclear warheads and their delivery systems. Thus our immediate need is not nuclear disarmament but nuclear junk disposal. This is the first essential step we must take towards security. If we follow this step with a transition to a ''third nuclear regime,''[†] in which *all* nuclear weapons are proscribed and dismantled (7), we might then be involved in complete nuclear disarmament, with all the difficulties entailed in preserving the balance and verifying compliance. At present, however, to argue about whether the remaining nuclear weapons have any military use, or would be moral or legal to possess or threaten to use, is irrelevant and divisive.

Three main views on how to achieve nuclear disarmament. People who want nuclear disarmament tend to see the problem in one of three ways. They either believe: 1) that *all* nuclear weapons are militarily useless—even for minimum deterrence; 2) that *most* nuclear weapons are useless—but a very few should be kept for minimum deterrence; or 3) that nuclear weapons *can* have a military purpose outside of minimum deterrence, and therefore reductions in arsenals must be balanced and bilateral or multilateral, so that one side won't gain an advantage during negotiations.

Those who believe that all nuclear weapons are militarily useless base their view on the fundamental immorality of using, or threatening to use, such weapons. They believe that nuclear deterence is incredible, inoperable and illusory—''the most dangerous collective fallacy of our time (8).'' For people with this view, the distinction between unilateral and bilateral disarmament is meaningless, since their goal is simply to get rid of all these useless and immoral devices.

[†]The ''second nuclear regime'' (essentially that of minimum deterrence) is that advocated by Garwin (7). The ''first regime'' is the current one, in which nations continue to possess nuclear weapons with declared purposes for them beyond simple deterrence or retaliation against nuclear attack. The ''third regime'' is one in which national possession of nuclear weapons would be proscribed.

Those who believe that *most* nuclear weapons are useless believe that disposing of most of them would not constitute disarmament. They do believe, however, that after disposing of ninety-five to ninety-nine percent of the existing nuclear weapons, the remaining weapons might be useful for deterrence (at the low levels of about 200 deliverable strategic warheads in each superpower's stockpile). People with this view do not make a distinction between bilateral and unilateral disarmament at the present nuclear weapon levels, but would make a distinction when it came time to dismantle the remaining one to five percent of the nuclear arsenal.

Those who believe in balanced multilateral disarmament think there are far too many nuclear weapons (as do the other two groups), and that the system is unstable. However, they believe that the way to reduce the nuclear arsenal is not simply to scrap all, or most, of it. They believe instead that reduction must be based on negotiation, and that a multilateral or bilateral freeze, stopping any further escalation, would be an important first step.

For the first two types of disarmament, the immediate requirement of nuclear garbage disposal does not involve defence, except in the sense that by disposing of useless and expensive hardware, along with illusions about nuclear defence, greater attention might be given to real defence issues. This, together with the relaxation in international tension that would follow from such massive reductions in nuclear arsenals, would increase national security.

Verifying this process would be simpler than verifying arms control or balanced arms reduction. The residual one to five percent of nuclear warheads retained from minimal deterrence would almost certainly be dispersed among several missile-launching nuclear submarines, so that each side would have at least one or two at sea at all times. All ICBMs and strategic bomber aircraft would be scrapped, as would all tactical nuclear weapons. A verification system capable of distinguishing between any and none has a much easier job than one that must count how many missiles, aircraft or whatever the other side has retained, and do so within the error limits called for by the principle of balance. Furthermore, this process of junk disposal starts with the premise that the hardware being disposed of has no military value. There could therefore be no problem about on-site inspection. Indeed, it would be in the interests of each side to make sure the other was confident that the garbage disposal was actually being carried out.

For the third type, bilateral or multilateral disarmament, the question is *how* to make the process actually happen. In this context, the debate about multilateral and unilateral nuclear disarmament centres around three questions. Is multilateral nuclear disarmament possible without unilateral (independent) initiatives? How can reciprocation be generated from independent initiatives? What is the role of negotiation in such a process ("Treaty first, implementation afterwards," or "Independent reciprocated implementation first, treaty afterwards")?

The 1984 Report of the Secretary-General of the United Nations, entitled *Unilateral Nuclear Disarmament Measures,* is of particular interest in this debate, as the following brief quotations show:

> During the past forty years the nuclear arms race has developed and escalated as the result of unilateral decisions by states taken in the name of national security. As decisions by one side were perceived to affect the security of the other side, an action/reaction process set in whose end is not in sight. The dynamics of the arms race can thus be traced to a series of unilateral and reciprocated steps. Conversely, its de-escalation and reversal could be facilitated by unilateral initatives of states aimed at reducing the level of international tension. . . .
>
> There is no either/or choice between unilateral and negotiated measures of disarmament. Both are needed. . . .
>
> There is an urgent need to inject new life into the multilateral negotiating process, if the present standstill is to be overcome.
>
> In such a situation, unilateral measures, which can have a valuable role to play in and of themselves, may acquire special relevance. They may serve as a means to initiate, stimulate or revive bilateral as well as multilateral disarmament negotiations. In particular, a unilateral action which invites reciprocation might do much to help revitalize negotiations. . . .
>
> Unilateral initiatives do not require confidence and mutual trust to exist before they are taken. On the contrary, confidence and mutual trust come about as a result of the unilateral actions.(8)

It is interesting to note the way in which the General Assembly of the United Nations voted to adopt this cautiously worded report (with an even more cautiously worded resolution): 126 for, 1 against (the United States) and 13 abstentions (which included France, the United Kingdom and Canada). The text of the resolution is as follows:

> The Thirty-ninth General Assembly of the United Nations:
> 1. *Takes note with satisfaction* of the study on unilateral nuclear disarmament measures;
> 2. *Expresses its appreciation* to the secretary-general and to the Group of Governmental Experts that assisted him in the preparation of the study;
> 3. *Takes note* of the conclusions of the study and trusts that they

> may encourage nuclear-weapons states to take the steps
> necessary to promote and orient adequately disarmament
> negotiations;
> 4. *Requests* the secretary-general to arrange for the reproduction
> of the report as a United Nations publication and, making full
> use of all the facilities of the Department of Public Information
> of the Secretariat, to publicize the report in as many languages as
> is considered desirable and practicable.

We need to recognize the three different ways in which people view the problem of nuclear disarmament and, if we intend to move forward, keep these differences in mind. "Nuclear disarmament" (with or without quotation marks) is not going to happen unless we put a great deal of public political pressure on governments, particularly those of the nuclear-weapons countries, and unless other governments put a lot of pressure on the nuclear-weapons states. Therefore, we must think about how to maximize the pressure.

Clearly, if we approach the problem assuming that peoples and governments fully accept the view that *all* nuclear weapons are immoral, illegal and militarily useless, we minimize rather than maximize the pressure, for the assumption is manifestly invalid. We need to form alliances across the whole spectrum of opinions on the nature of nuclear weapons and the nuclear arms race. We need to base these alliances on the common ground of immediate priority goals. For those who believe that most of, and those who believe that all of, the existing nuclear arsenal is militarily useless and immoral, the common ground is the elimination of at least ninety-five percent of the existing stockpiles, by an appropriate combination of unilateral and multilateral measures. These two points of view differ only in their perception of the *ultimate* utility (and acceptability) of nuclear weapons as a minimal deterrent, and that is hardly a matter of immediate concern.

Much harder to bridge is the gap between those who believe most nuclear weapons can simply be scrapped as garbage, and those who believe they must be removed through a carefully negotiated process. The difference here is that one side believes that these weapons have a usefulness outside minimal deterrence. This translates to a difference in opinion, not about whether there should be massive reductions in nuclear "weapons," but about *how* these are to be achieved—by independent (unilateral) measures and reciprocation, or by prenegotiated multilateral measures.

WHAT CAN GOVERNMENTS DO?
To properly discuss what governments can do to prevent nuclear war, I will divide them into two major categories: nuclear-weapons states and

non-nuclear-weapons states. As well, when one asks what governments can do, one asks two further questions: "What can the people of a particular country do to persuade or coerce their own government?" and "What can the peace movement in a particular country do?"

Nuclear-weapons states can take the following kinds of actions to promote disarmament:

1. Nuclear arms limitation and disarmament measures, whether independent or multilateral.

2. Confidence-building measures, both military and political.

3. Non-nuclear disarmament measures (for example, reductions in chemical weapons or conventional forces in Europe).

4. Disengagement measures, such as the establishment of nuclear-weapons-free zones.

It is necessary to distinguish between action and mere declamatory posturing. ("We are in favour of doing such-and-such, but we can't because you aren't"; "We would be prepared to do such-and-such, provided that you do the same.") A professed commitment to multilateralism has all too often served as cover for inaction.

Here are some specific examples of independent actions which the nuclear-weapons states, particularly the United States and the Soviet Union, could take. These would lead, through reciprocation, to multilateral nuclear disarmament:

1. A comprehensive test ban.

2. A freeze on the development and deployment of weapons with a significant counterforce capability.

3. Renunciation of any further development, testing and deployment of any anti-ballistic missile or anti-satellite weapon systems.

4. Withdrawal of specific counterforce weapons from specific zones of deployment (for example, Pershing II missiles, ground-launched cruise missiles and SS-20s could be withdrawn from the European zone).

5. Dismantling of counterforce weapons superfluous to the requirements of classical deterrence.

6. Withdrawal of *all* nuclear weapons from a zone 150 kilometres (approximately 100 miles) from the East-West European border, and a public guarantee not to reintroduce them in a crisis. (This measure, having been implemented unilaterally, could be formalized, if reciprocated, through the establishment of a nuclear-weapons-free zone 150 kilometres wide on each side of the border.)‡

7. Withdrawal of heavy armoured divisions in Central Europe to some

‡ Such a zone would include Kiel, Hamburg, Bremen, Hannover, Frankfurt and Nuremberg on the West; and Rostock, Berlin, Magdeburg, Leipzig, Dresden, Karl Marx Stadt and Prage on the East.

distance (for example, to one hundred kilometres or sixty miles) from the East-West border, and a public guarantee not to move these back into the border zone in a crisis unless and until the adversary does so (once the initiative has been reciprocated).°

8. Restriction of Anti-Submarine Warfare (ASW) exercises. The United States could promise to refrain from ASW exercises within a specified distance (for example, one hundred kilometres) of the Barents Sea and the Sea of Okhotsk; the Soviet Union could promise to restrict its own ASW exercises to the defence of these sanctuaries and to refrain from deploying their hunter-killer submarines in the Atlantic or Pacific oceans in peacetime. *

The nuclear-weapons states should consider the following confidence-building measures (CBMs). These could, again, be promoted by independent initiatives and incorporated in formal agreements after reciprocation:

1. A no-first-use commitment.
2. A guarantee that nuclear weapons will never be used against nuclear-weapons-free states.
3. A commitment to participate in the establishment of nuclear-weapons-free zones in specified regions, including the Balkans, Northern Europe and Central Europe.
4. Military information exchange and constraints on military activities in certain regions, particularly in Europe.
5. A commitment to freeze or reduce military expenditure.
6. A commitment to promote the negotiation of a treaty on the non-use of military force.
7. Economic, cultural and scientific exchanges and improved human contacts, information, communication and consultation.

Each and every one of the eight disarmament-related measures pre-

---

° Though this measure has no direct relationship to nuclear disarmament, it has relevance to the triggering of forward-based tactical nuclear weapons within range of such armoured divisions. Defensive preparations and weaponry (for example, anti-tank missiles would, of course, be maintained within this one hundred kilometre zone).

* The stability of "the second nuclear regime"(7) depends on the invulnerability of nuclear missile submarines, as does the argument that ICBMs are redundant. The present instability of the "first nuclear regime" is increased by anti-submarine warfare (ASW) developments that threaten nuclear missile submarines even in or near "home waters." Such limited restrictions on ASW exercises would not be reliably verifiable, but are probably the best that can be achieved in the short term. Their main value would be as confidence-building measures.

viously listed could be implemented independently by either the United States or the Soviet Union, without any loss in national security *irrespective of whether there is reciprocation by the other side or not.* The same is true of the seven confidence-building measures (with the possible exception of the fifth—the commitment to freeze or reduce military expenditure). Anyone who perceives most of the nuclear arsenal as militarily useless must also share this view. For people who think carefully negotiated multilateral disarmament is paramount, it would be extremely important that independent initiatives produce a reciprocal response from the other side, so that a genuinely multilateral process is assured. The Report of the Secretary General of the United Nations (8), from which I have already quoted, has some illuminating comments on how such a process could work:

> . . . Unilateralism is not one-sided disarmament, but it is a way in which through unilateral, or more precisely "graduated and reciprocated initiatives in tension reduction" (GRIT)(9) two or more countries can promote genuine arms limitation and disarmament agreements. In these terms, the arms race can be viewed as a kind of tension-increasing system which operates on the basis of unilateral, graduated and reciprocated measures. GRIT, on the other hand, is meant to be tension reducing—a flexible, self-regulation procedure in which the participants carefully monitor their own initiatives on the basis of their own evaluation of the reciprocate actions taken by the other side.
>
> Within this framework an "arms race in reverse" can be developed. From this basic principle a number of rules can be derived for maintaining security, inducing reciprocation and demonstrating the genuineness of intent. These rules include the following (10): a) unilateral initiatives must in no way impair the capacity of one party to meet aggression; b) they must be graduated in risk according to the degree of reciprocation obtained from an opponent; c) be so designed and conveyed to an adversary as to emphasize a sincere intent to reduce tensions and invite reciprocation in some form; d) be publicly announced in advance of their execution and identified as a deliberate policy of reducing tension; e) be executed on schedule, regardless of any prior commitments by the adversary to reciprocate; f) be persisted in over a considerable period of time regardless of the degree or even absence of reciprocation; g) be as unambiguous and as susceptible to verification as possible (8).

The underlying assumption of this approach, one might add, is incompatible with the view that negotiations can only succeed if they are undertaken and pursued from a position of strength.** That is a recipe for the arms race, in particular the nuclear arms race, which can hardly be defined as a strategy for survival in the nuclear age.

The United Nations Report makes no mention of a factor that could have a decisive effect upon the R in GRIT. The political pressure of the peace movement, particularly in the country being invited to reciprocate an initiative, as well as international political pressure at government level, would be considerably strengthened by such independent initiatives. For instance, consider the impact upon the freeze campaign in the United States of a unilateral Soviet decision to freeze all development and deployment of counterforce-capable nuclear missiles—a decision that would say clearly:

> We shall *not* deploy a new ICBM in response to your deployment
> of MX. We shall not deploy long-range cruise missiles in
> response to your deployments of air-launched, submarine-
> launched and ground-launched cruise missiles. We have taken
> this decision because we recognize that such counterdeployments
> would not increase our own national security but would reduce
> it. Our decision is unconditional and irreversible. We invite you,
> however, to reciprocate, in the interests of your own, as well as
> our common security, by some comparable measure of your own
> choice. While we shall retain and strengthen our capability to
> retaliate overwhelmingly in the event that we were to be attacked
> with nuclear weapons, we give notice that we shall not continue
> to participate in a competition in counterforce-capable nuclear
> weapons, because these do not, and can not, contribute to our
> national defence or security.

It requires little political imagination to appreciate that the impact would be considerable, even of such a limited unilateral measure, involving no actual *reductions* in nuclear weaponry.

The major American nuclear weapon system program, now being implemented at an estimated cost of over $300 billion, has been justified to Congress and to the American taxpayer as being an essential response to a first-strike threat from Soviet ICBMs. A simple calculation shows that, at best, if everything works according to design, the Soviet missile force might be capable of destroying just over half of the American ICBM silos, leaving the American nuclear strategic force with over one thousand warheads on the remaining ICBMs, as well as over five thousand warheads on nuclear submarines and over four thousand on long-range bombers (3). The threat is entirely fictitious, irrespective of what one be-

** To which I would add: "or from a position of so-called parity."

lieves about Soviet intentions. Yet there is practically universal belief in the existence of some such actual or at least potential threat. The political impact of an independent Soviet initiative that removed a substantial fraction, say one half, of the supposed threat would be dramatic. By proper attention to its presentation to the public, worldwide, the impact could be made spectacular. An invitation to international observers and media to witness *on site* the dismantling of, for instance, 520 SS-11, 60 SS-13, 150 SS-17 and 360 SS-19 ICBMs, and the destruction of their silos, would hardly be declined! These ICBMs currently carry over 4,000 nuclear warheads—about double the number on American ICBMs. If they were dismantled, the Soviet strategic nuclear force would still retain over 3,000 warheads on SS-18s, as well as nearly 2,000 on submarines and about 800 on long-range bombers—a vastly greater number than needed for an assured retaliatory capacity. Ironically, the SS-18 missiles retained would still be able to destroy (with luck) about half the American ICBM silos; that is, the Soviet ICBM force would still be about as useless for a first strike as it was before. Yet the *political* impact of such a unilateral disarmament measure would be enormous. It is hardly conceivable that American programs like MX, the B-1B and Stealth bombers, or Midgetman would survive—let alone the lunacies of Star Wars!

Such an approach to multilateral nuclear disarmament through independent initiatives and political pressures for reciprocation is, of course, unacceptable, even incomprehensible, to members of the military establishments (or of the general public!) whose mental frame of reference is that of nukethink. For instance, the Soviet defence minister, Marshal Dmitri Ustinov, commenting in an interview with *Tass* in 1982 on the American plans for deploying a hundred new MX missiles in superhardened Minuteman silos, said:

> If the current administration in the White House, in defiance of common sense and the popular desire for peace, provokes us by going ahead with the deployment of MX missiles, the Soviet Union will *respond by deploying a new ICBM of the same type that will not be inferior to the MX in any respect.* Similarly, the USSR will, if necessary, *react effectively and swiftly to other threats* emanating from Washington [my emphases].(11)

That such nukethink permeates much wider sections of the Soviet public (as it does in the United States or the United Kingdom) is clear from the following paragraph in an important appeal against the growing danger of war in Europe, issued by the Soviet Committee for European Security and Co-operation in August 1983:

Clearly, the Soviet people will let no one upset *the existing parity* in Europe and the rest of the world, for this would endanger their *security*. The Soviet public unanimously approves the measures taken in face of the now shaping situation *to maintain the defence capability of our country and its allies at the requisite level* [my emphases].(12)

On October 1, 1983, a mass antiwar demonstration in Moscow adopted the statement: "Let us avert the nuclear threat from Europe!"(13) It contained the immediate demands for no new medium-range nuclear weapons in Europe and a reduction in existing arsenals. These demands are, of course, widely supported by the peace movements throughout Europe as well as in the Soviet Union and the United States. However, the statement went on to make the same basic point about parity:

We are for a simple and clear principle—*equal security* for all! There is no difference between an American, British or French missile if they are targeted against and can hit the Soviet Union and its allies. It is our inalienable right to have defence against any of them! If the USA and NATO do start deploying new missiles, the Soviet government is duty bound to do everything necessary to take effective countermeasures [my emphases].

Commenting on these three statements in an article for *Scientific World*†† published at the end of 1983, I wrote:

Underlying all these statements is the "principle of parity and equal security" and imbedded in the "principle" itself is the unstated axiom that the existence of "parity" is a necessary condition for "equal security." I think the time has come to consider more carefully what is meant by the terms "parity" and "security" as used in this context, and also what is meant by "defence capability" and "effective countermeasures."(14)

The article concluded with these words:

There are clearly issues for serious analysis and debate here, debate animated by that critical spirit and freedom from dogma that is supposed to be characteristic of science and scientists. That is why I welcome the opportunity to open such a scientific debate through the columns of *Scientific World* and hope that colleagues from other countries, and especially Soviet colleagues, will take up the debate and examine critically and objectively the propositions that "military-strategic parity" and

†† *Scientific World* is the journal of the World Federation of Scientific Workers. It is published quarterly in English, French, German, Russian, and Esperanto.

"equal security" are not coterminous (except perhaps at an ever-decreasing level of security) and that therefore a *new* approach is needed to the problem of putting an end to the nuclear arms race before it puts an end to the debate, and the debaters.

The debate was, in fact, taken up in *Scientific World* by scientists from the Soviet Union, the German Democratic Republic and Denmark. Because of its relevance to one of the central themes of this paper—the paralyzing effects of nukethink— interested readers may wish to refer to my original article in *Scientific World* and subsequent correspondence relating to it (14).

I have so far suggested actions, both disarmament-related and confidence-building, that could be initiated independently by either of the nuclear superpowers. What of the other nuclear-weapons powers—Britain, France and China? All three claim to possess nuclear weapons as an independent deterrent—a claim that is almost entirely fictitious in the case of the United Kingdom, whose nuclear forces are really only a minor adjunct to those of the United States within the framework of SIOP.‡‡ The credibility of a French or Chinese nuclear deterrent is, to say the least, debatable; that of the British a palpable absurdity. For all three of the minor nuclear powers, the irrelevance of counterforce nuclear capability and strategy is even more obvious than it is for the nuclear superpowers. All three could take independent disarmament initiatives that would in no way decrease their defence capability or national security, and such initiatives could well have a political triggering effect upon the nuclear superpowers. In the particular case of the United Kingdom, the following independent measures could be undertaken:

1. Stopping tests of United Kingdom nuclear weapons.
2. Cancelling the program to replace Polaris submarines with Trident nuclear submarines and missiles.◊◊
3. Scrapping the Polaris submarines and missiles.
4. Denuclearizing British forces in Germany.

---

‡‡ SIOP stands for the Single Integrated Operational Plan, which "accounts for the nuclear weapons of all branches of the American military and embraces all the nuclear contingency plans of the United States' regional commands in the Pacific, the Atlantic and Europe, plus the lesser forces of America's closest and only real nuclear ally, Britain (15, preface)."

◊◊ The British Trident program—presented blandly as a "modernization of Polaris" or a "replacement" system, will, if it is implemented, be a major unilateral escalation. It will be able to destroy about twenty times as many independent targets as Polaris, and, with the much greater accuracy of the Trident II missiles, these will include hardened counterforce targets. For further details on the UK Trident program, see 16.

5. Denuclearizing all RAF and Royal Navy aircraft and all Royal Navy ships.

6. Closing down the American cruise missile bases in the United Kingdom.

7. Closing down U.S. Air Force nuclear bases in the United Kingdom and the American submarine base in Scotland.

8. Pressing within NATO for a revision of policy on "nuclear defence."

9. Supporting the creation of a nuclear-weapons-free zone in the North Atlantic and guaranteeing United Kingdom participation in it.

10. Promoting public information and education on nuclear weapons, defence and on nuclear-weapons-free zones.

The political impact of any one of these measures, and, in particular, its capacity to trigger initiatives by the major nuclear powers, would be enhanced by proper presentation, emphasizing that the purpose is to *increase* the security of the United Kingdom and to *improve* its defence capability, and suggesting that if the major nuclear powers are really interested in their own security they would do well to follow the United Kingdom's example.

ACTION BY GOVERNMENTS OF NON-NUCLEAR-WEAPONS STATES

Examples of actions that could be taken by these countries, whether they are members of the nuclear alliances or nonaligned, include the following:

1. Political pressure on the United States and the Soviet Union to initiate and reciprocate independent actions such as those listed above.

2. Independent adoption of nuclear-weapons-free zone status.☆☆

3. Reaffirmation and clarification of their own decisions not to acquire nuclear weapons, emphasizing their concern for national security and for *effective* defence.***

4. Pressure within the nuclear alliances (by those who belong to them) for defence policies and postures that are *effective* (and therefore non-

---

☆☆ The emphasis in this chapter (as indeed in this entire symposium), is upon *nuclear* weapons of mass destruction. Most of the points made about these apply also to *chemical* weapons of mass destruction. The problems of chemical and nuclear garbage disposal are similar and, indeed, interrelated. The adoption of chemical-weapons-free zone status would therefore have more than intrinsic significance and justification.

*** The political significance of this action would obviously be greater in the case of countries, such as Canada, with an evident technological capability to have acquired their "own" nuclear weapons.

nuclear) and unambiguously *defensive* (and consequently non-provocative).

5. Non-participation, as subcontractors or as testing grounds, in further developments of nuclear weapons by the United States or the USSR.[†††]

6. Public education, within their own countries and internationally through the United Nations agencies, on the nature of nuclear weapons and the significance of nuclear-weapons-free zone policies.

The time has perhaps come when the nonaligned, non-nuclear-weapons states should, in the interests of their own survival, be thinking of more effective co-ordinated actions than the mere adoption of resolutions at the General Assembly of the United Nations. It has been evident for some years now that a nuclear war between the United States and the Soviet Union would have catastrophic consequences not merely for them and their allies, but for most, if not all, other countries. The recent discovery that a nuclear war, even one in which a small proportion (perhaps as little as one percent) of the nuclear stockpile was detonated, could have serious, possibly catastrophic, climatic consequences affecting the whole planet, underlines the fact that no sovereign independent state should accept any longer the right of the nuclear-weapons states to behave unilaterally and independently in a manner that imperils the whole of humankind. The question that requires serious and urgent attention is what forms of political, diplomatic and, especially, economic pressures could be applied to the nuclear-weapons states. It may now be timely to convene a special conference of nonaligned and non-nuclear-weapons states to consider how to co-ordinate their efforts along just such lines. It seems most unlikely that many (or even any) of the actions suggested above will be taken by governments unless there is much more political pressure on them to do so, especially from their own peoples. Consideration of possible action by governments is therefore a somewhat academic exercise if it is not combined with some consideration of the question: what can the *people* of a particular country do to persuade or coerce their own government to take some action?

WHAT CAN THE PEOPLE DO?
The specific forms of action that are appropriate will obviously depend upon the specific circumstances of each country at any given stage. They may include national or local demonstrations, nonviolent direct action (which may involve civil disobedience or breaking the law), lobbying

[†††] The manufacture of the guidance system for the American air-launched cruise missile, and the flight-testing of these missiles, is an example of obvious importance to Canada.

(both public and private), electoral activity and combinations of any or all of these forms.

Flexibility and imagination in the choice of combinations of action, and confidence in the possibility of success, seem to be the two most important features of public political pressure of this kind. Of the two, the latter seems to present the greater problem. People may see the need for changing government policies, but greatly underestimate their power to do anything about it. This often reflects an ignorance of their own history; perhaps because they have forgotten it, perhaps because they were never taught it, or were taught some distorted version in which social and political change (sometimes called progress) is attributed entirely or mainly to the actions of "great men" (rarely, if ever, to those of great women). The people are merely at the receiving end of history, enjoying or suffering the consequences. Yet in reality, most political and social changes have been brought about by popular pressure, and this continues to be the main driving force of history. We are constantly being provided with new examples of the fact that popular pressure can and does frequently change government policy (or change governments) and that this can happen anywhere, even in the most unpromising places (Haiti is a recent example). The problem is to get this lesson of history across to the people.

This leads us naturally to consider the role of peace movements.

WHAT CAN PEACE MOVEMENTS DO?

If flexibility and imagination in the choice of combinations of action, and confidence in the possibility of success, are the most important features of effective popular pressure, then it follows that it is the primary responsibilty of the peace movement to give leadership to the people in precisely these two areas: choice of tactics and development of self-confidence.

It should be emphasized that it is the job of the peace movement to mobilize the people to take political action and to lead such action. This is *not* the same thing as taking action themselves, as peace movement organizations, setting themselves apart from the people.

A second, and in most circumstances secondary, function of the peace movement is to apply pressure to governments directly, through judicious lobbying activity and, where access to government is open, for instance through scientific and technical advisers, through briefing and advising members of government, politicians and the military.

If peace movements are to be effective in performing these functions, they must be politically independent, must be prepared to build alliances for the achievement of immediate common goals and must pay attention to imaginative education, especially on the basic case for nuclear disarmament.

Above all, peace movements must try to concentrate on priorities, and avoid divisive arguments about nonpriority issues, such as the best method of disarmament, pacifism, human rights, abolishing blocs and so on, important as they may be in the long run.

It is all very well to say that the peace movements have a responsibility to educate the public, but if their members are themselves entrapped in the assumptions of nukethink, they are going to have a difficult job freeing the public from them. I often wonder what proportion of members of the Campaign for Nuclear Disarmament, for example, who campaign vigorously and often with great courage for nuclear disarmament, and who are opposed to nuclear weapons on moral or religious grounds, or because they realize how dangerous they are, share the basic assumptions of the military-industrial-etc. complex that these things are "weapons" and that getting rid of them would therefore be "disarmament."

We are all guilty to some extent of perpetuating the nuclear myth. For convenience in writing or speaking we use accepted terminology such as "nuclear deterrence," "the strategic balance" and in so doing perpetuate the illusions that such terms reflect. It is all too easy to become entrapped in technicalities, to see the problems of ending the nuclear arms race in terms of concepts and language-models (and the premises they conceal) that are part of the process of entrapment of those who are within the complex itself.

I think that most, if not all, peace organizations also need to learn tolerance of diversity. This means not just being prepared to make common cause with people who have a different approach to the immediate problem, and a different view about what the following steps should be, but *actively* seeking to build working alliances with such people.

Finally, there is the crucial question of motivation. At the level of immediate short-range motivation, people take part in political activity, such as peace campaigning, because they feel better for doing so. Yet self-gratification can easily become an end in itself, and the aims of the campaign, such as nuclear disarmament, become lost from sight. At a group level, this often leads to sectarian behaviour that can become extremely disruptive. It leads also to confusion between ends and means, between strategy and tactics. There are examples of this from the experience of CND in Britain. For instance, maintaining the presence of a peace camp at Greenham Common, in the teeth of extreme hardship and harassment, requires a special kind of courage and concentration on the immediate task. It is easy, under such conditions, to lose sight of the political point of such activity, which is to maintain and enhance public awareness of the presence of American cruise missiles in Britain and to contribute to the mobilization of a majority of people in political action to have them removed. The same problem applies to all forms of nonviolent direct action. They are politically significant and useful to the degree that they are sensitive and mobilize public opinion. They can easily become ends in themselves that serve only to make the participants feel that they are "doing something," and may even alienate and demobilize the people.

Perhaps the most important of all learning processes that the peace movements now need to go through is that which will strengthen the rational, historical basis for believing that this campaign can actually be *won*.

References and Notes

1. *The Choice: Nuclear Weapons versus Security*, edited by Gwyn Prins (Chatto and Windus, 1984).

2. *The Prevention of Nuclear War*, Proceedings of a Symposium held at the University of British Columbia, March 5–6, 1983, edited by T. L. Perry, Jr. (Vancouver: Physicians for Social Responsibility, B.C. Chapter, 1983).

3. *Nuclear War: The Search for Solutions*, Proceedings of a Conference held at the University of British Columbia, October 19–21, 1984, edited by T. L. Perry, (Vancouver: Physicians for Social Responsibility, B.C. Chapter, 1985).

4. Robert S. McNamara, "The Military Role of Nuclear Weapons: Perceptions and Misperceptions," *Foreign Affairs* (fall 1983): pp. 59–80.

5. Owen Greene, Ian Percival and Irene Ridge, *Nuclear Winter* (Polity Press, 1985). (For more information on the nuclear winter, see the Further Reading list below.)

6. T. P. Turco, O. B. Toon, T. P. Ackerman, J. B. Pollock, C. Sagan, "Nuclear Winter: Global Consequences of Multiple Nuclear Explosions," *Science*, 222, 1283 (1983). (See also reference 3 above, pp. 25–43.)

7. D. C. Gompert, M. Mandelbaum, R. L. Garwin, J. H. Barton, *Nuclear Weapons and World Politics: Alternatives for the Future*, (McGraw Hill, 1980).

8. *Unilateral Nuclear Disarmament Measures*, Report of the Secretary-General of the United Nations (1984).

9. C. Osgood, *An Alternativie to War or Surrender*, (Chicago: University of Illinois Press, 1962).

10. *New Directions in Disarmament*, edited by W. Epstein, B. L. Feld, (Praeger, 1981).

11. Interview with *Tass*, December 1982.

12. From the text of the Appeal by the Soviet Committee for European Security and Co-operation, circulated on August 3, 1983.

13. From the text of the statement adopted by the mass anti-war demonstration in Moscow on October 1, 1983, circulated on October 14 by the Soviet Committee on European Security and Co-operation.

14. Michael Pentz, "The Nuclear Arms Race: a New Initiative is Urgently Needed," *Scientific World*, vol. 27, no. 4 (1983). (Responses to this article have appeared in *Scientific World* as follows: A. Kalyadin, "Checking the Nuclear Arms Race," *Scientific World*, vol. 28, no. 3; A. Brie, "Military Parity and Security," Ibid.; B. Boos, I. M. Jarvad, "Equal Security—a Basic Principle in the Nuclear Age," *Scientific World*, vol. 28, no. 4.)

15. Peter Pringle, William Arkin, *STOP—Nuclear War from the Inside*, (Sphere Books, 1983).

16. Malcolm Chalmers, *Trident—Britain's Independent Arms Race*, (London: CND Publications, 1984).

Further Reading

On nuclear winter:

1. *The Nuclear Winter*, Proceedings of the Conference on the Long-Term Worldwide Biological Consequences of Nuclear War, Paul R. Ehrlich, Carl Sagan, Donald Kennedy, Walter Orr Roberts (Sidgwick and Jackson, 1985).

2. *Nuclear Winter: The Human and Environmental Consequences of Nuclear War*, Mark A. Harwell (Springer-Verlag, 1984).

On "nuclear deterrence" (and other nuclear illusions):

1. *The Nuclear Delusion*, George E. Kennan, Hamish Hamilton, (1984).

2. *Nuclear Deterrence*, M. R. Dando, B. R. Newman (Castle House, 1982).

3. *The Death of Deterrence: Consequences of the New Nuclear Arms Race*, Malcolm Dando, Paul Rogers (London: CND Publications, 1984).

Ambassador Stephen Lewis

CHAPTER 28

Panel Discussion: Session V

AMBASSADOR STEPHEN LEWIS,
PAUL WARNKE, VITALY ZHURKIN,
AND MICHAEL PENTZ

Stephen Lewis (session chairperson):
Paul Warnke, last night Professor Galbraith suggested that the real power
on both sides is the military-industrial complex and that governments can
do little. What is your response to this?

Paul Warnke:
I hate to disagree with Professor Galbraith, but I do. I think, really, that
the problem is political rather than economic. There is not a single
weapon system that the United States has undertaken to develop during
the last thirty years that could not have been stopped by a brave American president. And I think his actions would have had the support of the
American people. Also, the fact is, the United States is going to spend a
certain amount of money on defence. The question is what the United
States will decide to spend this money on. The industrial complex does
not care whether this money is spent on conventional arms, or on something else. At present the industrial complex goes for strategic weapon

*Stephen Lewis is the Canadian Ambassador to the United Nations. After
election to the Ontario Legislature at the age of twenty-five, he became
the provincial leader of the New Democratic Party in Ontario in 1970,
holding that position until 1977. In 1984, after a successful career in
broadcasting on issues of public concern, Stephen Lewis was appointed
the Canadian permanent representative to the United Nations. There he
has raised Canada's profile, and earned a reputation as an eloquent
speaker and an ardent defender of the role of the United Nations in world
politics.*

297

systems like the Strategic Defense Initiative (SDI) for the same reason that Willy Sutton robbed banks. You recall he was asked, "Why do you rob banks, Willy Sutton?" and he said, "That's where the money is." If you had put the money in some other place, the industrial complex would have moved there too.

Lewis:
Dr. Zhurkin, please tell us about the relationship between the Soviet peace movement and the Soviet government. In the West we sometimes hear that no independence exists for peace movements in the socialist parts of the world.

Vitaly Zhurkin:
The Soviet peace movement certainly exists completely independently. It is a public movement where people participate voluntarily. It is subsidized by a peace fund, which has been created with the help of voluntary donations from millions and millions of people. Altogether, during the last thirty years, seventy million people have donated to this peace fund, according to the latest report. At the same time I would like to stress that the Soviet peace movement, in all of its major decisions, does support the foreign policies of the government. Therefore, it is not a separate peace movement in the Western sense of this word. It is a voluntary movement but it is not anti-government. This is the major difference between the Soviet and the Western peace movements.

Lewis:
Professor Pentz, a question has been put in a somewhat provocative fashion. Without scientists who *prostitute* their considerable intelligence to the military-industrial power groups, mankind would not be living under the threat of annihilation. Why do individual men in the scientific community put their egos and their inventions above their moral responsibility to their fellow man? If they collectively refused to bow to the demands of this military-industrial complex, surely all these international scientists, with their considerable intelligence, could initiate independent nonmilitary research programs. And perhaps when you answer you could remind the questioner that there is more than one gender in this world.

Michael Pentz:
Well, since you have done that for me, I shan't have to do it again. I would remind the questioner that he or she has singled out only two components of the military industrial complex: it is really a military-industrial-bureaucratic-scientific-technological-academic complex. And the factors which imprison people within this complex are not, in my

opinion, very different, whether these people are scientists, or generals, or admirals, or businesspeople, or professors or people in government offices. In a whole variety of very ordinary ways people get embedded in the process and find it very difficult to escape. We have had *one* such escaper speaking to us at this symposium—Admiral Eugene Carroll. But it took him a hell of a long time to escape. He could tell you, if he were on the panel, that he had doubts about the efficacy of nuclear weapons many, many years before he was eventually able to take his retirement, leave the United States Armed Forces, and speak out. And I heard the same thing a couple of years ago from a Canadian, Rear Admiral Robert Falls.

Quite ordinary, human considerations make escaping from the complex very difficult. This does not apply *just* to scientists. But, of course, it *also* applies to scientists. They are fascinated by the facilities they have in their laboratories. They believe that they are doing a good job: they believe that they are defending socialism, or the Western way of life, or I don't know what. They are not much different from you or me. And knocking these scientists is not going to get us anywhere. Even knocking businesspeople because they want to make a buck won't work. (Actually nowadays it's not a buck or even a mega-buck, it's a giga-buck. Giga is a thousand million, in case you didn't know.)

I don't believe it is profitable to pass moral judgments about people who have become caught in the complex. Instead, we have to mobilize a force which can intervene in the problem from outside, change government policies and liberate the military, the bureaucrats, the engineers and the scientists. Scientists can do some things; that is why we formed Scientists Against Nuclear Arms (SANA). Our goal is to help the peace movement, the politicians and other people, by giving them the tools they need to do the job.

Lewis:
As far as you know, what are the United States and the Soviet Union doing to reduce the very real risk of *accidental* nuclear war?

Pentz:
On the one hand, on the positive side (and I am sure Paul Warnke could elaborate on this), there is "the hot line." Attempts are made from time to time to update it, to make it a bit more sophisticated. However, these efforts are just drops in the ocean. In the meantime both sides are mostly engaged in activities which undercut whatever safeguards the hot line could create. In competition with each other, they are deploying systems which are increasingly complex and increasingly computer-dependent. Because of a number of characteristics, such as those exhibited by Persh-

ing II, the weapon systems are also operating on shorter and shorter time-scales. This is the way to vastly amplify the risk of accidental nuclear war. So, to answer the question: "What are they doing about accidental nuclear war?" on a grandiose scale—compensated for only by the most flimsy of other measures—they are *increasing* the risk of accidental nuclear war.

Zhurkin:

A number of agreements between the Soviet Union and the United States are aimed at reducing the risk of accidental nuclear conflicts. Professor Pentz mentioned the hot line agreement of 1963. The line was upgraded several times—the last time in 1985. There is also a so-called accident-at-sea agreement. This agreement aims at preventing accidents or collisions by naval vessels. It helps to prevent accidental nuclear war, because both navies have nuclear weapons on their boats. There was also an understanding reached in Geneva that experts should discuss the possibility of establishing risk-reduction centres. It is still a rather vague idea. But the idea is to create some centres for reasonable communication between the superpowers.

Despite the fact that these steps have been taken, I agree with Professor Pentz that these arrangements are only small achievements. Personally, I think that only by reducing the number of nuclear weapons can we seriously lower the danger of a nuclear war starting by accident.

Warnke:

If your question is whether these things will go off accidentally, there are a lot of scientific devices which prevent that from happening. So I don't worry about a true accident occurring. But what my colleagues have been describing is the risk that a nuclear exchange may start because of panic, because of desperation or because of the feeling that one can't afford to wait—that one has to fire first. From that standpoint, I certainly agree with Professor Pentz and Dr. Zhurkin. As we produce more and more nuclear weapons, with greater and greater accuracy, it becomes more and more likely that at some point the nuclear exchange may start because of panic, fear or desperation. This is the sort of accident that we ought to address. The gravest risk is not posed by the possibility of a mechanical accident; the gravest risk is that we might use nuclear weapons on purpose because of faulty thinking. There has never yet been a nuclear weapon exploded accidentally.

Lewis:

Professor Pentz, this question flows logically from what has been discussed. What do you believe would be the cause of World War III, were it to occur? Would it be caused by the escalation of a conventional war, by a nuclear accident, by a first-strike offensive or by something else?

Pentz:
Well, I would make a slightly different list of possible scenarios for the privilege of unleashing Armageddon. First on my list is that one side would incorrectly perceive the other side's intentions and capabilities. We are in a chronically dangerous situation at present, because both sides constantly apply, or misapply, worst-case analysis. It is one of the mechanisms, by the way, which actually drives the nuclear arms race. And it is also a mechanism which could trigger a nuclear war. If one side senses that the other side is contemplating a first strike there is a strong pressure—which the development of new weapon systems makes even stronger—to launch a preemptive strike. This situation could arise from a complete miscalculation or misconception based on misinformation or disinformation.

The second most likely cause of nuclear war is an accident, either of the kind Paul Warnke is talking about, or of the kind involving a simple failure of systems. Control systems have become so computerized and so automated that they eliminate even the possibility of constraint by human decisions. The near accidents which we have had (and Paul Warnke was quite right—we have not yet had an accident where a bomb actually exploded) have been prevented at the last moment on some occasions only because human beings could intervene. But as these systems become more complex and more computerized, the risk of accidents increases. Every engineer knows that the more complex a system is, the more likely it is to go wrong. Murphy's Law likes complex systems.

The third most likely cause is an unpremeditated escalation of a small, local conflict. The fourth cause—which I don't believe can be eliminated —is madness in high places. If anybody has the feeling that these last two possible causes may not be very likely, they should perhaps reflect, for a moment, about recent events in Libya. If the president of the world's greatest power of this century, and the prime minister of the world's greatest power of the last century, actually imagine that one can isolate Colonel Gadhafi from the Arab world—to take their own statements of their objectives at face value—and discourage terrorism by killing his baby daughter and injuring his infant sons, then I must say we have got to be afraid for the future of humankind! Such monstrous miscalculations—not to mention breach and disrespect of international law and plain immorality—could lead to the unleashing of a million Hiroshimas on this fragile planet. So I don't dismiss the last two candidates for unleashing Armageddon: escalation of a minor conflict and, let's be kind, misjudgment. [*enthusiastic applause*]

301

Lewis:
Dr. Zhurkin, does the Soviet government consider Canada to have a military and international economic policy distinct from that of the United States?

Zhurkin:
Yes. The Soviet Union considers that Canada—in spite of being a reliable American ally, a member of NATO, and closely connected with the United States—does have distinct features of its own policy. Or perhaps I should say that we think Canada has some distinct features in an embryonic state which, we hope, will be developed more fully in the future.

Lewis:
I would have thought this audience would explode in exultant pleasure at this confirmation of our independence!

May I add an addendum to the question, which might be put to all three panelists. Can you think of concrete ways in which Canada could help the United States and the Soviet Union achieve arms control goals? What is a role for a country like ours? Indeed, what is the role for middle powers generally?

Warnke:
The one thing that Canadians ought to make clear to the United States is that you don't think that the nuclear umbrella is useful for you. Both of the times that I have been in the United States government, members of the government have argued that we daren't move too fast on arms control, because we will panic our allies. They have argued that our allies will feel that suddenly they have been left alone—left naked in the world—without the American nuclear umbrella. And I must say that the discussions I've heard in international conferences, in NATO, and in the nuclear planning group do nothing really to dissuade the United States from feeling that it has to maintain the nuclear umbrella and make it bigger and bigger, to keep people such as you Canadians from panicking and leaving the alliance.

During the next couple of years it will be very important for the NATO allies, and particularly for Canada, to make it very clear that they would prefer to see *fewer* nuclear weapons rather than more; that they aren't in favour of the British and French exponentially increasing their nuclear forces; that they don't think that somehow security depends on having smaller, better and more accurate nuclear weapons; and that they could contemplate with total equanimity an American nuclear test ban. The United States does not get this message, and this is your fault, not mine.

Pentz:
I would like to add a couple of points to that. Canada would greatly help to pressure both the United States and the Soviet Union to make progress on arms control if it would firmly refuse to be used for the development of new, destabilizing, dangerous counterforce weaponry. What I am referring to, of course, is that Canada is allowing itself to be *used,* both as a sub-contractor for component parts of the cruise missile, and as a testing ground for these missiles. I think that Canada has an important asset which could help it in refusing to be used for this purpose. Immediately after the Second World War, Canada was in a very strong position to acquire its own nuclear weapons. It decided not to, as a number of other countries have done. It is significant that as a consequence Canada has *not* been occupied by the Red Army! And I think that point could be made more clearly by Canada, and more often. It would be a good idea for Canada to reaffirm its non-nuclear-weapons status, and to reaffirm the reasons for it—not only the moral and legal reasons, but also, above all, the security reasons. A country which possesses nuclear weapons is less, not more, secure. This leads to another action that Canada should take. It should exploit its non-nuclear position far more vigorously and impress upon other countries, including the old mother country, that they would have done much better to have followed Canada's example. Canada might even try this with the French. I wish you luck!

Zhurkin:
I agree with what has been said before, and want only to add that Canada could also contribute very much, if it desired to do so, to the process of reducing conventional weapons and conventional forces, be they in Europe or in the Pacific. If Canada did take such independent initiatives, it would carry a lot of moral weight.

Lewis:
Do you think that a country like Canada exercises a more effective role within NATO or without?

Pentz:
I think that a country like Sweden, promoting the peace-making role of the nonaligned and non-nuclear countries, is no less credible than Canada. And Sweden is not a member of either of the nuclear alliances. So I don't think that it actually follows, as night follows day, that if you get out of the club, you can't argue with your former fellow club members over the beer. The Swedes have helped to keep the peace as well, if not better, than Canada—not to mention Britain.
    On the other hand, since Canada like Britain is at the present time a

member of NATO, and since NATO constantly maintains that it exists only to defend the NATO countries, I think there might be some mileage to be gained, at least temporarily, were Britain to dispose of all its nuclear weapons, and to remove all those belonging to the United States from our territory, a thing which eventually we are certainly going to do. We should say to NATO: "We want to belong to a defensive alliance so long as we perceive the need for it, that is, only until we succeed in dismantling both the Warsaw Pact and NATO alliances, as has already been proposed several times by the Warsaw Treaty side. So we want to have an effective defence policy, but that means one without nuclear weapons, because they are *not* effective. The nuclear umbrella is useless." Let us call upon NATO to revise its defence strategies, and agree that we will stay in to help NATO do it. If we are unsuccessful in this demand, then we want out. And I think that might offer a way to proceed which would be useful both for Canada and the United Kingdom—perhaps for the United Kingdom, of course, if we can reach the stage when we are as sensible as Canada, and no longer have any nuclear weapons of our own, nor any based on our territory.

Lewis:
I presume this is a prophecy of a prospective Labour government.

Pentz:
Perhaps.

Lewis:
Do you dare make a comment, Dr. Zhurkin, about NATO and Canada's involvement in it?

Zhurkin:
As far as I remember, the Soviet Union is *not* a member of NATO! [*waves of laughter*] Although, to recall history, as Michael Pentz just reminded me, the Soviet Union originally offered to join NATO. NATO was created in 1949. In 1953, or maybe in 1954, the Soviet Union proposed to Great Britain, France and the United States that it would join NATO, and NATO would then be transformed into a regional defence organization, as envisaged by the United Nations charter. But this proposal was declined. It is a historical fact. And only one and a half years after that the Warsaw Pact was created.

Lewis:
Mr. Warnke, please tell us your opinion of the effect of the peace movement on American arms negotiators.

Warnke:

First, I would want a definition of what we mean by United States arms negotiators. Essentially, the people who sit across that green felt table in Geneva are not influenced by anything except their own instructions. So, really, it is necessary to influence the actual principles, rather than the negotiators. This is why I feel that until the top leadership gets together, the negotiators have no role to perform at all. They can sit there forever and exchange prepared statements. But until there is some sort of an outline, some sort of a foundation, some sort of an agreement in principle at the top level, the negotiators are not going to make any progress whatever.

This is where the influence of the peace movements can be felt. I really believe that negotiations would not have been started back in 1982 had it not been for the peace movement in the United States, in Canada and in Western Europe. The Reagan administration came into office feeling that it did not want to negotiate arms control agreements. As a matter of a fact Eugene Rostow, who was the first head of the United States Arms Control and Disarmament Agency under President Reagan, said during his confirmation hearings that he couldn't find anybody in the administration who knew of anything they wanted him to negotiate about. I believe that the peace movement in Europe gave rise to the Intermediate-Range Nuclear Force talks at the end of 1981. And the freeze movement in the United States inspired the beginning of the so-called START talks—which never really started—in June 1982. So I think the peace movement has made a difference, and I think it should keep the pressure on. It should make very clear what the people want: they are tired of all this sparring; they are tired of this idea that somehow you can build better, safer nuclear weapons. Take that phrase, "safer nuclear weapons." What is a safe nuclear weapon? It is a dud. [*laughter and clapping*] So as a taxpayer, I'm against building duds. I think the peace movement has really made a tremendous difference.

Lewis:

I have a question addressed to the professor from the Soviet Union. "I am a person who, driven by my strong hope for world peace, will soon be visiting the Soviet Union for three weeks on a friendship tour. I hope to spread the message of world unity in the country which is so wrongly deemed the opposition. What do you feel that I could do while there to play my part in helping to achieve this goal—one that is shared by all who are here tonight?"

Zhurkin:

I think the answer is already contained in the question. You should meet

Soviet people and talk with them about what should be done to strengthen peace.

Lewis:

Professor Pentz, if the nuclear arms race and SDI are essentially useless, do you think that these programs to produce "junk" are designed to encourage the Soviet Union to expend its time and money in similar useless pursuits, while the United States secretly develops more diabolical weapons?

Pentz:

Frankly, no. However, some people have suggested quite seriously that the name of the game is precisely to try to induce the Soviet Union to indulge in yet another upward spiral of the arms race, including very expensive systems like space weapons, which could cripple the Soviet economy, and thus win the conflict with "the evil empire." I don't know whether or not these people should be taken seriously. However, I think that questions like the one just put to me—which look for a clean, neat, rational explanation—miss the point. The most important fact about the whole of the nuclear arms race is that it is irrational. To answer the question of how it could come about, one has to get right into the nitty-gritty of the inner mechanisms of the military-industrial-et cetera complex. It is a mistake to expect to find a rational explanation, such as: one side is trying to bankrupt the other; it exists only so that some sectors can make money; or it's the generals—they like to have big weapons; or, it's the scientists—they like inventing nasty things in their laboratories. All of these simplistic explanations are wrong, precisely because they are too simplistic. But I think that they are also wrong because they assume a rational answer. The sooner we face the facts—that we are dealing with a machine driven by an irrational process—the sooner we will be able to cope with the problem.

Lewis:

Dr. Zhurkin, Paul Warnke gave an American view of Western Europe's attitude toward American nuclear disarmament. What are the views of the Warsaw Pact countries, and of the Warsaw Pact generally, on Soviet disarmament?

Zhurkin:

Several times lately the Warsaw Pact has presented a number of ideas on how the Soviet Union and the United States, as well as the Warsaw Pact and NATO, could reduce armaments. For example, it has called for military budget freezes on both sides, maybe as a beginning, just by the

Soviet Union and the United States. It has also called for a freeze in both sides' conventional forces. The Warsaw Pact supports the idea of creating a chemical-weapons-free zone in Europe. So, the Warsaw Pact has developed an impetus of its own towards balanced but radical disarmament on both sides.

Pentz:
This question has arisen because of Paul Warnke's observation—to caricature it slightly (and with apologies)—that "the United States has been dragged protesting into continuing the nuclear arms race because those idiots in Britain, France and Germany insist on a nuclear umbrella. They asked us to put Pershings in Europe. They asked us to put cruise missiles in Britain. And we just *had* to." The United States frequently described the situation in these terms when all those tremendous efforts were being made to get the Pershing II's into Germany, and to get the cruise missiles into Britain and a number of other European countries. But if you actually look into the history of the cruise missile, you will find that it bears no relationship at all to such a process. The United States was trying to solve the problem of where to deploy its cruise missiles long, long before poor Chancellor Schmidt of Germany, who gets blamed for all this, was supposed to have said: "For God's sake, give us these new missiles, or we will be defenceless again—let's get better coupling between the strategic deterrent and the local nuclear weapons." The United States faced the problem of where the devil to put ground-launched cruise missiles with a range of 2,500 kilometres (1,550 miles). This kind of weapon is not useful in most places: Britain stands out a mile.

The truth of the matter is that the Pentagon sent a letter (which is on file) to all NATO governments. It more or less said: "Since you guys say you are so concerned about the umbrella and all that, how about having some of these nice new missiles we have got on the production lines?" And it wasn't poor old Schmidt who said yes first. It was the foreign minister of a British Labour government. All of this was because something had to be done with the damn things. Of course, now that the cruise missiles are deployed, no one has the foggiest idea what they could be used for other than a rather good nuclear holocaust.

Warnke:
I would have to say that is not a caricature, it is a corruption. I was in the government which decided to deploy the ground-launched cruise missiles and the Pershing II, and it was at the request of the Western Europeans. The Pentagon had no real interest in deploying either weapon system. All you need to do in NATO is to tell us to take them back, and we'll take them back.

Lewis:
Go ahead, Professor Pentz, you are poised.

Pentz:
You may have noticed, Paul, that two-thirds of Britain's population said in several successive opinion polls that they want those things out. And the government of Britain will make this request before long, I hope.

Warnke:
I would welcome that request.

Lewis:
I wish I knew which part of history to believe. I have noticed that it was a socialist prime minister in Spain who recently presided over a referendum keeping that country in NATO, and I have noticed that it is a socialist president of France who tests nuclear weapons. This world, and life, is not entirely without complication.

I have a delicious question for Paul Warnke to bring this session to an end. What are the chances for the election of a more pro-arms control administration in the United States in 1988?

Warnke:
Since there is no way in the world of electing an administration less in favour of arms control, I welcome the verdict of 1988. And I would love to serve under the next Democratic president!

PART VI

The Ability of Human Beings to Save
the World

PHOTO: DAN KEETON

Dr. Helen Caldicott

CHAPTER 29
Commit Yourself to Saving the Earth

DR. HELEN CALDICOTT

What I want to talk to you about tonight is the present situation in the United States. It is very serious. I want you to understand the situation because you are very close allies of the United States. You are almost another state of the United States because you allow yourselves to be that.

COMMITTEE ON THE PRESENT DANGER

In the early seventies President Richard Nixon and Henry Kissinger went to China and made friends with the largest communist nation in the world. Now, in truth, the United States has more communists on its side than the Soviets have on theirs. That was done overnight--from enemy to friend. We could do that tomorrow with the Soviets. They are not the enemy, they are the excuse for making money. They have been the excuse for internal domestic policies in the United States for many years. Nixon also established détente with the Soviet Union and negotiated SALT I

Dr. Helen Caldicott has probably moved more people to become active in the peace movement than any other person in North America. As a passionate opponent of nuclear war, she has made outstanding contributions to the physicians' and women's peace movements. The author of two best-selling books, Nuclear Madness *and* Missile Envy, *Dr. Caldicott has drawn wide popular attention to the Reagan administration's policies on fighting a winnable nuclear war. Many North Americans will have seen Dr. Caldicott in the Oscar award-winning film,* If You Love This Planet, *which was produced by the Canadian National Film Board. This chapter is an abridged version of a speech by Dr. Caldicott given on April 3, 1986, at the University of British Columbia.*

and the Anti-Ballistic Missile Treaty. The Bolshoi Ballet came to America, scientists went to the Soviet Union and we established a co-operative effort in space. People felt better.

But a group of right-wing intellectuals in the United States didn't like détente. They were bipartisan Democrats and Republicans who hated the Soviet Union. Senator Henry Jackson and others established a committee called the Committee on the Present Danger. The name of the committee came from a judgment which was made by Oliver Wendell Holmes, the Supreme Court justice in the United States early in the century. He interpreted the First Amendment in the Bill of Rights of the United States Constitution as protecting freedom of speech—except in certain instances. For instance, one may not cry "fire" in a crowded theatre, because that would create a clear and present danger.

The Committee on the Present Danger believes that the present danger is communism—not Chinese communism, but Russian communism. They believe this danger is greater than the danger of nuclear war. Very intelligent people, 140 of them, joined this committee by invitation. Their philosophy, which they write a lot about in the press, including in prestigious journals such as *Foreign Affairs,* goes like this: you can't trust the Russians because they cheat on treaties. If the Soviets cheat on treaties, you can't have arms control, and if you can't have arms control, nuclear war becomes inevitable. If nuclear war is inevitable, then America has to prepare to fight and win a nuclear war.

This committee allied itself with the American Security Council, which is a private organization consisting of about half a million people, funded by major corporations, including defence contractors. They have private files on six million Americans. The American Security Council was founded during the McCarthy era when they were hunting communists in American society. The Committee on the Present Danger has provided the thinkers, and the American Security Council has provided the propaganda. They have made two major films. One, called the SALT Syndrome, says that the Russians cheat on treaties—that they built more nuclear weapons than America during the seventies, and that during that time the United States had actually been disarming. This isn't true. America had built more nuclear weapons than Russia. I know the person who has been responsible for many years for monitoring violations of the seventeen treaties on nuclear weapons between the United States and the Soviet Union. According to this source, there have been, and are now, no major Soviet violations of those treaties.

In 1979, President Reagan was asked to join the Committee on the Present Danger. After his election, President Reagan appointed fifty members from this committee to his administration. Among them were Jeanne Kirkpatrick, the United States ambassador to the United Nations;

George Shultz, secretary of state; Caspar Weinberger, secretary of defense, Eugene Rostow, who headed the Arms Control and Disarmament Agency; Max Kampelman, who leads the arms control team in Geneva; his colleagues Edward Rowney and Paul Nitze; Lane Kirkland, the former head of the AFL-CIO; and others. They became the Reagan administration.

FUNDAMENTALIST CHRISTIANS
The fundamentalist Christians are another group of people who helped to get President Reagan and other like-minded politicians elected. Approximately 100 million Americans watch their spokesmen on TV evangelical shows and listen to them on radio. You know who these people are: Pat Robertson, who was recently featured on the front of *Time Magazine* and is thinking of running for the presidency in 1988; Jerry Falwell, who is very influential in this movement, and many others. These evangelists have become so powerful that poor little people mortgage their homes and take out bank loans and bankrupt themselves in order to send in money to get a velvet-covered Bible which will get them to heaven. They preach very right-wing politics: they are against abortion—I respect people who are against abortion but they use this opinion as a political tool; they are for capital punishment; they talk a lot about support for the Contras, who are trying to overthrow the Sandinista government of Nicaragua; and they define the Soviet Union as the evil empire.

These fundamentalists masquerade themselves behind the cross and the flag. Jerry Falwell believes, as do the others, in Armageddon. If you read Revelations, the last book of the New Testament, you will read that the earth will be consumed in fire. When this happens, the people who have the mark of God on their foreheads are going to go to meet Jesus in the sky. This upward elevation of the human body is called *the rapture*. I saw Jerry Falwell on television talking about nuclear war. He said to his audience: "Look, I don't know what is going to happen to you, but I've got my bags packed, and when nuclear war comes, I'm going straight up to heaven to meet Jesus."

There are now many fundamentalist Christians within the administration with high-level positions. Remember James Watt who wanted to give all the national parks to the oil companies to develop them? He was a fundamentalist Christian. He used to get down on his knees every morning in his office and pray about the rapture and Armageddon. He said that we don't have to worry about the national parks, because they are not going to be around much longer.

People have turned to religion in other ways. When the Catholic bishops in America wrote that wonderful pastoral letter on nuclear war, they were trying to live up to the teachings of Jesus. Many other religions in the United States are doing the same thing, including the Jewish religion. So there are two ways people are reacting to the extremely anxiety-provoking situation with which science has endowed us, that of living so close to nuclear annihilation.

Indeed, Sir Martin Ryle, the astronomer-royal, who discovered radar, and was a Nobel laureate, became profoundly concerned about nuclear war at the end of his life. He said: "I wish I had been a farmer." He believed that the pursuit of pure science should now stop. He contended that we know enough now to help everybody on the planet, to feed them, clothe them, house them, educate them, control the population, prevent pollution, and keep each other happy and healthy. Even the pursuit of science in medicine is a little aberrant at the moment, with heart transplants costing an enormous amount of money, and putting baboon hearts in little babies. So we need to think about that. I know what I am saying is heresy to scientists, but I say it because I think it is true.

RIGHT-WING THINK TANKS
As well as the fundamentalist Christians, who have had an enormous influence on the Reagan administration, there are also right-wing think tanks like the Heritage Foundation, the American Enterprise Institute, the Hoover Foundation, and others. They are funded by people like Richard Scape from the Mellon family; David Packard from Hewlett Packard, one of the biggest arms manufacturers in the country; Bechtel, who make nuclear reactors; Amway; *Reader's Digest;* Hunt Oil; Holiday Inns; Hertz Rent-a-Car; Coors Beer; Sears-Roebuck; Marshall Field Company; Ocean Spray Cranberries; Johns-Mansville; General Electric; Proctor & Gamble; Rockwell International; and many others. These right-wing think-tanks employ brilliant people to pump out op-ed pieces, the articles opposite the editorial page in the newspaper. At the *Boston Globe,* they receive hundreds of these articles a week. They are well-written, intelligent and well thought out. Legislators use them to formulate bills. But their fundamental premise is evil; based on hatred and death and destruction.

THE MEDIA
Right-wing think tanks also manipulate the electronic media. We just did a study in the United States, which cost $160,000, to find out why the nuclear freeze campaign failed. We did a national poll of the American people which showed that thirty-one percent of them think that nuclear war could happen within ten years. Ninety-six percent of them know that nuclear war would mean the end of their country and probably of the earth. Eighty percent of them support a nuclear-weapons freeze. Eighty-six percent of them believe that the Russians cheat on treaties. Yet most

of them also say that if Russia launches weapons first, of course we should retaliate and destroy the Soviet Union, although this would induce nuclear winter and destroy all life on earth. So there is a tremendous ambivalence in the American population toward the nuclear threat; the average American's position fluctuates between knowledge, ignorance and superstition. People are terribly confused.

We discovered, when we went through all the transcripts of all the news for five years, that the freeze movement was a phenomenon never seen before in the history of the United States. Eighty percent of people supported it across the board: grandmothers, children, all classes of society, rich and poor, black and white, lesbians, conservatives.

But when the freeze got to Washington, who did the media go to for advice about the freeze? They went to the "experts." Men like Edward Teller, the father of the hydrogen bomb and the father of Star Wars, and two former secretaries of defence, James Schlesinger and Harold Brown. Did they interview Randall Forsberg, the brilliant woman who initiated the freeze? No. Not one article was written objectively analyzing the freeze, not one, in the whole of the literature of the United States in four years. It was simply written off. In fact, the *New York Times* wrote an editorial saying that the freeze was a wonderful movement but a stupid idea. The media killed the freeze.

In truth, the fate of the earth lies at the feet of the media. In the United States because of time constraints, television newscasters have little opportunity to do good investigative journalism. The Pentagon and the White House hold press conferences *just* before news deadlines so that there is no time to go elsewhere to search for the truth. Their presentations are well-packaged and attractive. Every morning members of the administration hold a conference in the White House to define one theme for the day. They only talk about that theme. The networks told us that the White House is on the phone from 7:00 a.m. in the morning until the nightly news, manipulating and orchestrating the news. The journalists admit that their coverage is somewhat biased.

CONGRESS

What about the Congress? We interviewed twenty senators and representatives to find out what they thought. They voted for the freeze because their constituents were screaming at them to do it. But they thought it was a stupid idea. Why? Because they thought the Russians would never go for it. (Meanwhile the Russians had put the freeze on the negotiating table in Geneva. I went to Russia in 1979 and met with the two ambassadors who negotiated SALT II [the second Strategic Arms Limitation Treaty]. They were deeply attached to it, very proud of it and anxious that it be ratified by the United States, but it was not). When we first presented the freeze idea to these senators and representatives, they had never heard of it. They argued for hours with us. They were like children running in and out making phone calls, discussing, and finally they said: ''Well, we'd vote for that with both hands.'' In 1979, the Russians presented a freeze resolution to the United Nations, and it was endorsed by the whole world except for the United States and a couple of its allies.

THE PENTAGON AND THE CORPORATIONS

A number of right-wing think tanks are funded by the military-industrial complex. They are really the propaganda wings of the corporations building the weapons. In the Pentagon, there is intense rivalry between the Army, the Navy, and the Air Force. One of the reasons we have an arms race is because these three branches of the military all want their own aeroplanes, their own missiles, and their own hydrogen bombs.

The men in the Pentagon can retire at the age of forty-two with tremendous pensions; but while in the Pentagon, they feather their own nests. They are very nice to the corporations who manufacture weapons, making sure they get their contracts. Then, when these people retire, at forty-two, they are immediately employed as high-salaried executives in these corporations. Because they know the inside workings of the Pentagon, they know how to give the corporations everything they want. This also happens when congresspeople or their aides retire: corporations employ them and learn the inside workings of Congress. This system is called the ''revolving door,'' in and out, in and out, all the time. The relationship between the Pentagon, the Congress and the corporations is incestuous. The Pentagon has 1,500 lobbyists who are paid for by the American taxpayers. Then there are the ''beltway bandits.'' There is a beltway around Washington, D.C., where most of the defence corporations have their lobbying offices, funded to the tune of millions of dollars. Only six percent of Pentagon contracts are competitively bid. All the rest are straight government handouts to the corporations. It is socialism for the corporations and capitalism for everyone else; socialism for the corporations and capitalism for all the little people who need health care, and education, help when they are mentally sick and food for their babies.

It is a complex situation. You have the religious people, the think tanks, the corporations and their control, the Pentagon, and the Congress. Let me give you an example of how the Congress is controlled. The B-1 bomber has three major contracts, and I think minor contracts in 252 Congressional Districts. Two hundred and fifty-two congresspeople are captive to jobs in their districts for the B-1 bomber. Then what about Star Wars? President Reagan is going to spend over $1 trillion building Star Wars. Seventy-five percent of government research and development funding now goes to military research—not to medical research, or ways to stop pollution, or ways to stop the forests from being cut down and thus saving the oxygen in the air, or ways to feed the people of the world. This money is going to build weapons to kill the world. What is happening is that the universities are short of funds for research, so the money is coming into the universities from the Pentagon. The scientists are prostituting themselves before the altar of annihilation. It is very sad for me, because I am a scientist and a doctor. It is unethical behaviour. Most of the scientists in America who are working on Star Wars admit it won't work. It is being set up for profits for corporations and so that scientists can do research. But they know they are prostituting their souls and their lives. The corporations already are making huge profits from Star Wars.

THE REAGAN ADMINISTRATION: WINNING NUCLEAR WAR
Let's go back to the Reagan administration again to see what their policy is on nuclear war. Until recently the West and the East believed in deterrence. If the Soviets bomb the United States, the United States has enough bombs to kill all of the Soviets; that is deterrence. But in 1982 the Reagan administration switched from deterrence to a strategy based on making a first strike and winning a nuclear war. This means the United States has built very accurate missiles that can silently go over and knock out the Russian missiles before they can press their button and retaliate. According to people who believe in fighting a nuclear war, if you knock out all the Soviet's missiles, you win the war. When Caspar Weinberger was told by doctors that a nuclear war cannot be won, he said: "Oh, I didn't really mean win; I meant prevail."

When you launch a first-strike nuclear war, you must first knock out the "enemy's" eyes and ears so that he can't see the bombs coming. America is working very hard on anti-satellite warfare, despite the fact that the Soviet Union has put a unilateral moratorium on testing anti-satellite weapons for the last two years. If the United States launches a first strike and misses a few Soviet missiles, Star Wars is intended to knock out these few remaining Soviet missiles after they are launched. That is really what Star Wars is about: it is the *shield* behind which the first-strike nuclear war will be launched.

Unfortunately for these strategists, we have just discovered nuclear winter. If bombs were exploded in cities and over forests, they would create a tremendous, raging fire, and a huge cloud of black smoke, which would rise high up in the atmosphere. Within weeks it would cover the earth with a pall of smoke so thick that the sun would not be able to penetrate it for months. Without sun, and with darkness even in the middle of the day, the plants would all die. (They need sunlight for photosynthesis.) The temperatures might fall to as low as minus forty degrees Celsius, even in the middle of the summer. If a few of us were to survive the immediate effects of a nuclear war, we still would freeze to death in the dark, along with all the plants and other life forms.

A Trident submarine has twenty-four missiles. Each missile has ten hydrogen bombs. That makes 240 hydrogen bombs, enough to destroy every major city in the Northern Hemisphere. The weapons from a single submarine could vaporize hundreds of millions of people. The Pentagon plans to build thirty of these submarines.

Another missile I want to describe is the Pershing II. It is deployed in West Germany. It takes only six minutes to reach Moscow, whereas an intercontinental ballistic missile would take thirty minutes to get from America to the Soviet Union across Canadian territory. In an eighteen-month period recently there were 151 errors in the early warning system when American radar observers thought the Russians had launched missiles, and they put the world on red alert. In November 1979, one of these errors lasted six minutes, because someone plugged a war games tape into the fail-safe computer in the Pentagon. The computer made a mistake and said we were under attack. The men in the missile silos were ready to insert the keys into the locks to launch the missiles. Three squadrons of B-52s, armed with nuclear weapons, took off and headed toward the Soviet Union. At the seventh minute, they tried to find President Jimmy Carter to tell him, but they couldn't find him. Maybe he had gone to the bathroom? When the mistake was realized, we were only thirteen minutes from nuclear war. That particular instance was reported in a tiny little paragraph near the obituaries in the *New York Times*. It should have been in headlines blasting across the whole of the world's press.

Now, the Pershing II has a very short flight time. It is very accurate and is to be used for decapitation of the Soviet leadership. This means that we intend to try to kill them before they have time to press their buttons. There is no time in six minutes for Mr. Gorbachev to say: "Oh, my God, we are about to be decapitated. I had better press the button." Because the Russians obviously don't want to be killed before they get a chance to press their buttons to kill all of us. That is how the thinking goes.

So they will find it necessary to computerize their buttons. When the satellite sends a message to the computer, the computer will press the button with no human decision having taken place. That is called launch-on-warning. And because the Russians were so upset that America put these Pershing IIs in West Germany, they have now put submarines just off the Atlantic coast of the United States with missiles that would take only six minutes to hit Washington, D.C.

A mathematician has recently done a study to show that as the number of computer errors increases in the early warning system, and as the transit times for the new missiles decrease, it is only a matter of time before accidental nuclear war occurs. That is why there are very senior people now saying that they think nuclear war could happen within the next ten years. Every year five thousand men who handle nuclear weapons in silos in the United States and in Europe are discharged from the American military because they are alcoholics, or they take drugs like LSD or heroin, or they are mentally unstable. How else could nuclear war start? How did the First World War start? You remember, two nations armed themselves and someone shot an archduke in Sarajevo. And then millions and millions of beautiful young men were killed, for no reason.

HOW CAN WE SAVE OURSELVES?
How are you going to save yourselves? You must use the political process to put pressure on your member of Parliament and the government of Canada. What do you demand? You insist that Canada get out of NORAD, which is linked to Star Wars and is essential for a first-strike. [*tumultuous applause*] You demand that Prime Minister Mulroney stop allowing America to test cruise missiles on your soil. [*applause*] You prohibit American B-52s from practicing terrain flying in the north of your country, where they train to fly underneath Soviet radar to drop their bombs silently during their first strike. You get rid of the DEW (Distant Early Warning) line. The United States is building big hangars up in the north of your country for their aeroplanes and big landing strips. You have a bay near here, Nanoose Bay, where there are American submarines practicing with nuclear-tipped torpedoes.

If nuclear war happens it is about money, greed and comfort. *Comfort!* But we are not comfortable. We are repressing the most incredible fear and discomfort. We are having nightmares about it. How did you feel when the Americans sent their warships into the Gulf of Sidra, or to within ten miles of the Russian coast? Eighty percent of their ships carry nuclear weapons. We are relying on Russian restraint and sanity.

Slavery is obsolete. Cannibalism is obsolete. Sacrificing children to the gods is obsolete. *War must be made obsolete.* Because now any war at any time and in any place in the world could bring in the superpowers and destroy the products of evolution and the fruits of our cultural heritage. It will destroy the blossom trees, the lichen, the moss, and the whales. It will destroy the music of Bach, Handel, and Haydn, the paintings of Renoir and Picasso, and the poetry of Shakespeare. And it will destroy humanity with its capacity for love. Let me close with a beautiful love poem, Shakespeare's 18th Sonnet, because it epitomizes what I am talking about: it is about emotions. It's not about numbers, it's about people.

> Shall I compare thee to a Summer's day?
> Thou art more lovely and more temperate
> Rough winds do shake the darling buds of May,
> and Summer's lease hath all too short a date:
> Sometime too hot the eye of heaven shines,
> and often is his gold complexion dimm'd
> And every fair from fair sometimes declines
> By chance or nature's changing course untrimm'd:
> But thy eternal summer shall not fade
> Nor lose possession of that fair thou owest;
> Nor shall Death brag thou wanderest in his shade,
> When in eternal lines to time thou growest:
>   So long as men can breathe, or eyes can see
>   So long lives this, and this gives life to thee.

Go home tonight, and before you go to bed, get out a pen and a piece of paper and write a letter to your children, born or unborn. Tell them how you are going to commit your life to save their lives. And commit your total life, your money, your fortune and every day until you die, to save the earth. We were *born,* you and I, for only one reason: we were conceived and born to save the earth—and we will know in our lifetime whether we have done it. *It is up to you.*

CHAPTER 30

Technology, Science and Preparations for War

PROFESSOR DAVID SUZUKI

THE CAPACITY OF HUMAN BEINGS TO CHANGE THE WORLD

As a biologist I spend a lot of time thinking about the evolutionary roots of our species. And when you look at the history of our species from this viewpoint, you find it is a wonderful story. I look at human beings the way I study fruit flies: I don't listen to what fruit flies say to one another, I don't read the books that they write, and I don't watch their television programs. I just watch what fruit flies *do,* and that shows me very clearly what fruit flies are all about. Well, if you look at human beings this way, you find that we are not a very impressive species. We are not very big: a lot of animals are much bigger than we are, and so certainly are a lot of plants and trees. We are not very strong: lots of animals are much stronger. We are not very fast: even an elephant can outrun the fastest human being alive. We are not gifted with armour, claws, fangs or sensory acuity. As biological creatures we simply are not very distinguished. The only feature that has distinguished our species is a huge brain—the most complex structure in the known universe. And it is the ratio of our brain to brawn that has been the secret of the great success of our species.

It was with this magnificent organ—our brain—that we were able to recognize that we are different from the other creatures. We also were able to recognize that certain cycles, irregularities or patterns repeat themselves over and over again: we recognized that day follows night, that the seasons follow each other, that there are tides and lunar cycles, that animals migrate in certain ways, that plants succeed each other through the seasons. The capacity of human beings to recognize and remember these patterns allowed us to do something that no other creature

Dr. David Suzuki

does—*organize* the world around us and create sense out of chaos. This sense of regularity allowed us to predict the various aspects of the world's behaviour. We could predict in what seasons animals would be in a certain area; we knew when to look for certain edible plants; and we knew where to shelter in different seasons. We, unlike any other creatures, had a sense of the future. We were unique in having the ability to predict the future from past patterns—and we used that ability to survive.

We were also unique because when we realized that the future could be affected by what we do today, we created options for ourselves. When we found out that by deliberately choosing a particular path today, we could influence the future tomorrow, we found that we could avoid doing things that would bring future risks. That has been the secret of our survival.

It is the greatest of ironies that today, with all the amplified brain power of computers, science and technology, we now seem incapable of doing the one thing that got us to where we are today: taking a deliberate action today to avoid difficulties or dangers tomorrow. And that is why we are all here—because we are all concerned about the greatest hazard that faces all of humankind and much of the natural world. Yet for the most part our ability to do anything about the terrible situation that we're in seems paralyzed.

TECHNOLOGY, SCIENCE AND THE BOMB
Why are we incapable now of doing anything about the present escalation in weapons? If we look at the history of our species, we will realize that the secret of our advancement has been that the human brain created technology. Other animals do use instruments; they do use tools. But generally they just pick them up from where they are lying around and

Dr. David Suzuki, a prominent geneticist, is a professor at the University of British Columbia, and an outstanding science broadcaster on television and radio. During the past decade Dr. Suzuki has won many awards for his successful efforts to popularize science among ordinary Canadians. He is a member of the Order of Canada, and in 1986 he received the prestigious Royal Bank Award for his distinguished public services. Dr. Suzuki is deeply concerned about the misuse of science and technology, and the scientific illiteracy of Canadian members of Parliament and government policy makers generally. He has long been an opponent of all preparations for nuclear war. He has also strongly condemned the mistreatment of Japanese Canadians in Western Canada during World War II. David Suzuki spoke in Vancouver on April 14, 1986, at a fundraising banquet for the 1986 Walk for Peace. This chapter is an abridged version of that speech.

use them with their bills or their hands. We do more than that. We *create* technology. From the time we tamed fire to the time we recognized how to use clay, pottery, glassware and metals, we were tool- and technology-inventing creatures. Our ability to make things to add to our arsenal of tools has more than compensated for our lack of physical power. In the past, until this century, we developed technology through trial and error. Technology always *preceded* scientific understanding of what that technology was about. Long before we knew the chemistry of glass, we had invented glass. Long before we knew the science of metallurgy, we had invented metals. Technology always preceded science or scientific understanding.

Hiroshima was a very important landmark in human evolution. It signaled that in this century this general principle had changed. For the first time, science preceded technology in a major event. The greatest scientists of the day conceived of the nuclear bomb, the greatest scientists of the day sold it to politicians, and the same great scientists built the machine successfully. From Hiroshima on, science and the military have been inextricably linked.

SCIENCE AND WARFARE INEXTRICABLY LINKED

Today over half of all scientists in the world carry out work directly for the military under military contracts. Science without military funding would not exist as the science that we know, and modern warfare today is inconceivable without science and technology as its basis. Science and warfare have become inextricably bound up in an unholy alliance. The great power of science to understand nature has now become the source of most new technology in this second part of the twentieth century. In large part, this explains the escalation in the arms race. Neither Mr. Reagan nor Mr. Gorbachev, nor their generals nor their military advisers came up with the terrifying new weapons that we face today. Scientists proposed the use of neutron bombs—which are supposed preferentially to destroy animals and human beings and to leave property relatively undamaged. Scientists proposed and designed binary chemical weapons— where two innocuous compounds are driven together inside a shell, where they react chemically to produce a deadly nerve gas. Scientists are now engineering biological weapons. I am ashamed to say that a geneticist proposed ethnic weapons in 1970—a cocktail of chemicals that would selectively eliminate one ethnic group, and leave all others untouched. And scientists, some of the great physicists of the day, are now promulgating the notion of the Strategic Defense Initiative, or Star Wars.

David Suzuki

SCIENCE PRESENTS A FRACTURED VIEW OF NATURE

The problem we face today with this unholy alliance between science and the military is that science provides only a fragmented view of nature. The great strength of science, the secret of its success, has been that scientists have said: "Look, the universe and the world around us are far too complex for us to gain a definitive, comprehensive explanation. As scientists, we can only give you little insights into tiny fragments of nature." Scientists have not attempted to give comprehensive explanations. They have taken tiny parts of nature, isolated them from the rest, brought these into the laboratories and looked at them under their microscopes. What scientists try to do is to control all of the factors impinging on that fragment of nature, measure everything about it that they can, and then try to understand the nature of the particular fragment which they are looking at. This process has provided us with some very profound insights into fragments of nature. Most scientists have assumed that if we look at enough fragments of nature, *eventually* we will be able to piece them into a comprehensive explanation of the universe. By reducing nature to its smallest parts, the hope has been that we could put them back together and reconstruct an understandable picture of the whole.

As I am sure you are well aware, modern physics has put the lie to that. Physics has shown in this century that in order to see nature at all, we have to change it. By interposing ourselves to look at nature, we have to control it and affect it. We can never know nature as it really is. Scientists have shown that when you take two fragments of nature and put them together again they interact synergistically. They have effects that are greater than the sum of their individual parts. So if you said to a physicist: "Tell me all the physical properties of atomic hydrogen," he could tell you everything there was to know about atomic hydrogen. If you said: "Tell me everything there is to know about atomic oxygen," you could learn everything about that. But if you asked: "What happens if I take two atoms of hydrogen and combine them with one atom of oxygen to make a molecule of water?" the physicist would say: "Damned if I know." Knowing the individual properties of atomic hydrogen and oxygen does not help to explain what happens when you combine them into a molecule. And this is true of the whole of nature. By looking at its isolated bits and pieces you cannot gain a comprehensive understanding of the whole picture, because the pieces interact synergistically and lead to effects that are not predictable from the individual parts. Science provides us with a *fractured* view of the world.

I believe that we have become intoxicated with the insights we have gained by examining nature in this way. Now we believe that through science we are in fact coming up with a comprehensive world view. I think the scientific community has failed to understand the very basis of science's methodology: it cannot provide comprehensive views; it can provide only a fractured, fragmented view of the world.

I think that those who work to invent ever more terrible weapons have become caught up in the notion that they understand the world, and that science provides them with this all-explaining view. They are caught up in the exuberance of discovery. They live in a fractured society in which they can disconnect their studies on the production of weapons from the end result—the ultimate destruction of human beings. The very nature of science leads us to live in a fragmented world—a disconnected world, where we can disconnect what we're doing now from other events in other parts of the world.

THE HIDDEN COSTS OF NEW TECHNOLOGIES

When I began broadcasting in 1962, I had perceived that there were often deleterious consequences of technology. So I felt that, before we put new technologies into place, we had to have a way of analyzing their costs and benefits. If the costs of a new technology were high, and its benefits low, I thought we would decide not to develop that particular technology. For the last twenty years, this assumption has impelled me to work in the media. I really thought that I could make a more scientifically literate public that would be better able to assess the costs and benefits of new technologies, including weapons technology.

It has only been in the last two years that I have recognized that my assumption was completely wrong. The reason is as follows: throughout history, when a new technology has been invented, the benefits have always been immediate and obvious. We *love* technology because it immediately does wonderful things for us. The problem with a new technology is that its costs are usually hidden and unpredictable. Let me give you two examples.

When DDT was first synthesized in a chemistry lab, its benefits—as a powerful insecticide—were obvious and immediate. It was a very powerful way of killing insects. If its ecological and genetic costs had been analyzed, some of these would also have been obvious. Any good ecologist would have said: "Hey, listen, this doesn't make sense. It is a crazy way to manage pests. There are a lot of other insects that are friends or allies of ours and not enemies. You don't try to get rid of every criminal in New York City by killing all of its inhabitants." Any geneticist would have said: "Well, that is a very powerful way of killing insects, but in a very few years you will have rigidly selected for resistant strains. You can expect that in a few years the insect population will have recovered its original size, and you'll need new, more powerful pesticides to control them." Before DDT was used no one could have predicted the phenomenon called "biomagnification." Biomagnification describes what happens when low concentrations of a chemical are sprayed into the environment. Little organisms eat the chemical and concentrate it. They are then eaten by bigger organisms, and so on up the food chain, until there is a concentration in birds and animals, in the mammary glands of people and in the shell glands of birds. These concentrations may be hundreds of millions or billions of times greater than that when the chemical was first sprayed into the environment. We couldn't predict biomagnification because we only discovered it by using DDT. Only when birds began to go sterile because their egg shells broke, did we realize, or infer, that it had something to do with DDT.

The same problem is evident in my second example: nuclear energy. When scientists went to work on the atomic bomb, the benefits were obvious. If the Nazis got the atomic bomb before we did, we'd be in trouble. So, we had to get it first. And it worked—we beat them to it. Then, once the bomb was there, people argued that the benefits of using it would far outweigh the costs of not using it: they argued that the bomb dropped on a Japanese city might end the war; that by using it, the bloodbath caused by the deaths of millions of allies and Japanese soldiers might be avoided. Again it worked. The war ended very quickly. (I don't know why they had to drop two bombs, but anyway, they did.) Had there been a cost-benefit analysis before those bombs were dropped, no one could have predicted the thing called radioactive fallout; radioactive fallout was only discovered in 1946, when they blew the bomb up in Bikini. It was years after the Hiroshima bombing that scientists discovered that a bomb exploded in the atmosphere punches holes in the ozone layer, letting in ultraviolet radiation. Years later, the military discovered that an atmospheric explosion sends out an electromagnetic pulse of gamma rays over a broad area which destroys electrical circuits. Forty years after Hiroshima we now discover there's a thing called "nuclear winter."

I am sure that's not the last cost of this technology we will encounter. The problem with these new technologies is that the benefits are immediate and obvious, while the costs are simply not predictable. But we have reached the point where we must accept, as history informs us, that every technology has a cost; there is no such thing as a cost-free technology. The more powerful the technology, the greater the probable cost, and the more likely it is to be unpredictable. Can we then go on asking our scientists and technologists to give us more and more technology for the benefits, and keep hoping to clear up the costs later, by inventing more technology?

VALUES AND SHORTCOMINGS OF SCIENTIFIC TECHNOLOGY

So, what I come down to then, is that the issue of nuclear weapons and the armaments race is only the most obvious and immediate hazard we face coming from this terrible alliance between science and the military. In fact, there is something even more fundamental that we have to face. We can no longer afford to go on accepting the benefits of technology and delaying the costs until we discover what they will be later. But we are in a real pickle, because politicians have finally discovered there is a thing called "science policy," and that scientific research pays off in technological dividends. So an enormous amount of pressure is being exerted on young scientists today from both the federal and provincial governments to do scientific research that is socially relevant, that can be applied, that is mission-oriented. I think what we face is the terrible recognition that science's great strength and its capacity to move us profoundly lies in its ability to describe nature. There is nothing more exciting and wonderful than the view which we get from scientists of the structure of an atom, of a cell, or the nature of DNA, or the existence of black holes. That is science at its finest. But we make a great mistake in rushing to apply the knowledge that we gain in fragmented bits and pieces. We seem to be intoxicated with the amount of knowledge that we have gained, and it has been great in the last few decades, compared to what we have known throughout human history. But I think we are looking at it the wrong way. Sure we have gained tremendous insights in the last two or three decades, but compared to what we don't know, what we are gaining is just a little tiny insight.

Let me give you an example of the difficulty we get into. You know four-fifths of the planet is covered with water. We describe the ecology of the ocean, and we set up these grand computer programs, and we have all kinds of models of what the ocean is really like. How do we sample the ocean? We drag these little tiny plankton nets through the ocean at different levels and we drag them for an hour and pull them up and look at all the beasts in there and say: "Oh, now we know the nature of the ecosystem at that particular level." I would say, it is like being in a rocket ten miles up off the surface of the earth and dragging a net which would be maybe a hundred feet wide on the surface, and then judging what is present on the surface of the planet by what you catch in the net. But we make all of these models of the ocean based on these puny sampling methods. Up until five years ago, it was always accepted that the base of the food chain in the ocean was plankton: phytoplankton and zooplankton (tiny plants and animals). They are the smallest creatures in the ocean, and they are the base of the whole food chain. About five years ago it was discovered that there are creatures a hundred times smaller than plankton. They are so small you can't see them with a light microscope; you have to use an electron microscope. They are called microplankton. They are so small they go through the finest plankton nets. Now that we know of the existence of microplankton, we have done re-analyses of our data and find that microplankton are so numerous they are probably the major source of oxygen in the atmosphere of the planet. Yet, up until five years ago, we didn't even know they existed.

Each time we gain a little bit of knowledge we become so infatuated with what we have gained that we want to rush to apply it immediately. I think that we have reached a terrible point in history. The sad thing we face is that history informs us that never have human beings invented a technology from which they have been able to pull back or which they can get rid of. Once you have a technology, you are stuck with it and have to live with it. Yet we now live with a technology which inevitably, it seems to me, will create a situation of its open abuse. We now for the first time face a technology that is so powerful we have to do what we've never been able to do in all of human history.

THE MORALITY OF SCIENCE

As a once practicing scientist, or as my peer group now call me, a heretic, I believe that more and more a great deal of the responsibility for the terrible arms race we face lies with scientists. Most of my scientific colleagues would say to this: "Look, scientists just search for truth. What you do with it is *your* responsibility. It is up to the public and politicians to decide, and in those decisions scientists have no greater responsibility than any other voting member of the public." But it is scientists who continue to provide the knowledge and ideas that make new weapons possible. It is scientists who are peddling them to politicians, and it is scientists who're doing the work to build them. Yet we scientists have no code of ethics. Even the medical profession, one of the most—well, I won't say that [*laughter*]—even the medical profession has a code of ethics, but science doesn't. Most scientists today, because of the extreme pressure to specialize early in their education, have little knowledge of the history of science, the social context in which science is carried out and applied, the limitations of the scientific enterprise or any sense of responsibility that accompanies becoming a scientist. Scientists must be a target for education. The general public must put pressure on the scientific community. How do you do this? You have to become more scientifically literate yourself.

Our illiteracy in science reflects itself in the people we elect to public office. The people we are now electing to public office in fact show an abysmal lack of understanding of science. Science is by far the most important issue that faces us today. Science is at the base of the nuclear arms race, pollution and many of the other problems which affect us. Until we elect people to office who can take science seriously, and make decisions in an informed way, we will not control our own destiny. But what we need first is a public that takes science seriously. Then we'll begin to elect people who also take it seriously.

[audience interjection: "Do we have time to wait for that?"]

You can't ask questions such as whether or not we have enough time. We all have to act to the best of our ability. The issue is not whether or not we make it. The important thing is that we have to try. [*applause*]

A PARABLE ON SURVIVAL

I'd like to conclude with a little parable that I wrote the other day. I call it "A Grim, Grim Fairytale."

My daughters love the Royal Ontario Museum in Toronto. Fortunately, their dad never tires of it either. Our favourite displays, of course, are of the dinosaurs and other prehistoric animals. The other day as we approached the awesome display of *Megaloceros giganteus,* the long-extinct Irish Elk, with its spectacular eleven-foot antlers, Severn marvelled at their size and asked what had happened to them. Taking a bit of paleontological liberty I told her the following story:

"Thousands of years ago, one gargantuan bull elk ruled all of the others of his species throughout Europe. He was the most magnificent elk ever seen, with an immense set of antlers, a powerful bellowing voice, and a majestic, muscular body. As he strolled across the vast plains, the ground shook and all of the other elks trembled with fear and envy. With his strength and antlers he was invincible and overwhelmed any who dared challenge his power. Those who shared his territory accepted his authority. Each day he surveyed a different part of the vast expanse of his range.

"One day he ventured further than he had ever gone beyond his own terrain. But he was confident in his might. After all, his antlers were the greatest weapons ever developed. Presently he spotted another huge elk in the distance. 'Who could be so impudent as to encroach on my turf?' he wondered, and hurried toward the figure. The foreigner was every bit as big and carried a set of antlers as impressive as his own. Trembling with fear and rage, he ran at the stranger and bellowed with all his might: 'This is *my* territory. I rule it. Submit! Back away or be destroyed!' He was shocked to hear the reply that rang through the air: 'No, this is *my* land! And *you* are trespassing. *I* am the commander here.' Pawing the ground and shaking their antlers, the two giants stood facing each other threatening and yelling all day, while the smaller elks caught between them cringed in fear of being crushed by these two superb animals.

"When night fell the two bulls retreated to their respective camps and called for their scientists and engineers. 'I have met a mighty force,' each told their minions. 'And I need reinforcements and advantage to overcome my enemy's strength. Do everything you can, or else he will overwhelm me and subjugate you in slavery.' And so a great effort was made. One had many long, sharp spines added to his antlers to stab his opponent, while the other had a huge, heavy club placed up front to deliver a knock-out blow.

"The next day the two bulls hurried back to the border only to discover the ingenious changes added to each other's antlers overnight. Once again they stood shaking and roaring, but each feared the enemy's possible advantage. When night fell, they rushed back for additional reinforcements and defences against the enemy's clever inventions. Antlers were armoured with flat surfaces to blunt the other's blows, and embellishments were added at the edge to probe the weaknesses in the other's defensive shield.

"And so it continued day after day. Each night the bulls required more help and demanded that those under their control contribute more resources, more muscle power, and more imagination, because a victory by the other male brought terrifying possibilities. But each new addition to those giant antlers had other repercussions. The weight of the racks grew so great that the bulls' necks had to be shored up with more muscle than bone. But now they couldn't turn their heads as quickly, so they needed other elks to provide an early warning of danger and possibly even absorb the first blow. Legs had to be increased in diameter to support the massive weight and to generate the driving power to wield the antlers. Their bodies were increased in girth to provide more lung power and stomach volume to fuel the muscles. More and more material, effort, and creativity went into supporting those magnificent antlers. Inevitably rumbles of discontent spread from the lower ranks of elk. 'Those antlers are draining resources from everything else,' they grumbled. 'Wouldn't it be better to sit down and discuss a way to coexist? Perhaps we could share space and maybe even co-operate?' some suggested. But the two males bellowed at such treachery. 'How dare you consider coexistence with a tyrant? The best protection is a superior offensive capacity and an invincible defence. We have to develop cleverer ways to gain an advantage.' And when some asked: 'Is it worth the expense?' both of the great elks replied: 'Of course it is. There will be enormous spin-offs. You will have more shade from my antlers on hot days, and birds will find greater space to sit on. . . .'

"And so it went. Each new development led inevitably to more complex and contrived inventions. Those antlers were an obsession to the two bulls and came to dominate every other elk's life."

"And then what happened, Daddy?" asked Sarika, my three-year-old.

"Well, dear," I replied, "eventually the smaller elks realized that the two opponents had put all their faith in massive antlers that looked impressive but were completely unreliable and impractical. So they simply left the two giants alone to roar and threaten each other. Eventually the sheer weight and cost of those antlers broke their backs, and they both died. The other elks were grateful that they hadn't developed such useless structures. Their antlers were quite big enough. So they lived together in herds and turned their attention to the important business of living."

"Oh," said Severn, "That's why Canada shouldn't get involved in Star Wars!"

"Yes," I said. Even a six year old can see the obvious!

Postscript

As this book goes to press, five months have passed since the Vancouver Centennial Symposium on Peace and Disarmament took place. The Vancouver Proposals for Peace which were formulated and endorsed by the symposium participants were transmitted by the Vancouver City Council to the heads of government of the NATO and Warsaw Pact nations, to the leaders of the six countries (India, Sweden, Greece, Tanzania, Mexico and Argentina) who issued the Five Continent Appeal, and to various agencies of the United Nations. The following excerpt from a reply received from the United Nations is indicative of the response to this document.

> Through the approval by the City Council of the Vancouver
> Proposals for Peace, your metropolitan area joins countless other
> cities and smaller municipalities around the world in calling for
> the cessation and reversal of the spiralling arms race with its
> negative effects on international security and human well-being.
> As articulated by the Secretary-General:
> "The threat of nuclear catastrophe is not one issue among many.
> Preventing such a horror is the pre-condition of all our
> endeavours. The great tasks before this world Organization — the
> challenge of economic and social development, progress in
> human rights, the construction of a world of justice and human
> dignity — all will be in vain if we fail to prevent nuclear
> disaster.''

The Vancouver Proposals for Peace emphasized the importance of joint adherence by the United States and the Soviet Union to a moratorium on nuclear weapons testing and an early completion and ratification of a comprehensive nuclear test ban treaty. The arguments in favour of a test ban have been eloquently expressed in a recent statement by International Physicians for the Prevention of Nuclear War (IPPNW), the recipients of the 1985 Nobel Peace Prize. According to their physicians' prescription for 1986–1987 (1):

1. A ban on nuclear explosions is a clear focal point for rallying world public opinion behind a single, important, readily achievable arms control proposal, thus sidestepping the paralysing complexity of most other proposals.
2. A ban on nuclear explosions is verifiable. Both the United States and the Soviet Union have agreed to on-site inspections. Even without them, however, modern seismic techniques can distinguish earthquakes from underground explosions as small as one kiloton. Trust in this matter is no longer an issue.
3. A ban on nuclear explosions will impede the development of new generations of nuclear warheads, including those designed to power space-based systems, those capable of acting as first-strike weapons, and those that are so small and mobile that future arms control verification might be rendered impossible.
4. Leading scientists, East and West, have stated that test detonations are not necessary to ensure the reliability of nuclear arsenals. In fact, few nuclear test explosions have ever been conducted for this purpose.
5. A ban on nuclear explosions would not decrease the security of any country, but would increase the security of all.
6. A ban on nuclear explosions would strengthen the non-proliferation treaty, which seeks "to achieve the discontinuance of all test explosions for all time and to continue negotiations to this end..."
7. A ban on nuclear explosions provides a litmus test for distinguishing those political leaders who are committed to ending the nuclear arms race from those who tolerate its continuation.

Until recently, opposition to a nuclear test ban has focussed on the alleged unverifiability of compliance with such a treaty. It is now clear that modern seismic technology is sufficiently sensitive to detect and identify underground nuclear explosions as small as one kiloton. In fact, an adequate network of monitoring stations could detect nuclear explosions as small as 0.1 kiloton anywhere in the world (2), which is much smaller than that which could be useful for weapons development.

During the last five months, the Soviet government has responded to an informal proposal from the United States Geological Survey by indicating its willingness to permit the installation of as many as eighteen sophisticated seismic monitoring instruments on its territory, manned by American technicians, in return for a similar system in the United States (3). A private group of American scientists already is being allowed to deploy seismic detection instruments near the main Soviet test site at Semipalatinsk, as well as near the United States test site in Nevada, in order to demonstrate the feasibility of verifying compliance with a nuclear test ban (4).

Hence objections to a nuclear test ban on the grounds of its alleged unverifiability are no longer tenable. In spite of claims by Pentagon spokesmen that continued testing is required to confirm the viability of existing weapons stockpiles, and to devise "safer, more reliable" weapons, it is evident that their only real objection to a halt to nuclear weapons tests is that it would prevent the development of new, more dangerous, and more readily concealed offensive nuclear weapons, and that it would prevent the perfection of X-ray lasers powered by nuclear explosions for the space-based weapons envisioned by the Strategic Defense Initiative (Star Wars) program. This is precisely the most cogent argument in favour of a comprehensive nuclear test ban agreement.

As these paragraphs are being written, circumstances seem particularly propitious for an agreement to stop nuclear weapons tests, offering a unique opportunity which may not recur and which must not be lost. The Soviet Union has not tested nuclear weapons since August 6, 1985, and has promised to continue its moratorium throughout the remainder of 1986. Although the United States has conducted at least nineteen nuclear tests in Nevada during the Soviet test moratorium, the latest on September 30, 1986, both houses of the United States Congress have adopted resolutions urging the conclusion of a comprehensive test ban agreement, and the House of Representatives has been resisting further appropriations to finance nuclear weapons tests as long as the Soviet moratorium remains in effect. The forthcoming meetings between President Reagan and General Secretary Gorbachev, starting in Iceland later this month, have raised hopes for significant progress toward relief from the onerous burden of the arms race, and for the redirection of the vast human and material resources which it now wastes so that they can be turned to solving the massive social and health problems which now beset most of the world's people.

Nevertheless, meaningful reductions in the huge arsenals of strategic offensive nuclear weapons seem unlikely as long as the Pentagon insists that United States national security requires the continued development and testing of new types of weapons in the belief that political dominance can be regained through attempts to achieve military superiority. On the other hand, a comprehensive nuclear test ban could interrupt the momentum of the arms race and provide an atmosphere conducive to the negotiation of serious arms reductions and the creation of a safer world, more secure for everyone.

We hope readers of this book will translate their knowledge into constructive political activity. The government of Canada has been strangely reticent about encouraging the United States to respond positively to the Soviet moratorium on nuclear testing. Canadian readers ought to be pressuring their MPs and Prime Minister Brian Mulroney on this issue. By the same token, we hope that American and British readers will urge their governments to pursue a comprehensive nuclear test ban agreement without delay.

October 1986
Thomas L. Perry, M.D.
James G. Foulks, PhD., M.D.

References

1. IPPNW, International Physicians for the Prevention of Nuclear War's Medical Prescription for 1986–87, *Lancet*, 2 (1986): 585
2. R. A. Scribner, T. J. Ralston, and W.D. Metz, *The Verification Challenge*, (Birkhäuser, Boston, 1985): 67–86.
3. R. J. Smith, "Soviets agree to broad seismic test," *Science*, 233 (1986): 511–512.
4. J. Palca, "Seismic monitoring: Private diplomacy emergent," *Nature*, 321 (1986): 638.